T0202795

Springer Series in Public Health and Health Policy Ethics

Series Editors
Bruce Jennings, Center for Biomedical Ethics and Society
Vanderbilt University
Nashville, TN, USA

Lisa M. Lee, Scholarly Integrity and Research Compliance,
and Department of Population Health Sciences
Virginia Tech
Blacksburg, VA, USA

The *Springer Series in Public Health and Health Policy Ethics* and its companion compact-book series, the *SpringerBriefs in Public Health and Health Policy Ethics*, are designed to foster diverse and innovative research and critical analysis of health governance, with particular emphasis on the role of normative frameworks, such as ethics, political theory, and law. Both series focus on normative theory and the practice of public health, with its emphasis on the health and well-being at the population level and the social determinants of health.

The Series also welcomes submissions focusing on normative theory and the practice of health policy analysis, with its focus on the politics, economics, and institutional design of health systems. This Series aims to foster innovative critical scholarship and research in these two fields, and cognate areas, such as environmental health, justice, and climate change, that are converging with public health and health policy. Such new scholarship is needed for two reasons. First, the global pandemic of COVID-19 has brought transformative challenges and changes to public health and health policy and the time is right for a reexamination of the normative and the social scientific aspects of these fields. Second, the pandemic has exposed significant vulnerabilities in all societies that grow out of the convergence of health emergencies, altered patterns of risk and adaptation emerging from climate change, and a growing loss of legitimacy and public trust that is undermining the democratic foundations of all governance, including health.

This *Springer Series in Public Health and Health Policy Ethics* welcomes original works that explore the connections among human health, ecosystemic integrity and health, and social justice and rights. The Series aims to publish full-length volumes emerging from philosophical, historical, and cultural analysis as well as empirical research emerging from biomedical and social sciences. Comparative analysis of historical and intellectual development of the fields of public health and health policy analysis, and the similarities and differences among these fields, can find a home in this Series. This Series is open to volumes of 150 pages or longer, to single or co-authored monographs, and to edited and multi-authored collections of content of significant interest for scholarship and teaching.

Andrew Sola

Ethics and Pandemics

Interdisciplinary Perspectives on COVID-19
and Future Pandemics

 Springer

Andrew Sola
Amerikazentrum, e.V.
FOM University of Applied Sciences
Hamburg, Germany

ISSN 2731-0124   ISSN 2731-0132   (electronic)
Springer Series in Public Health and Health Policy Ethics
ISBN 978-3-031-33209-8   ISBN 978-3-031-33207-4   (eBook)
https://doi.org/10.1007/978-3-031-33207-4

This Springer imprint is published by the registered company Springer Nature Switzerland AG
The registered company address is: Gewerbestrasse 11, 6330 Cham, Switzerland

For Anna

Series Editorial Advisory Board

Preface

The sun set on the year 2019 with little to indicate what was to come next. People around the world were heralding the bright dawn of a new decade, drinking, dancing, and making merry. Little did we know that 2020 would not bring yet another normal, boring old year.

Within weeks everything changed. The whole planet went into lockdown, people died by the thousands, millions more became sick, factories were shuttered, entire sectors of the economy collapsed, workers couldn't work, parents couldn't feed their children, families were thrown out of their homes, lines for food banks stretched for blocks, borders were sealed, politicians rattled their sabers, the price of oil went into negative numbers, minorities suffered even more from pandemic-inflamed discrimination, conspiracy theories took root in the minds of many, and people looked at each other with increasing suspicion behind their homemade masks.

But some optimists began to see rays of hope. People started being kinder to their neighbors, postal workers and grocery couriers were hailed as modern-day heroes, doctors and nurses were applauded for their selfless sacrifice, dolphins returned to the Venetian lagoon to frolic by Saint Mark's Square, wild sheep strolled through Welsh villages, wealthy nations sent struggling nations ventilators and PPE, communities shared their resources, politicians hailed a post-epidemic future of mutual understanding and perpetual peace, and a spirit of good will permeated every nook and cranny of the globe.

Observing these events, I couldn't help but think about the famous opening to Charles Dickens' *A Tale of Two Cities* (1859), a novel set during the French Revolution in 1789 but written with the benefit of hindsight many years later. The book begins by describing the emotional extremes that people experience when living through world-changing crises:

> It was the best of times, it was the worst of times, it was the age of wisdom, it was the age of foolishness, it was the epoch of belief, it was the epoch of incredulity, it was the season of Light, it was the season of Darkness, it was the spring of hope, it was the winter of despair, we had everything before us, we had nothing before us, we were all going direct to Heaven, we were all going direct the other way—in short, the period was so far like the

present period, that some of its noisiest authorities insisted on its being received, for good
or for evil, in the superlative degree of comparison only.

Many of us probably drew similarly extreme conclusions during the height of
COVID-19 pandemic. We wondered if it was the best of times or the worst of times.
Were we living in a time of unprecedented opportunity or unprecedented crisis?
Was it a time of great good or absolute evil?

It has always been difficult to answer these questions, but maybe Dickens was on
to something, way back in 1859. Perhaps he was right to pause for a moment, survey
the course of human history, and argue that we have a tendency to hold extreme
views about the world no matter what era we are living in. It happens all the time.
Superlatives are the order of the day—just listen to the noisiest authorities in our
own hyperactive media. And looking back at the world in December 2019, surely
we were just as extreme as we became shortly afterwards at the start of 2020. There
were similar grounds for hope and despair, the best of times and the worst: Trump
was still President! Brexit was really happening! It was the hottest year on record!
For some, it was the best of times; for others, the worst.

And much as Dickens might have predicted, both the years 2020 and 2021 continued to be years of superlatives. Recall both the elation and skepticism on 11
December 2020 when the US Food and Drug Administration granted emergency
use authorization for the Pfizer/BioNTech mRNA vaccine after the advisory panel
voted 17-4 with 1 abstention to permit its use.[1] The vaccines were meant to be a
game changer that marked the beginning of the end of the pandemic. Universal vaccination would lead to the inevitable defeat of the virus and a return to normal. On
4 July 2021, Joe Biden, the newly elected President of the United States, announced:

> So, today, while the virus hasn't been vanquished, we know this: It no longer controls our
> lives. It no longer paralyzes our nation. And it's within our power to make sure it never does
> again. And for that, we can thank the scientists and researchers, the educators, and all the
> other frontline and essential workers, like many of you here today who became the light to
> see us through the darkness.[2]

The heavy mood was lifting and the clouds were parting. A light could be seen at the
end of the tunnel. It was the time of hope.

Other world leaders shared Biden's conviction. Boris Johnson, then Prime
Minister of the UK, announced that 19 July 2021 would be "freedom day," a day
that marked an end to most pandemic restrictions and a symbolic return to normal
life. Unfortunately for Johnson, he was forced to spend freedom day in isolation
after coming into contact with one of his cabinet ministers who tested positive for
COVID-19. Fast forward a year and President Biden, on 18 September 2022,
declared the pandemic to be over, despite the fact that 400 Americans continued to

[1] See the FDA website for all of the official memoranda and approval documents for the various
vaccines. This, the first EUA, is available at https://www.fda.gov/media/144416/
[2] See the White House website for transcripts of presidential speeches. This speech is available at
https://www.whitehouse.gov/briefing-room/speeches-remarks/2021/07/05/remarks-by-president-biden-
celebrating-independence-day-and-independence-from-covid-19/

die from COVID-19 every day and despite considerable scientific objections to that claim. Even as of April 2023, the daily death rate in the US exceeds 300, raising further doubts about the "end" of the pandemic.[3]

Indeed, these freedom days—like the joy about mRNA vaccines and Biden's optimistic declaration that "the virus no longer controls our lives"—proved to be premature celebrations, for here I write in April of 2023, having faced down two additional waves of deadly variants: Delta and Omicron. Countries like China have reinstated various types of lockdown, before canceling them altogether, and global COVID-19 deaths are rapidly approaching seven million.[4] To make matters worse, a rare illness with the frightening name of monkeypox started spreading around the globe and polio reappeared in New York City's wastewater. It is, again, the worst of times. Furthermore, as Dickens may have predicted, skepticism and mistrust of politicians and public health authorities remain high in many parts of the world. It is the epoch of incredulity, the winter of despair.

It may be wise to remind ourselves periodically of the great novelist's insight about common emotional reactions to crises: They tend to be noisy and extreme. Was COVID-19 really any different from any other crisis, any other earthquake, hurricane, pandemic, depression, war, or revolution? Did it even surpass the ongoing challenge of climate change? Did it really mark the dawn of a new era, like the French Revolution, the Spanish Flu, World War II, AIDS, the fall of the Berlin Wall, 9/11, or the war in Ukraine? Or were we just being hysterical and peddling in extremes all over again?

This book does take a stance on these questions. Yes, COVID-19 was really something revolutionary and new. It was a proper, world-changing, epoch-making crisis. It changed everything—industry, society, politics, international relations, nature. However, it might be wise to keep our hyperbolic emotions in check and view the pandemic through a more thoughtful and nuanced perspective. For me, as a teacher of ethics, I have been greatly encouraged by the increasing interest that students have shown in philosophical topics as they came of age during a global pandemic. I hope that most people have become more thoughtful as they reflect on the fundamental life changes wrought by the pandemic and increase their awareness of the ethical dimension of life.

Fortunately, philosophers have been studying ethical behavior—as Socrates said, *how we ought to live*—for a very long time. They have asked for thousands of years, "How should I live ethically with my family, my friends, my neighbors, my community, my country, and the world as a whole? And how should I live as myself? How should I be the best me I can be?" These questions needed to be addressed before the onset of COVID-19, but they are no less important to consider right now as we prepare for the inevitable outbreak of the next global pandemic.

---

[3] See the CDC for constantly updated data about COVID-19. These figures come from the CDC's COVID Data Tracker Portal at https://www.cdc.gov/coronavirus/2019-ncov/covid-data/covid-view/index.html

[4] Many sites offer statistics about the pandemic, updated daily. Johns Hopkins University provides particularly effective data and visualizations on COVID-19 mortality. See https://coronavirus.jhu.edu/data/mortality

At its heart, this book is meant to help you think through questions about ethics and pandemics in a patient and careful way—without lapsing into noisy extremes.

Hamburg, Germany   Andrew Sola
April 2023

Acknowledgments

Since this book has been developed over several decades teaching philosophy and ethics courses, I would like to thank my students at the University of East Anglia, Loyola University Chicago, University of Maryland Global Campus, as well as the FOM University of Applied Sciences for sharing their unique perspectives on the subject matter. This book would never have been written without the lifelong support of my parents and the care of my wife, who is the most patient and gracious pandemic-lockdown companion a husband could desire. Also, I would like to thank the staff and my colleagues on the board of directors at Hamburg's German-American Institute, the Amerikazentrum, e. V., who have given me a happy harbor to explore the interdisciplinary subjects that appear throughout the text. Finally, I am grateful to Springer Nature's editors and reviewers, who provided superb guidance throughout the research and writing process.

Contents

About the Author

Andrew Sola earned his Ph.D. from the University of East Anglia in Norwich, England. From 2004 to 2018, he was Professor of Philosophy and English at the University of Maryland Global Campus, where he taught philosophy, ethics, and English at a variety of locations in the UK, Italy, and Germany. His publications include scholarly articles on military ethics as well as philosophy. He is the co-author with PGA Professional Bruce Loome of *The Philosophical Golfer*, a two-volume history of philosophy. He is currently Professor of Business English at the FOM University of Applied Sciences in Hamburg, Germany, where he also teaches business ethics. He is a member of the board of Hamburg's German-American Institute, the Amerikazentrum, where he produces the interdisciplinary podcast, The Trans-Atlanticist.

Abbreviations

AIDS	Acquired immune deficiency syndrome
BIS	Behavioral immune system
CDC	Centers for Disease Control and Prevention (US)
COVAX	COVID-19 Global Vaccine Access Program (UN)
COVID	Coronavirus disease
DNI	Office of the Director of National Intelligence (US)
DOD	Department of Defense (US)
DOJ	Department of Justice (US)
DOT	Department of Transportation (US)
EPA	Environmental Protection Agency (US)
EUA	Emergency use authorization
FDA	Food and Drug Administration (US)
FOMO	Fear of missing out
GAVI	Global Alliance for Vaccines and Immunization
GNI	Gross national income
HHS	Department of Health and Human Services (US)
HIV	Human immunodeficiency virus
ICU	Intensive care unit
ISIS	Islamic State in Iraq and Syria
MERS	Middle Eastern respiratory syndrome
NHS	National Health Service (UK)
PPE	Personal protective equipment
QALY	Quality-adjusted life year
SARS	Severe acute respiratory syndrome
SEYLL	Standard expected years of life lost
STD	Sexually transmitted disease
TRIPS	Trade-Related Aspects of Intellectual Property Rights
UN	United Nations
UNICEF	United Nations Children's Fund

VSL	Value of a statistical life
WHO	World Health Organization
WTO	World Trade Organization
YOLO	You only live once

Chapter 1
An Introduction to Ethics and Pandemics

1.1 A Note on the Main Title

The COVID-19 pandemic has transformed all of our lives to such an extent that no single book will ever be able to capture its complexity. This book acknowledges the complexity of this life-changing epoch by attempting to embrace as many perspectives as possible. It strives for openness and interdisciplinary dialogue. It is open to diverse points of view, open to different ethical systems, and open to a wide variety of academic disciplines. The main title, *Ethics and Pandemics*, is meant to capture this open approach. The word *and* suggests three broad approaches to exploring the subject: ethics for, in, and of pandemics.

Ethics for Pandemics
This theme addresses the following questions: What ethical systems are helpful *for* pandemic life? What concepts are useful *for* pandemic living? How can I live a good life during a pandemic? These questions are for people as people, not as healthcare professionals or bioethicists, but for people as neighbors, citizens, students, colleagues, family members, and friends. In many respects, this theme cannot be separated from the general question of how we should live our lives when a pandemic is *not* raging. Indeed, are there lessons that the pandemic teaches us about how we ought to behave in "normal" times? Should there be differences? Are there different, higher standards of behavior for pandemic life? Or is a good person a good person in any and all circumstances? How do we define this good person?

Ethics in Pandemics
This theme addresses the question: How are long-standing philosophical and ethical concepts, theories, and problems revealed *in* pandemics? Having taught philosophy for 20 years, I was struck in 2020 by how quickly the subject of ethics came to the fore. People who rarely contemplated complex ethical problems—such as resource scarcity, compulsory vaccination, healthcare equity, and the balance between

A. Sola, *Ethics and Pandemics*, Springer Series in Public Health and Health
Policy Ethics, https://doi.org/10.1007/978-3-031-33207-4_1

personal freedom and the public good—began to take a keen interest in these rather discipline-specific topics. In many respects, COVID-19 sparked an ethical reawakening in the broader public. For this, we can all be grateful. In one sense, then, the pandemic strengthened ethical discourse in general. After all, there is nothing like a crisis to make us reexamine our lives, our beliefs, our behaviors, and our attitudes. Long-standing ethical problems come to the surface during pandemics, making ethics revealed *in* pandemics another key theme of this book.

Ethics of Pandemics
The book is not focused exclusively on living a good life during a pandemic nor on the ethical dilemmas revealed in pandemics, since it also focuses on the ethics *of* pandemics, a specialized subject suited for public health authorities, political scientists, policy makers, medical professionals, as well as students in these fields. This theme, therefore, addresses a more subject-specific question: How should medical professionals and policy makers craft ethical policies to manage pandemics? These are the people who make life-and-death medical decisions and craft pandemic management policies on a daily basis. This theme is also important for students who might be interested in pursuing a career in healthcare, so they can better understand theoretical and practical approaches to crafting ethical policies when managing a pandemic.

1.2   The Importance of Interdisciplinary Perspectives

We have already seen in the discussion above that the concept of ethics *and* pandemics cannot be fully understood through the lens of a single academic discipline such as philosophy, hence the subtitle: *Interdisciplinary Perspectives on COVID-19 and Future Pandemics*. Interdisciplinary perspectives allow one to gather information from a variety of fields, providing a fuller picture of the ethical problems raised by the pandemic. Twenty interdisciplinary perspectives appear throughout this text (see Table 8.1 for a full list). Here are some examples:

Medicine and Public Health
Obviously, a book about pandemics will dive into the fields of medicine and public health. For example, we know that viruses can spread much more easily in a globalized, highly interconnected world, in which an infected human on one continent can hop on a plane and transfer the virus to another continent in a matter of hours. No one has really suggested that we completely restrict travel to other countries (although countries like New Zealand, Japan, China, and Australia implemented very stringent travel rules for both foreigners and their own citizens). So, is this form of globalization a public health problem? In the future, should we continue our carefree world travel despite the dangers that it entails? Should travelers be screened not only for COVID-19 but also for HIV/AIDS, TB, and other infectious diseases as some countries have required in the past (see the section on HIV/AIDS in Chap. 6 of this book)? Although this is not a specialized book for highly specialized medical

professionals, there will be passages to help you expand your knowledge of COVID-19 and other historical pandemics.

History
COVID-19 was neither the first pandemic nor will it be the last. So what can past pandemics teach us about both COVID-19 as well as future pandemics? In the subsequent chapters, there will be a discussion of a historical pandemic, namely, typhoid, smallpox, the Black Death, HIV/AIDS, and polio. I'll briefly note here that our modern concept of the nation state with its public health institutions is directly connected to the Black Death as is the concept of quarantine (from *quaranta giorni* or 40 days in Italian). It is worth reminding ourselves that the development of human societies over time—the creation of our nations, governments, laws, and institutions—is deeply intertwined with our experience of battling horrific pandemics.

Economics
The COVID-19 pandemic had profound effects on the global economy. It also transformed industries and changed the nature of how we work. However, the field of economics helps us understand how the illness is treated, how healthcare systems are designed, how vaccine research is funded and monetized, and how vaccines are distributed to both the rich and the poor. Although economic questions are raised throughout the book, Chap. 4 on utilitarianism focuses heavily on the question: Given the fact that resources (money, ventilators, ICU stations, doctors, etc.) are finite, what is the ethical way to allocate them? As we prepare to face the next global pandemic, have we committed enough resources to build pandemic-resilient economies and healthcare systems?

Evolutionary Sciences
The evolutionary sciences help us to understand characteristics of the human body and the origins of human behavior, such as disease-avoidance strategies, the emotions of disgust and shame, and other impulses. The discipline provides a scientific basis for philosophical questions about human nature. Are humans essentially selfish or altruistic? Are we driven primarily by reason or biology? Evolutionary biology and psychology provide some useful frameworks for explaining human nature, vaccine skepticism, and mechanisms of social control during a pandemic, which are discussed in Chap. 2.

Political Science
As I argue throughout this book, pandemics are as much of a political phenomenon as they are a public health phenomenon, for they raise fundamental questions about the relationship between the individual and society. COVID-19 challenged us with a number of deep, fundamental, and painful political questions: To what extent should we sacrifice individual liberties in the name of pandemic control? Does compulsory vaccination violate our civil rights? What entities should have the power to determine pandemic controls, public health authorities, local governments, and national governments? These questions are raised regularly throughout the text, but Chap. 5 on the social contract theory deals with them extensively. In short, the

discipline of political sciences forces us to ask if our societies are robust enough to withstand the next global pandemic.

Climate Science and the Environment

COVID-19 has deflected attention from another, potentially deadlier, crisis facing human beings and the planet: climate change. If climate change is an existential threat, then no book about ethics can avoid talking about it. Even before COVID-19, scientists indicated that human activity—such as the general degradation of natural areas, the illegal wildlife trade, and the encroachment of humans into the wild— made pandemics much more likely. So, sure, being kinder to the natural world will help us prevent pandemics. However, should we protect the environment *only* in order to prevent pandemics? Or are there other compelling ethical reasons to do so?

As stated earlier, no single point-of-view is adequate for understanding the complexities of the COVID-19 pandemic or any other past or future one. These interdisciplinary perspectives are meant to provide openings for students with diverse interests to engage with the subject. Indeed, students pursuing any course of study— from history to political science and from medicine to business—can find places in the book to apply their own specialized knowledge. Each new perspective will add to the richness of the pandemic conversation. By no means am I suggesting that the perspectives that I chose in this book are the only ones that ought to be pursued. For example, art or literature or religion could also provide a valuable lens through which to understand pandemics. Faced with the endless possibilities, I chose the ones with which I am most comfortable. However, I would encourage students and scholars to explore those possibilities in their future studies since this book provides a framework for further interdisciplinary pandemic research.

It is also important to note that the book is written for a broad audience of conscientious people whose interest in ethics—how to be a good person—was awakened by COVID-19. But it is also written for people who are concerned about our preparedness for the next inevitable global pandemic. For you as a reader, remember that the discipline of ethics has always had a profound influence on our understanding of the weighty issues raised simply by being a thinking person living on earth. So, in turning to the discipline of ethics, students will learn that the issues we are grappling with every day are not new. Indeed, they have been pondered for millennia. Perhaps we can take some comfort in the fact that our pain and sorrow, as well as our hopes for a better future, have been shared by generations before us and will be experienced by generations yet to come.

Lastly, the reality of living through a pandemic also requires putting the pandemic itself to the fore. Pandemics force us to acknowledge the ethical dimension of life in unique ways. COVID-19 increased our interest in "the right thing to do." Furthermore, the discipline of ethics helps us to think more clearly about the issues that pandemics awaken in ourselves. During a pandemic, what are our obligations to our family, our neighbors, our friends, and strangers halfway around the world? And what are our obligations to ourselves? Well, if the pandemic has forced you to ask yourself these questions, then the long history of ethics is a great place to begin to find answers.

1.3   Structure and Method of the Book

The book combines theory with practice—ethical theory with lived practice. It presents you with the key themes in the history of ethics. However, unlike other philosophical books, it applies the themes to problems that you—the next generation of leaders—will face. It engages you in a dialogue and asks you to develop a set of values and principles that will form a firm foundation for your decision-making in the present and in the future. This process-driven approach is not new to philosophy. Teachers might recognize it as a Socratic dialogue, Hegel might call it the dialectical development of Spirit (*Geist*), Marx might call it *Praxis*, Heidegger might call it the Conversation, and the Pragmatists might call it the Pragmatic Method. These precursors are important, but our way of understanding the world needs to be renewed with each generation—with each war, depression, earthquake, tsunami, hurricane, plague, and pandemic—and there is no time more pressing than now to renew and reinvent the philosophical conversation. After all, this conversation defines our humanity.

After this introductory chapter and Chap. 2, which examines assumptions about human nature, each of Chaps. 3 through 7 introduces you to one major ethical theory; then, you will be encouraged to apply the theory to the real world of this pandemic. There are five chapters that cover the following theories:

- Kantian Deontology
- Utilitarianism
- Social Contract Theory
- Ethical Egoism
- Virtue Ethics

Throughout each chapter, you will be introduced to various interdisciplinary perspectives that will help you apply the ethical theory to the pandemic through the lens of a specific academic discipline.

As you work through each chapter, you will be encouraged to begin formulating your own ethical theory by evaluating the strengths and weaknesses of each moral theory. Also, you will be asked to decide which key values are the most important for your own life. For example, should animals be included in your moral community? Should there be exceptions to moral rules? Should there be a clear separation between public ethics (the law) and private ethics (personal morality)?

In the final chapter in Sect. 8.4, you will be given the opportunity to join your own assessments of the theories with your own core values in order to create your own theory of ethics—let's call it "My Ideal Ethical Theory." This theory will provide a firm foundation on which to base ethical decisions throughout your life.

Afterward, in Sect. 8.5, you will be offered guidance about how to formulate your own ethical system for public health and pandemic management.

I hope this book will serve as a guide to help you navigate the complexities of the problems facing the world in the present and in the future. At the end of the book, you will have a strong sense of your own values, which will serve as an anchor for many problems you may face in life.

1.4   Using the Anchor of Ethics to Understand Past, Present, and Future Pandemics

It is important to bear in mind that the strategies, concepts, and theories used by politicians and health authorities to create policies that manage (or mismanage) pandemics have been around for a very long time. For example, debates about mandatory quarantine go back at least to the Black Death (see Chap. 5), when armed soldiers were stationed outside of homes to prevent the infected families from flight, a policy that was essentially a death sentence for everyone in the home even if they had not contracted the disease. Another example would be the thorny problem of resource allocation, which does not merely touch upon pandemic management—for example, the allocation of oxygen and ventilators during COVID-19 or access to antiretroviral drugs for HIV patients—but wider issues of resource inequality when it comes to even more basic and timeless issues like access to shelter, fresh water, and food.

In a certain respect, there is no original thinking to be done about ethical theories related to any specific catastrophe, such as COVID-19, a drought in California, a war in Asia, a famine in Africa, or global climate change. However, with each new crisis, the *specific* features of the crisis change. Is it a localized crisis or a global crisis? Does it affect the young or the old, men or women, Asians or Africans, gay or straight? How easily can the spread be contained? What specific measures are needed to control the spread? Do those measures infringe upon the basic rights of citizens? What resources are needed to save as many lives as possible? If resources are scarce, who should be saved first?

None of these questions is easy to answer. Fortunately, ethics provides a *general* theoretical framework to address all of these *specific* issues. I would further argue that ideas about pandemic management that are not anchored in theory risk being swept away by the specifics of every new crisis that comes our way. This book focuses heavily on the five major ethical theories for this very reason: to serve as an anchor to help us understand past pandemics, to provide analysis of COVID-19, and to prepare for future pandemics.

And this is also a point where you—conscientious and caring students, citizens, friends, and human beings—have an extremely important role to play. Perhaps one lesson that COVID-19 taught is that each of us, as individuals in a community, plays an important role in pandemic management. We can—through our carelessness, ignorance, or selfishness—infect other people. But we can also prevent infections in ourselves and others through adopting different behaviors. To my mind, this is an important bedrock of ethics: personal choice.

And the consequences of personal choice extend far beyond our potentially trivial decisions to wash our hands thoroughly or wear masks properly. Indeed, what are the decisions of presidents and prime ministers to open and close borders and businesses if not personal choices? Of course, these choices affect the lives of many more people than our private hygiene decisions, but still they are personal choices—to allow some to die and others to live, to send some vaccines to one country but none to another, to give the ventilator to a child but not to a grandpa.

In between the highest political level of shutting down the economy and the lowest personal level of washing one's own hands are countless additional levels of choice that are extremely significant. During COVID-19, the personal choices of university presidents and school principals to reopen classrooms had profound effects on the health of communities. Restaurant and bar owners made personal choices to decide to what extent they would protect their staff and customers.

Although this book is addressed primarily toward students and readers without a broad understanding of general ethics, I know not only that you are currently making personal choices that affect others but also that you *will* make choices in the future that will have profound consequences. You will be the leaders facing crises in the future. Although the specifics of a future crisis might be different from COVID-19, I hope that the general framework of ethics, which this book provides, will serve as a secure anchor for the storms yet to come.

1.5   A Note on the Politicization of COVID-19

It is perhaps no longer possible to discuss the COVID-19 pandemic without being dragged into political controversy. Mask-wearing was politicized, vaccines were politicized, lockdowns were politicized, and even declarations that the pandemic has ended were politicized. Therefore, it is important to explain some reasons for the politicization as well as my own approach to the topic.

First, it should be obvious by now that the COVID-19 pandemic was not simply a medical circumstance divorced from political, social, and historical factors. Consider, for example, what it means for the pandemic to be "over." First of all, who is vested with the authority to declare that a pandemic is over? The WHO, politicians, epidemiologists, you, or me? No one seems to know. I certainly don't know. And how do we define the end point? With a disease like smallpox, it was fairly easy to identify the end point. The last known case was discovered in Somalia in 1977, and the WHO proclaimed smallpox to be eradicated in 1980. If a new case of smallpox were to occur, then the eradication claim would be factually false, and we would presumably set about eradicating it once and for all. With other diseases, such a precise and objectively identifiable end point might never come. Consider, for example, HIV/AIDS, which still affects millions of people, and polio, which is reemerging in places that were thought to be free from it. The COVID-19 pandemic further complicated the problem of defining an end point. Politicians like Boris Johnson and Joe Biden said at various times that the pandemic was ending or, indeed, had ended. At exactly the same time those declarations were being made, millions of people remained in lockdown in China. Since it appears that COVID-19 will not be eradicated, the end of the pandemic will be defined and redefined from a variety of political, scientific, and social perspectives; furthermore, it is safe to predict that declarations about the precise point when the pandemic ended will continue to be fervently disputed.

The second reason for the politicization of the pandemic comes from something seemingly as harmless as the careless use of language. In ethics, scholars deploy a useful distinction to help identify two primary uses of language that often are confused: *descriptive* language and *normative* (or prescriptive) language. Descriptive language simply describes phenomena. For example, *some people believe that abortion is immoral* and *other people believe that abortion is not immoral* are descriptive uses of language. Normative language, on the other hand, tells us how we ought to behave and what we should believe. For example, *you should not have an abortion* is clearly a normative statement. But a statement like *abortion is immoral* is tricky. At first glance, it seems to be descriptive because of the use of the word *is* (compare it to statements like *the earth is round* or *two plus two is four*); however, *abortion is immoral* is really a normative statement masquerading as a descriptive statement because immorality presupposes the normative idea that *something should not be done*. It is extremely important to recognize these complicated uses of language, especially when dealing with controversial subjects related to pandemics.

Consider the imperative sentence: *follow the science*. The phrase was often used in pandemic policy debates both to shame critics of public health advice and also to criticize pandemic policies requiring masking, lockdowns, and vaccination. The phrase suggests that anyone who objects to advice from scientists is somehow anti-science. However, a student of ethics sees a great deal of confusion in the use of the phrase *follow the science*. First, it is grammatically a normative statement; it commands that you *should* follow the science. Second, it presupposes that science is a normative pursuit, even though the activity of science doesn't actually tell us what we *should* do. Science might tell us what can be done, but it never tells us that we *should* do it. For example, science tells us that nuclear fission is possible and shows us how to make it happen, but it does not tell us that we should build nuclear weapons let alone use them to destroy people. Similarly, science might tell us that COVID-19 is spread via respiratory droplets, but it never tells us how we should behave once we have that information. I would suggest that science is best understood as a descriptive pursuit, a process of accumulating knowledge. Ethics, on the other hand, is a normative pursuit, a process of determining whether or not we should do one thing and not another. In short, the phrase *follow the science* confuses descriptive and normative uses of language, and deploying it in pandemic debates is counterproductive.

There is a second confusion in the use of language that has further inflamed political divisions about the subject. Some have insisted that pandemics should be understood exclusively as a scientific phenomenon; however, pandemics are experienced by real people living their real lives, so they are as much sociopolitical events as scientific ones. Regarding the use of the word *science* in pandemic policy debates, it is therefore of utmost importance to distinguish between science as a process (i.e., the scientific method) and science as an instrument of political power (i.e., the enactment of public health restrictions).

Oftentimes, these two concepts become confused in public debate. For example, at the start of the pandemic, the CDC changed its advice about masking multiple times. First, masks were deemed to be ineffective and then effective; afterward only a certain type of mask was deemed to be effective, but since supply was scarce masks were to be reserved for frontline health workers (Schulman, 2022). Eventually, restrictive mask mandates were enacted, but the science about the effectiveness of masks kept changing over time (as you would expect because science is a process of revising errors and perfecting knowledge). As the science evolved, critics of masking attacked both *science* and scientists, arguing that mask mandates were an authoritarian overreach. However, these critics weren't really attacking science as such, but the way in which immature science became often-restrictive public policy. Defenders of public health officials then argued that the anti-mask brigade was afraid of *science*. This is not necessarily an accurate characterization of their objections because anti-maskers were afraid of and angry with science being used as an instrument of political power. What happened here—and all sides can be accused of misusing the word *science*—was a slippage between the concept of science as a process and science as a system of authority.

I would suggest that there is a virtuous middle ground in these positions. First, people should use the term *science* with care. Also, it may be appropriate to criticize scientists for claiming to know more than they do; furthermore, it may be appropriate to criticize flawed policies drawn from immature science. However, it is also appropriate to recognize, first, that science does evolve and that public health officials might give advice that proves to be inaccurate or faulty at a certain moment in time, and, second, that pandemic policies will evolve along with the science.

Nevertheless, at this point in history, it seems unlikely that one can depoliticize any pandemic-related topic. As long as there are these two linguistic confusions between (1) science as a descriptive pursuit and science as a normative pursuit and (2) science as a process and science as an instrument of political power, tensions will persist.

As you read this text, you might be tempted to extrapolate my own beliefs about the COVID-19 pandemic and paint me as a liberal or conservative or whatever and thereby find reasons to discredit me or support me. However, I have done my level best throughout this text to avoid categorical statements about right and wrong, to avoid critique of political parties or any other group, and to avoid pronouncements on moral or immoral pandemic policies. Indeed, my role in this book—which is the same as my role in the classroom—is not to tell you what is right and wrong. My role is to provide a framework for you to learn about the five major ethical theories and then build your own robust and mature sense of ethics independently from my personal point of view.

In short, the book will be a success if you forget about me as an author and focus on the ideas of the philosophers that are presented. To that end, I have indicated where I am providing an objective exposition of philosophers and their concepts and where I am providing my own subjective analysis. Of course, I do have my own views on ethics and pandemics which I refrain from discussing until the final chapter. However, remember that my general attitude, which I share with my students in the classroom, is this: In an ethics class, it is not important *what* you think, but *how* you think. Some of my students will never be convinced that I grade their papers with a relentless focus on fairness and control of my own biases (and some would reject the concept of objective critiques anyway). Anyway, as you read this book, you will slowly begin to realize that I do avoid taking a stand on issues, preferring instead to illuminate the strengths and weaknesses of a number of positions and then to work beyond them. (There is more on this dialectical methodology below.)

In sum, there is no place for political dogma in ethics or pandemics. Ethical issues are often so complicated that they defy simple solutions. Indeed, if ethical dilemmas were simple to solve, they wouldn't be dilemmas at all. So the more we all focus on intellectual nuance, the better off we will be. Ethics provides the perfect way to develop a richer, broader, and deeper understanding of our complex world. If I do have one dogmatic view that you can find me guilty of, it is this: I strongly believe that the more people think about ethics in general, the better the world will be in the long run.

1.6 Guidelines for Students

Before we jump in, it is important to understand some of the broad philosophical positions of the book, namely, the straitjacket of names, dialectical thinking, the limits of knowledge, and Bloom's taxonomy of knowledge.

The Straitjacket of Names
An important first step is to give yourself permission to be a free and unencumbered thinker. Specifically, the book requires that you break out of "the straitjacket of names." What does this mean? Many view the current state of the intellectual climate in the United States, Europe, and the rest of the world as being counterproductive because of an undue focus on the power of oppositional name-pairs, such as Republican-Democrat, conservative-liberal, capitalist-socialist, Christian-Muslim, Sunni-Shia, hawk-dove, interventionist-isolationist, globalist-protectionist, extractionist-environmentalist, individualist-collectivist, and us-them. These oppositional name-pairs are easy to master, and they help to organize thoughts and value systems along clear lines. They help to simplify our own views and caricature the views of our opponents. They help us to immediately recognize whom we like and whom we don't like without really thinking about complexity or nuance. A problem arises when we uncritically adopt these names ourselves and choose to live our lives based on the simplicities expressed by them.

However, the continual use of these oppositional name-pairs in language only inflames differences in reality. Instead of promoting dialogue, the straitjacket of names promotes monologue. Instead of promoting productive discussion, the strait-jacket of names promotes entrenchment and isolation. The outcome is stagnation, stale thinking, and a lack of progress.

Many people who embrace their own name-category view maintaining the principles associated with that name-category to be honorable, principled, and virtuous. Sticking to one's values is a commendable trait. However, there is a point at which one must acknowledge that there are alternative points of view, views that are not merely ridiculous, wrong, or stupid. Perhaps this tenacity to hold to one's own straitjacket at all costs reveals a yearning for authenticity, a state that is difficult to attain in a hyperactive social media environment that tends toward inauthenticity. However, authenticity can be achieved through alternate means, such as through practicing the virtues of patience, tolerance, and intellectual bravery (see Chap. 7). As the first important step in this book, therefore, you are encouraged to abandon your name- straitjacket and embrace the freedom of starting anew, with a blank slate.

Dialectical Thinking

In his seminal book *The Phenomenology of Spirit* (1807), G. W. F. Hegel discussed the progression of thought in human history. He called the process the dialectic. The word is a technical term, but it is easy to understand. Hegel believed that human thought—and truth itself—developed along historical lines according to a triple stage of thesis-antithesis-synthesis. In any stage of history, people hold idea A to be true (thesis), but it is opposed to not-A (antithesis). This contradiction cannot survive, so a new idea has to be conceived, an idea that *supersedes* or overcomes or moves beyond the existing contradiction (synthesis). The new truth that is created represents the defeat of the old contradiction and the existence of a new harmony. However, Truth for Hegel is historical. The new thesis is opposed by a new antithesis, creating an opposition that must yet again be resolved in a new synthesis. As these contradictions are worked out, Truth eventually unfolds, and human beings, Hegel believed, would eventually arrive at a stage of Absolute Truth.

Hegel was perhaps overly optimistic that Truth would develop over the course of human history and that there could be a time when no contradictions would remain. Indeed, he could scarcely conceive of the fact that the environment in which we live is a precursor to thought itself, and perhaps the greatest contradiction of our time is that between human beings and the environment. The new philosophy of environmentalism is powerful because it reminds us that thought cannot take place if we do not have an environment in which we thinkers can actually exist. As such, sustaining the environment can be thought of as a primary concern for all people who are concerned with philosophy itself.

More importantly, Hegel reminds us that a strong intellect should seek out contradictions and attempt to resolve them. As you read this book, you should be thinking about all of the thorny contradictions that face the world today. However, rather than choosing a side, you should attempt to find the common ground that allows for synthesis[1]; you should be searching for the insights that might help us move beyond simple contradictions.

For example, many people see a fundamental conflict between (1) shutting down the economy during an epidemic, which has serious short- and long-term disadvantages but saves lives, and (2) letting society operate almost as normal, which reduces economic damage but increases the death toll. This is certainly a thorny problem. How can one balance the interests of public health with economic well-being? Are they really even separate issues? Rather than picking a side, the dialectical thinker tries to find a position beyond the existing opposition.

Another example involves politics. The opposition between left and right has become so rigid, so entrenched, that it is difficult for many people to move beyond. Rather than picking a side, the dialectical thinker attempts to find a synthesis.

Yet another example involves international relations. The opposition between isolationism and interventionism frames many security situations in black-and-white terms. However, rather than picking a side, the dialectical thinker seeks a synthesis that moves beyond the simple contradiction. Another primary goal of this book is to create a critical mass of thinkers who are willing to seek out new syntheses and move beyond the stale contradictions that constrict our thinking today.

The Limits of Knowledge
Another important principle of the book is humility with respect to our claims to knowledge. In the academic discipline of philosophy, the term *epistemology* refers to the study of knowledge itself. What do we know? What don't we know? How can we be certain that we know what we know? What are the real limits of our knowledge? The discipline itself is quite complex, but ex-US Secretary of Defense Donald Rumsfeld explained the problems of knowledge with uncanny clarity: "There are known-knowns, known-unknowns, and unknown-unknowns."[2] Some ridiculed him for his comment, but he was touching upon one of the most basic epistemological problems that we face.

Perhaps Secretary Rumsfeld was intentionally echoing Socrates, who skewered one of his philosophical opponents in Plato's *Apology* (c. 4th C. BCE) by saying, "For he knows nothing, and thinks that he knows. I neither know nor think that I know. In this latter particular, then, I seem to have slightly the advantage of him" (para. 7). A developed intellect understands what one knows and what one does not know. In other words, a developed intellect understands the limits of knowledge. Having an overly confident view of one's own knowledge leads to real problems in the real world. Indeed, one could write a complete history of human civilization around the central theme of catastrophes caused by people not knowing the limits of

---

[1] Note that the word *synthesis* is preferred to the term *compromise*. *Compromise* implies both sides in an argument "winning" some points but "losing" others. *Synthesis*, on the other hand, implies the creation of a new position beyond winning and losing, a position that has advanced beyond the original disagreement.

[2] Rumsfeld, during a press conference at the US Department of Defense in February 2002, was responding to a request from a journalist to provide evidence that Saddam Hussein had supplied WMD to terrorists.

their knowledge. The term I use for this phenomenon is *epistemological overreach*. We have often thought we knew things that we did not know. We only realized when it was too late that we did not know what we did not know. Consider, for example, the unforeseen negative effects associated with acid rain, mercury, greenhouse gas emissions, thalidomide, smoking, nuclear fallout, or, say, gain-of-function research in virology labs.

COVID-19 highlighted this problem considerably, and epistemological problems proliferated as quickly as the virus itself. Yet another positive result of COVID-19 was that many people became much more interested in the fusty academic discipline of epistemology. We not only began to ask factual questions like, "Where did the virus come from?" but also epistemological ones like, "*How do we know* where viruses come from?" We asked, "What is the best way to reduce the infection rate?" and also, "*How do we know* this or that measure reduces the infection rate?" We asked, "How many people are infected?" and also, "*How do we know* that we can even count how many people are infected when many people aren't tested and many more are asymptomatic and tests are at times unreliable?" At their essence, these questions are philosophical questions—epistemological questions about the nature of knowledge itself.

In the book, I do my best to indicate the limits of knowledge where appropriate. After all, I am going through a historical learning process too, and this book can only represent facts available to me at this moment. I also attempt to sketch the limits of scientific, economic, and political knowledge more broadly. It is important that you also recognize the limits of your knowledge and embrace those limits, not in order to criticize yourself but in order to develop a firm foundation for your knowledge.

Bloom's Taxonomy of Knowledge
The book guides you through this process because there are no quick fixes or easy answers to the problems that the planet faces. Patient thinking is required. Let us, then, remind ourselves of *how thinking works*. This is admittedly a vague philosophical statement, but we can make it more concrete by remembering Bloom's taxonomy of knowledge. Benjamin Bloom (1913–1999) was an American educational psychologist who helped to develop a highly influential system of explaining and categorizing the objectives of education. He divided learning into these widely cited categories, presented here in order of lower to higher:

- Knowledge—The ability to recall facts
- Comprehension—The ability to understand the importance of facts
- Application—The ability to apply knowledge to different scenarios
- Analysis—The ability to make logical inferences based on facts and the ability to provide specific evidence to support generalizations
- Synthesis—The ability to take different facts and different theories and then combine them in new ways in order to develop new and different conclusions
- Evaluation—The ability to defend subjective judgments with logic and research as well as the ability to reconcile conflicting points of view

This book works on all levels of the taxonomy, but it focuses on the "higher" thinking functions, namely, application, analysis, synthesis, and evaluation. These functions are important for leaders and decision-makers to master.

This book introduces you to the five main ethical theories and then asks you to think through the consequences of those theories by going through the various levels of Bloom's taxonomy. For example, you will learn about the theory of deontology developed by the great German philosopher Immanuel Kant.

- Knowledge: First, you will develop your knowledge of Kant's theory. You should check your mastery of his theory by your ability to explain it to a friend.
- Comprehension: Then, you should be able to show your comprehension by putting his theory in the wider context of philosophical history and different ethical systems.
- Application: Next, you should apply Kant's theory to a variety of dilemmas (e.g., lying versus telling the truth, helping versus not helping strangers, etc.), including ethical problems that have arisen since his death, problems that he could not have conceived of (atomic weapons, stem-cell research, environmental degradation, drone warfare, etc.).
- Analysis: As you apply Kant's theory, you should be able to construct logical arguments and provide specific evidence to support your applications.
- Synthesis: Next, you should be able to synthesize Kant's ideas by connecting his theory to other theories you have learned about in the book.
- Evaluation: Lastly, you should be able to evaluate Kant's theory by judging both the strengths and weaknesses of it. How do his ideas relate to your own knowledge and experience? Does his theory meet all of your criteria for a solid ethical theory? Why or why not?

You can perform a final check on your grasp of the information and the usefulness of the theory by asking the following pragmatic question: What difference would it make? This question asks you to reflect on the theories you are reading. For example, regarding Immanuel Kant's theory, you should ask yourself the following questions: What difference would it make if I were to believe Kant's theory and implement it in my daily life and decision-making process? How would I have made different decisions in the past if I used Kant? For issues I am facing right now, what difference would it make for me to make a Kantian decision? How would I make different decisions in the future if I were to follow Kant's theory? If I am creating pandemic policies, how would I create them to align with Kantian values? You will learn more about this pragmatic line of questioning in Chap. 8.

1.7 Additional Suggestions for Doing Philosophy

This introduction has provided a broad framework for the pedagogical theory behind the practice. We have already discussed the importance of four key points:

1. Reject the straitjacket of names: Try to approach all of the ideas in this book from an open mind. Start with a blank slate. Read it as a free thinker.
2. Think dialectically: Do your best to try to move beyond simple contradictions, and actively think about ways to move beyond them.
3. Recognize the limits of knowledge: We know a lot, but we also know very little. A careful and mature thinker recognizes the limits of his or her knowledge.
4. Focus on the higher functions in Bloom's taxonomy: Do not settle with mere knowledge and comprehension; try to develop your higher levels of thinking, namely, application, analysis, synthesis, and evaluation.

Here are six additional suggestions to help you more effectively develop your critical thinking skills as you read the book:

5. Remember that understanding precedes criticism: Refrain from passing judgment on ideas before you have fully understood them and fully absorbed them. You may prematurely dismiss ideas that contradict views you have held for a long time. Having negative emotional reactions to ideas that make you feel uncomfortable is natural, but I ask you to be aware of the tendency to reject ideas prematurely. *Defensive reasoning*—the tendency to find reasons to summarily reject ideas that do not conform to our own established worldviews—prevents us from seeing issues clearly and objectively. Your first reaction to many ideas will not be the most measured, so give yourself time to consider every idea patiently and maturely.
6. Remember that philosophy is not always fun: Many people enjoy philosophy, but the enjoyment that philosophy brings is not the same as other enjoyments that provide instant gratification. Oftentimes, only after a long period of confusion and bewilderment will you experience an insight that clarifies many questions and that might be considered enjoyable. These insights, when they come, are exhilarating.
7. Develop a technical vocabulary: You may come across words and phrases in this book that come from a specialized academic discipline. Make sure you spend some time understanding these terms, so you can use them in your own life.
8. Do not seek all the answers: The book raises critical questions and provides strategies for answering them. However, it does not provide definitive answers. The world is too complex for simple, stable, and permanent solutions. Many people have a tendency to seek definitive answers, to seek a worldview that explains all problems, but this book encourages you to be continually on your toes—ready to adapt and adjust to evolving circumstances. So avoid seeking answers that allow you to rest easy.
9. Give yourself permission to change: One fact of life is that our thoughts grow and develop over time, but sometimes it is difficult to acknowledge that we are changing. Our beliefs are very much like habits; they may be good or bad ones. Because we have these habits of thought, it is difficult to break out of them. The first step of growth, then, is to acknowledge those habits, and the second is to give yourself permission to change them.

10. Develop a network of open-minded thinkers with diverse interests and special-
ties: Philosophy is easiest to practice in a community, so make connections with
mature and patient thinkers who are receptive to and knowledgeable about different disciplines. If you prefer quantitative analysis, seek people who prefer
qualitative analysis. If you are an engineer, befriend a musician. If you are an
accountant, befriend a painter. If you are an entrepreneur, befriend a philosopher. Surround yourself with open minds and learn from them.

1.8   Why?

One final question must be addressed openly before departing on this journey:
Why? Why have I written this book and why should you read it? The answers are
very simple:

- The COVID-19 pandemic represented an unprecedented crisis to public health,
the global economy, domestic politics, international relations, and global security; it also changed our thinking and values. However, in every crisis one can
find an opportunity. As we extract ourselves from the crisis and encounter the
new post-COVID world, we have a unique opportunity to reorganize the world
in closer alignment with our values.
- The next global pandemic is waiting for us around the corner and will arrive
much sooner than many of us expect. So how can we increase the resilience of
our societies in order to manage future pandemics better than past ones? This
book attempts to provide some possible paths to prepare for the future.
- If we as a species do not address the great problems facing our planet, we will no
longer be able to ask the question, *why?* If we lose our environment, we will also
lose ourselves. Philosophy itself dies as the livable environment dies.
- If we do not develop a more productive way of working together to solve problems, the future will not be an improvement on the present. One aim of the book
is to reboot our brains, so we can more effectively work with others who have
opposing points of view.
- If we do not create a critical mass of people who are dedicated to improving the
future, then the future will be lost.

Still, we may have some lingering doubts about our ability to shape world events.
As the famous and controversial philosopher Karl Marx (1852) once remarked,
"Man makes his own history, but he does not make it out of the whole cloth; he does
not make it out of conditions chosen by himself, but out of such as he finds close at
hand. The tradition of all past generations weighs like an alp upon the brain of the
living" (para. 2). Just as people have made decisions that have helped to create the
circumstances that we now face, we will make decisions that create the circumstances under which future generations will live. At its heart, this book is also about
decision-making. It is about the considerations you make—consciously or

unconsciously—when making decisions that shape the future and affect future generations.

Let us return to the ideas expressed in Dickens' quotation in the preface: It may be the best of times, or it may be the worst; it may yet be the age of wisdom, or it may become the age of foolishness. Whatever future generations may say about us and the world we have left them, do not forget that we have all played our part in creating that world. Maybe we can make it a better one.

References

Marx, K. (1852). *The eighteenth Brumaire of Louis Bonaparte*. Project Gutenberg. 1998. https://www.gutenberg.org/files/1346/1346-h/1346-h.htm

Plato. (c. 4th C. BCE). *Apology* (B. Jowett, Trans.). Project Gutenberg. 2020. https://www.gutenberg.org/files/1656/1656-h/1656-h.htm

Schulman, A. (2022, August 30). Why many Americans turned on Anthony Fauci. *New York Times*. https://www.nytimes.com/2022/08/30/opinion/why-anthony-faucis-covid-legacy-is-a-failure.html. Accessed 30 Aug 2022.

Chapter 2
Evaluating Assumptions About Human Nature Pre- and Post-COVID-19

2.1 Three Questions About Human Nature

Before COVID-19 swept across the planet, many of us had already established—perhaps unconsciously—our most profound beliefs about the world. These beliefs are based on our *assumptions* about human nature: Human beings are fundamentally good or bad, unselfish or selfish, trustworthy or not. The COVID-19 pandemic provided a convenient laboratory to test these fundamental assumptions.

Perhaps you saw store shelves emptied of toilet paper, flour, sugar, yeast, and wheat. Selfish! And then you saw people donating food and clothing to homeless people and the elderly. Altruistic! Maybe you saw a group of kids intentionally coughing on old people. Evil! And then you saw some other kids singing to pensioners outside of a retirement home in order to lift their spirits. Kind! The wealthy fled to their country homes and yachts. Villains! At the same time, nurses, doctors, postal workers, grocery store clerks, and firefighters went to work every day without personal protective equipment at great risk to themselves. Heroes!

Do these epidemic events confirm or contradict your previous view of humanity? Did COVID-19 alter your beliefs about human nature?

And what about yourself? Being locked down perhaps gave you the opportunity to analyze your own behavior both before and during the crisis. Were you a good person before the crisis? Did you change your behavior?

Our fundamental beliefs often remain hidden even from ourselves, clouded by the disjunction between what we profess to believe and how we actually behave in our day-to-day life. All of us might profess to believe that human beings are fundamentally good and trustworthy, but our habits of behavior in our daily interactions with other people might reveal the opposite. Those daily habits, when examined, reveal our actual core beliefs. They reveal what we really think about ourselves, other human beings, and the world as a whole.

Like all crises, the COVID-19 crisis revealed much about human behavior, and in this section we will explore three questions related to our basic assumptions about human nature:

1. Are human beings selfish and egoistic or unselfish and altruistic?
2. Are humans driven primarily by biological impulses or by reason?
3. Will human beings be forever alienated from each other or do we have the ability to reconcile our religious, social, economic, and political differences?

This chapter introduces you in the broadest possible terms to the fundamental issues that have shaped the development of dominant philosophical systems in Western thought, namely, Kantian deontology, utilitarianism, social contract theory, egoism, and virtue ethics. Those systems, which will be discussed at length in subsequent chapters, are briefly introduced below. In this chapter, it is sufficient to begin to reexamine some of your most basic assumptions about what it means to be a human being.

The framework through which we will analyze these questions comes from the great German idealist philosopher, G. W. F. Hegel, who wrote in his *Philosophy of History* (1831): "To him who looks upon the world rationally, the world in its turn presents a rational aspect." Implied in this comment is this: When we choose to look at the world with a specific point of view, the world will provide us evidence to support that perspective. Hegel's concept here is something like an early form of cognitive bias theory. At any rate, if the world is cunning enough to convince us that our preconceptions are always true, perhaps we need another way to evaluate our preconceptions.

2.2 Egoism Versus Altruism

Many political philosophers in the Western tradition have consistently argued that human beings are essentially bad. For example, the great political theorist Niccolò Machiavelli (1517) asserts in *Discourses on the First Ten Books of Titus Livius*, "They who lay the foundations of a State and furnish it with laws must, as is shown by all who have treated of civil government, and by examples of which history is full, assume that all men are bad, and will always, when they have free field, give loose to their evil inclinations" (III, para. 1). Were he alive today Machiavelli would point to panic-buying and empty store shelves during the COVID-19 pandemic as further proof of our vicious nature.

Machiavelli is known for his pessimism (or realism, depending on your inclinations) regarding human beings, but other philosophers held a similar view. In his seminal work on human beings and government, *Leviathan*, Thomas Hobbes also argued in the seventeenth century that human beings are essentially egotistical creatures who are selfish, greedy, and power-hungry. In his view, the lust for power, the craving of wealth, and the desire for status are the most basic human drives. Without a strong government that moderates these urges, human beings live in a dreary and depressing *state of nature*. Hobbes (1651) writes:

> In such condition, there is no place for industry, because the fruit thereof is uncertain; and consequently no culture of the earth; no navigation, nor use of the commodities that may be imported by sea; no commodious building; no instruments of moving, and removing, such things as require much force; no knowledge of the face of the earth; no account of time; no arts; no letters; no society; and which is worst of all, continual fear, and danger of violent death; and the life of man, solitary, poor, nasty, brutish and short. (XIII, para. 9)

Plenty of modern examples can be provided to support Hobbes' view even before the COVID-19 pandemic. In the absence of strong centralized governments, civilized society breaks down, as one can see after the US-led invasion of Iraq in 2003 and the subsequent ouster of Iraq's Leviathan Saddam Hussein. The ongoing mayhem in Afghanistan, the civil wars in Syria and Libya, the protracted conflict with Boko Haram in Nigeria, and the rise and fall of ISIS or ISIL also indicate the consequences of living life in a society without a government "to overawe them all," as Hobbes says. However, even in countries with strong central governments, such as the United States, civilized life is remarkably fragile. After Hurricane Katrina struck New Orleans in the summer of 2005, law and order swiftly broke down, and citizens resorted to looting and violence. Hobbes would argue that the residents of New Orleans returned to the state of nature, which is the natural state of human beings when they are not overawed by a strong government. Perhaps, COVID-19 provided further evidence to support Hobbes' view.

History provides many examples of both the vicious nature of human beings and also the role that strong centralized governments play in moderating those urges. It seems that human beings are indeed naughty by nature. But Hobbes goes even further. He argues that even when we are living in a "civilized" society, we still behave according to the assumption that people are essentially nasty and untrustworthy. Having taken such a pessimistic view, he insists that he himself is not trying to be pessimistic; he insists he is merely being realistic. He further argues that he is honest enough to publicize his low opinion of human beings, whereas others show their low opinion of humanity in their routine daily behavior. How, then, does the average person behave? Hobbes (1651) notes again in *Leviathan*:

> [...] when going to sleep, he locks his doors; when even in his house he locks his chests; and this when he knows there be laws, and public officers, armed, to revenge all injuries shall be done to him: what opinion he has of his fellow-subjects, when he rides armed; of his fellow-citizens, when he locks his doors; and of his children, and servants, when he locks his chests. Does he not there as much accuse mankind by his actions, as I do by my words? (XIII, para. 10)

We too might claim that we trust in the goodness of our fellow human beings, but we lock the doors to our homes and cars, install surveillance cameras, and hire security companies to guard our valuables; we keep handguns under our pillows, baseball bats and axes under our beds, and rifles in our cars; we treat strangers with suspicion and tell our children not to talk to them. When dealing with work and money, we insist on having contracts—enforceable in courts of law—that hold our fellow human beings to account. Newspapers overflow with stories about the selfish and immoral acquisition of wealth through insider trading, interest rate manipulation, currency exchange collusion, Ponzi schemes, and outright fraud. During the COVID-19 pandemic, greed led unscrupulous people to sell false virus tests, faulty PPE, and quack medicines. Others bought legitimate products and marked up the price to gouge extortionate sums of money from desperate hospitals and governments.

These examples show that greed is perhaps the predominant human vice. White-collar crime cases highlight the basic avariciousness of human beings, and the laws that are meant to prevent and punish financial fraud illustrate the need society has to check the egotistical urges that make up who we really are. Practically the entire legal system—with its armies of lawyers, judges, clerks, police officers, prison guards, wardens, and sheriffs— is a labyrinthine institution created to serve as a check against our uncontrollable desire for wealth, inappropriately gained. The legal system also reveals a basic lack of faith in the reliability and trustworthiness of our fellow human beings—even within the framework of a robust civil society. Hobbes wonders: If we really believed that people are good, why do we have such a gigantic legal system? Laws, he argues, are only proof of our viciousness not our virtue.

Based on the traditional view of humans as being vicious at their core, two important theories have been constructed: social contract theory and egoism. Social contract theory—with its roots in the thought of Hobbes, Locke, and Rousseau—is the predominant tradition that set the foundation for the political world in which we live today (if we live in functioning liberal democracies). It can be partly explained as follows: If human beings are essentially nasty, then a system needs to be put in place to control our base instincts. This system is known as the *government*, whose role is to check egotistical impulses and to provide a framework in which civilized society can flourish. Social contract theory is a political philosophy with a rich and diverse intellectual history, but it also includes a system of ethics; its complexities will be discussed in detail in Chap. 5.

Whereas Hobbes insists that human beings are selfish and egotistical by nature, another branch of philosophers, the egoists, do not make such an assumption. Instead, they argue that human beings have the free choice to be egotistical or altruistic but that it is *morally right* for human beings to pursue their own self-interest exclusively: to be greedy, if that is in their self-interest; to acquire power, if that is in their self-interest; to increase their social status, if that is in their self-interest. Ethical egoists insist that we should always pursue our own self-interest. In the past 60 years, a number of thinkers, particularly Ayn Rand in *The Virtue of Selfishness* (1964), have endorsed this doctrine, and the strengths and weaknesses of this view will be discussed in greater detail in Chap. 6.

Let us, however, return to Hobbes' assertion that human beings are selfish by nature. Indeed, one can provide innumerable examples of egoism, but one can counter each of them with an example of altruistic or selfless behavior. Yes, people may often be evil, but we have unmatched capacities for good as well. Just look at the long list of charities, foundations, and NGOs committed to helping both humans and non-human animals in countless ways. Members of these institutions have dedicated themselves to protecting the environment, educating historically marginalized and underserved people, lifting people out of poverty, fighting injustice, and curing disease. And look at the countless small acts of kindness that are never reported—you, perhaps, donate food to the local food bank or pay your tithe to the church or build homes for the poor or pick up trash at the local park or donate blood to the sick or mentor troubled youth at the local school. As already mentioned, during the COVID-19 pandemic, there were just as many examples of good deeds as bad.

Yet another extremely influential philosophical system has been developed that demands that we not pursue our own self-interest at the expense of others; instead, we should pursue the greatest possible happiness for all, even when doing so goes against our own self-interest. This moral system, utilitarianism, insists that the *telos* or final goal of human beings is to alleviate suffering and simultaneously increase pleasure for both humans and non-human animals alike. All moral, social, and political decisions should be made based on calculations of happiness achieved and suffering eliminated. Utilitarian thinking has profoundly influenced policy decisions that affect every level of society—economic, environmental, and cultural.

Indeed, utilitarian thinking remains the most entrenched mode of thought in the minds of civil servants, policy makers, and politicians before, during, and after the COVID-19 pandemic. How do we allocate scarce resources to maximize benefits? Is it better to give a ventilator to an old person or a young person? How do we measure the suffering caused by an economic shutdown against the happiness gained by saving people's lives? These are weighty matters that will be discussed in greater detail in Chap. 4.

But let us return to the critical question of this section: Are we, then, fundamentally egoistic or altruistic? The evidence does not conclusively prove either side, so perhaps we are somewhere in between. Maybe it depends on our own perspective. Hegel said the world looks back at us rationally if we look at it in a rational way. Maybe the world looks at us selfishly if we look at it in a selfish way; and maybe the world looks at us altruistically if we look at it in an altruistic way.

But what difference would it make if you take a side when making decisions about your own life? The egoism-altruism dichotomy has profound implications on your personal morality and your political views. If you believe people are fundamentally evil, then you may live your life with extreme caution. On a personal level, you will be wary of both strangers and friends. You will seek to preserve your own life, wealth, power, and status at all costs—and at the expense of others. You will only give your time and money to charities if doing so would further your self-interest in some way. Since you have no faith in the kindness of others, you might be what is now called a "prepper." You will have already stockpiled food, water, a medical kit, weapons, ammo, and gold coins in order to be ready for the next breakdown in social order. Understood in this pessimistic way, the COVID-19 pandemic might have been just one of a number of potential crises that you have always been ready and waiting for. On a political level, if you believe people are fundamentally egotistical, then you will support institutions that maintain the status quo and the fragile equilibrium of civilized society—as long as they preserve your self-interest.

So, is this a "bad" way to live your life? Not necessarily. It is the only *reasonable* way to live based on this fundamental view of human nature. Machiavelli and Hobbes would certainly approve.

If, on the other hand, you believe people are fundamentally altruistic, then you may feel an obligation to help your fellow human beings even if helping others is not in your self-interest. After all, if people are fundamentally good, then you would naturally want to help them in their time of need, just as they would help you in your time of need. During a pandemic, you might look after your neighbors, give supplies to the poor, and donate your time and money for the good of the community. If you believe in human altruism, then you may also gravitate toward a utilitarian outlook. On a personal level, you may leave the door to your home unlocked, give to charity, and tell your children not to be afraid of strangers. You will sacrifice your own self-interest for the greater good of others. On a political level, you may seek to reform institutions in order to redress grievances and ensure a just, equitable, and happy life for all human beings.[1]

Is it "good" to live your life believing in the altruism of others? Not necessarily. Perhaps, you may find life more rewarding living this way, but you might also be subject to fraud and abuse if bad people choose to take advantage of you. Furthermore, if you are the only nice person in a community of degenerates, perhaps you are just a fool.

The distinction between altruism and egoism is important, but it is also simplistic. Maybe this dichotomy is not a fruitful one to pursue. Maybe human beings are somewhere in between the two sides, and the most important fact about human nature is that we are *animals who think*. Before addressing the importance of reason, let us assess examples of egoistic and altruistic decision-making during the COVID-19 pandemic.

Box 2.1 Interdisciplinary Perspective #1: Public Health

Using Public Health Statistics to Determine Risk to Self and Others
The CDC (2022a) reports that approximately 75% of COVID-19 deaths are in the 65+ age-group, 21% in the 45–64 age-group, and only 4% in under-45s. As a result of these data, many young people developed a devil-may-care attitude about COVID—partying in large groups, ignoring mask mandates, avoiding vaccines, etc. The Child and Adolescent Behavioral Health Foundation (n.d.) explored some common reasons why the younger generation developed this thought process. First, the statistics clearly show that young people do indeed have a much reduced risk of dying from COVID. Naturally, they would perceive strict limitations on their social lives as disproportionate to their personal risk.

(continued)

---

[1] There is a third option: You could opt to be a "free-rider." After all, if everyone is good, and you choose to be evil, then you could take advantage of all of the good people out there.

FOMO is another reason cited by the young for their questionable behavior. FOMO or fear-of-missing-out refers to the psychological pressure that people put on themselves when they see other people having fun. The FOMO phenomenon is prevalent among Millennials and Gen-Zers—in other words, children who grew up with the Internet, social media, and the constant pressure to compare their own experiences with others through digital media. So, when they saw their friends having fun, oftentimes defying public health orders, they developed FOMO and wanted to have fun themselves.

FOMO connects to another phenomenon with the young: YOLO or the you-only-live-once attitude. Many students were negatively affected by school shutdowns as well as the cancellation of graduations, proms, concerts, and sporting events. These were important life events that they were deprived of, and many reacted with a YOLO attitude. Many important rights-of-passage were taken away from them, so they wanted to experience the joys of life in any way they could.

Many older people, of course, took an opposing view. Regarding the first point, public health officials and parent killjoys remind the younger generation of two things. First, although their risk levels are indeed much reduced, the young are not immune. Many young people died from COVID, and many others who contracted it developed long-COVID. Indeed, Lewis (2021) notes that " 9.8% of children aged 2–11 years and 13% aged 12–16 years reported at least one lingering symptom five weeks after a positive diagnosis" (p. 483). Second, the older generation reminded the younger that they should follow the rules not only to protect themselves but also to protect others by preventing further community spread in general. Young people could infect their parents or grandparents, their elderly friends, or their neighbors. Indeed, I urged my students to be COVID-careful so they did not infect their teachers, namely, me (although some might have actually desired this outcome).

Here we see the egoism-altruism come clearly into focus. Egoists only worry about themselves. Altruists worry about others. Egoists do not wish to sacrifice their own lives and their own potential—after all, we only have one life to live. Altruists believe that personal sacrifice in service of the community is the right thing to do. Egoists remind us that if we spend our whole lives sacrificing our happiness for others, then we are left with no life at all. Altruists disagree.

However, this is not really a black-and-white issue; it's not all or nothing. Of course, there are gray areas. During a pandemic, you could, for example, party with your friends, but then get tested and avoid contact with your grandparents until you know you have not been infected. You could choose to party with a small group of tested friends whom you trust. You could travel, but quarantine. You could only party outside. These decisions came to be defined as the COVID risk budget, which was recommended by many health authorities, including the CDC (2022b), in order to help both the young and the old

(continued)

cope with the stress of not being able to see friends and have fun anymore. According to this model, you should choose to participate in a certain risky activity if and only if you minimize the risk by not participating in others. If you wished to attend a high-risk event, you could still attend, but you would have fewer events in your overall risk budget in the future. A low-risk event of course would change your budget in different ways. The overall idea here was to balance the benefits of social interaction with the risks of infection.

Throughout the COVID-19 pandemic, people were forced to make countless decisions to balance the risk of infection with living a normal life. It is perhaps useful to evaluate your decisions consciously in order to determine where you would put your past behavior on the egoism-altruism spectrum.

Discuss
- **Describe your own thought process about socializing during COVID-19. Would you describe you and your friends as being mostly altruistic or egoistic? Provide examples to support your position.**
- **Generally speaking, should young people sacrifice their own social lives for the benefit of the broader community's health?**
- **From a broader public health perspective, what are some arguments for and against having age-specific pandemic prevention measures? Indeed, is the single demographic category of *age* an appropriate measure for any community-wide public health regulation or would such age-specific regulations constitute age discrimination? Explain your position.**
- **Lastly, is statistical analysis an ethical way to make decisions about how everyone in a certain demographic group should behave during a pandemic?**

2.3 Reason Versus Biology

We have already examined the tension between egoism and altruism, so let us now move to another tension, that between reason, the uniquely human capacity for systematic thought, and biology, the qualities we share with animals. The history of reason and truth—or we might say the history of human thought on the subject of reason and truth—is long and complex. Reason and truth are central themes that run throughout the book. We begin telling the story of reason in Chap. 3, with the great champion of reason, Immanuel Kant. However, in this section, let us focus on whether or not our capacity for reason places us above nature. This question became particularly important during COVID-19 because the pandemic illustrated both our biological helplessness in the face of a zoonotic illness and our human superpower to force nature to bend to our will with the aid of scientific reasoning.

So, is our reasoning capacity simply a product of evolution? Are we, at a fundamental level, simply animals who also, by cosmic coincidence, think? To what extent is human behavior shaped by evolution and biology? Is reason itself a direct consequence of natural selection? Are the mistakes in peoples' lives a consequence of biology, or were they failures of judgment, failures of reason? Is reason actually *Reason*? Is it a superhuman tool that we can use to discover the truth?

Before the Darwinian revolution, Western thinkers consistently placed human beings both in and above the natural world. The Ancient Greeks, particularly Aristotle (384–322 BCE), developed a hierarchical view of humans at the summit of the natural order. In the passage below from *Politics*, he justifies the dominion both of certain men over others and also of human beings over animals (he also assumed, rather problematically, that men were more rational than women and hence superior to women). The critical difference between the two is the capacity to reason. Aristotle (350 BCE) notes:

> For the soul governs the body as the master governs his slave; the mind governs the appetite with a political or a kingly power, which shows that it is both natural and advantageous that the body should be governed by the soul, and the pathetic part by the mind, and that part which is possessed of reason; but to have no ruling power, or an improper one, is hurtful to all. (I, Part 5)

Aristotle here implies that humans are a curious combination of reason and biology, the "kingly power" and the "passionate." The more rational a person is, the more suitable he is to rule; the more animalistic, the more suitable to be ruled. Aristotle's dichotomy has had a profound effect on the development of our basic attitudes about human nature, and his ideas have been used to justify a large number of racist, sexist, and *speciesist* attitudes, all based on the theory that certain people possess a more developed "rational element" than others.

After the Greeks, many Christian thinkers also insisted that humans were at the summit of the natural world because God made humans in his own image and gave them dominion over the earth. In a certain sense, human beings were separate from the biological world. Religious leaders created dogma to support this view, but scholars also pointed to the human capacity for language and thought to prove the supremacy of the human animal. Early Christian thinkers were profoundly influenced by the Aristotelian dichotomy between the rational and animal elements. Human vices (sloth, greed, gluttony) were associated with animalistic tendencies, and the virtues (temperance, courage, justice, prudence) were associated with rational qualities. The virtues coupled with both God's grace and the gift of reason provided mortal sinners the opportunity to achieve eternal life, and these qualities also separated us from our furry friends in the animal kingdom.

Charles Darwin's work on natural selection, first presented in *On the Origin of Species* in 1859, profoundly altered these orthodoxies. After Darwin, it became increasingly difficult to draw such a clear line between human beings and animals (except, of course, if one steadfastly maintains orthodox religious beliefs). In the Darwinian view, humans are simply clever apes with unique capabilities, such as reason and language, which have been developed through the process of natural selection. In the strong Darwinian view, virtues are not virtues and vices are not vices. Human behavior can be described descriptively and scientifically, but there are no values to be assigned to that behavior. There is no "correct" or "incorrect," no "right" and no "wrong." After all, if human behavior is determined by our DNA and evolutionary history, virtues and vices can only be explained empirically, objectively, or scientifically—in terms of patterns of behavior that are evolutionarily successful or unsuccessful. With Darwin and the subsequent development of existential philosophy and the rediscovery of nihilism, the foundations of traditional morality eroded. What does being a "good" person mean if the universe itself is meaningless? On what foundation can a system of values be built if humans are simply special animals who think?

The tension between reason and biology has only increased over the years, reshaping and challenging traditional views of human nature in helpful ways. More complete biological explanations for behavior that was once described as "deficient" or "flawed" are gaining acceptance. For example, in the modern view, struggling students are no longer intellectually challenged; instead, they have diverse ways of thinking and learning that make traditional forms of learning difficult for them. This is certainly a helpful development for countless diverse learners around the world who have been discriminated against for far too long. Also in the modern view, criminals are no longer regarded as simply being bad people; instead, they have special conditions in their brain chemistry or have faced past traumas that have made them aggressive or impulsive or susceptible to harmful behaviors. When treated appropriately, they can improve their conditions and reintegrate into civil society.

Other academic disciplines have explored the reason-biology dichotomy even more. The field of behavioral economics, with its focus on evolutionary psychology, attempts to show the biological basis for economic decisions and investment behavior—illustrated through experiments with pigeons, rats, capuchin monkeys, and toddlers. Techies and philosophers are working on artificial intelligence that might help us further refine and develop our reasoning capacities, solving problems about morality and the meaning of life, problems that have plagued philosophers for millennia. Simultaneously, scientists and medical doctors are trying to overcome biology and cheat death through life-extension research. And at time of writing, nearly every vaccine lab in the world is trying to unlock the secrets of mRNA in order to find treatments and create even more effective vaccines for all sorts of diseases, from cancer to the next novel coronavirus. In short, understanding the relationship between reason and biology may be the central problem of the current moment in history.

Why do these questions about the relationship between reason and biology matter? What difference do they make? For starters, these questions profoundly affect beliefs about freedom and free will. On the one hand, if human behavior is determined to a large extent by biology, then the very notion of free will is called into doubt. After all, how can we make "free" choices if our behavior and thoughts are predetermined by our DNA, hormones, and brain chemistry? If, on the other hand, we accept the view that (at least most) human beings do have the ability to reason and ought to be held accountable for their actions, then we can also make a case for free will. The truth of the matter might rest somewhere in the middle.

The Darwinian paradigm shift has had profound consequences on a central philosophical area, namely, ethics and value theory.[2] With the ascent of Darwin and the subsequent and marked decline in religious belief in the West, human beings have been thrust into a new world of cosmic meaninglessness. If death marks the end, if there is no Heaven, no Hell, no afterlife at all, then you might feel a cosmic sense of insignificance and purposelessness. Your life and indeed all life is merely a cosmic accident. How would such a belief affect your day-to-day life? For some, the accident that is one's life can lead to the denial of the existence of values. And so, one might become a hedonist and seek to maximize pleasure. Others might choose to follow their self-interest, maximizing their power, wealth, and status. Examples of these choices were common during COVID-19. Some people took the hedonist's path, holding COVID parties, attending illegal raves, and abusing alcohol and drugs. Others took the path of power. Following the basic rule—every crisis is an opportunity—politicians of all persuasions the world over used the crisis as an opportunity to concentrate their own power. Transparency International (2021), an NGO devoted to ending corruption, reported in 2021 that "the global COVID-19 pandemic has […] been used in many countries as an excuse to curtail basic freedoms and sidestep important checks and balances." Pandemic measures even tarnished the "clean image" of Western democracies as bastions of civil liberty. Furthermore, the disorientation of the pandemic led others to turn away from secular values, and many people returned to religion as a source of comfort in uncertain times.

There is another group of people—let's call them humanists—who seek to find alternative ways to live outside of the traditional framework of religion, outside of the nihilist framework of hedonism, and outside of the egotistical framework of capitalism. Humanists wish to create "moral values" in a universe that is fundamentally devoid of meaning. They wish to create a just and equitable society on earth, but not because God wants us to. God, the law giver, is removed from the equation. But what, then, can take God's place? If the universe is meaningless and if human beings are a cosmic accident, how can one derive values that insist on creating equality and justice? Humanists tend to join reason and biology in order to answer this question. From reason, humanists derive the concept of *rational consistency*; from biology, they recognize basic animal experiences. Since I know that I feel pleasure and pain, I know that others must too. Since I would not want to be mistreated, I know that others would not want to either. Since I want to be treated fairly, I know that others want the same. Therefore, my values correspond with the values of others, and I should work to make those values real on earth. (Note that these statements neatly echo the Christian concept of the Golden Rule—treat thy neighbor as thyself—and also Kant's categorical imperative.)

The moral consequences of the relationship between reason and biology are, as has been shown, both fascinating and complex. This book attempts to provide some clarity to the conversation. Three chapters deal with these complexities. In Chap. 3,

---

[2] Of course, Darwin's thought has implications that reach much further, but we will focus only on two areas here.

we explore the thought of Immanuel Kant, who was a staunch advocate for reason. He believed that reason could be used to discover the truth of morality through the development of a rational system of moral rules. He summed these up in his famous categorical imperative: *Act only according to that maxim by which you can, at the same time, will that it should become a universal law.* In Chap. 4 on utilitarianism, we explore the biological equality of humans and non-human animals. In Chap. 7, we discuss virtue ethics, which provides an alternative to the two dominant reason-based moral systems proposed by the utilitarians and Kant. Virtue ethics attempts to create virtuous people and a virtuous society in which everyone can fulfill their full potential as thinking, valuing, self-directing people.

But now let's explore the complex relationship between reason and biology through the discipline of evolutionary psychology, which helps us to understand the significance of disease-avoidance strategies in social interactions.

Box 2.2 Interdisciplinary Perspective #2: Evolutionary Psychology

Emotional Responses to COVID-19: The Science Behind Disgust and Shame

On 20 December 2020, a group of men were photographed being paraded through the city of Jingxi in China (BBC, 2021). Dressed in hazmat suits with face coverings, they were forced to carry posters showing their names and faces. This public shaming was their punishment for violating local pandemic rules. Reactions to the scene were mixed both locally and internationally. After all, public shaming has been frowned upon, at least in the West, for many years. Although citizens of Western democracies disapprove of such humiliating displays, not everyone thought that this spectacle was immoral, arguing that the pandemic was a burden shared by all and a crisis that could only be overcome through shared sacrifice and pandemic rule-following. Those who violated the social contract should, therefore, be publicly humiliated for being bad citizens.

The President of France, Emmanuel Macron, stated as much during an interview on 4 January 2022 when he stated that he wished to put people who chose not to be vaccinated "in the shit" by making life for them as difficult as possible (Chrisafis, 2022). His political decision was to remove them forcibly from social life by preventing them from visiting bars, restaurants, museums, and concerts (although he would not subject them to fines, imprisonment, or forced vaccination). He further remarked that it is irresponsible when people use their freedom to harm others, noting that "someone who is irresponsible is not a citizen" (as cited in Chrisafis, 2022). Macron's public shaming of those who chose to avoid vaccination is not unlike the shame-parade in Jingxi, although Macron did not identify individuals by name. Still, one might wonder what the intent of public shaming is, and why it is thought to be an effective method to change behavior.

(continued)

Anecdotally, my belief is that the emotions of shame and disgust rose drastically after the onset of the pandemic. People who were not vaccinated complained about being shamed for their choice—banned from public events, forced to be hermits. Both people who wore masks and those who did not complained about finding themselves in a situation where they were either the only ones wearing masks or the only ones not wearing them. They all experienced shame as a result. Some people were disgusted by their fellow citizens wearing their masks incorrectly—nose hanging out, mask under the chin. Coughing and sneezing and spitting in public drew looks of horror and disgust. "Have you been tested?" and "Are you vaccinated?" and "Could you please wear a mask?" became incendiary questions that ended in violence and death. For example, a gas station attendant in Germany was murdered for asking a customer to wear a mask (Oltermann, 2021). In short, the general atmosphere was one of public suspicion and mistrust.

We can debate the merits of public humiliation later, but these examples are meant to highlight the slippery nature of the reason-biology distinction. If, according to the Darwinian paradigm discussed above, human beings are a product of evolution and not fundamentally reasoning creatures, then what are the evolutionary advantages of emotions like disgust and shame?

Researchers have developed some interesting theories about these emotions—and, yes, the evolutionary advantage of these emotions is connected to our long relationship with disease and the advantage of having robust disease-avoidance strategies. These evolutionary strategies are referred to technically as the behavioral immune system (BIS)—the behaviors creatures adopt to protect themselves from disease—as opposed to the physiological immune system (white blood cells, antibodies, bone marrow, etc.).

Let's look at each of these two emotions individually. Why do we feel the emotion of disgust? Scholars note that disgust is not culturally specific; people in all societies feel it. It is a universal emotion (Terrizzi & Shook, 2020). So why did it originate? One suggestion is that disgust originates from our desire to protect ourselves from illness and disease (Oaten, Stevenson and Case, 2009). Bad smells—from feces or decaying food—lead us to feel disgust, and that emotion is basically a warning sign that we need to stay away. However, visual signs of sickness in others (e.g., coughing and sneezing) also lead us to experience disgust. Researchers have quite clearly shown that disgust is a disease-avoidance emotion that actually forces us to avoid interacting physically with the object of our disgust (Schaller, 2006). During the pandemic, perhaps we all experienced this emotion and also avoided the source of our disgust. Evolutionarily speaking, avoidance of contagion is always a safe bet for ensuring survival.

There are wider implications for disgust too. Disgust acts as a mechanism of social control within a society and establishes which behaviors are appropriate and inappropriate. For example, let's say you are walking around in

(continued)

public covered in your own vomit and urine. Most people will feel disgust and cross the street to avoid you. The message being sent by society is that your appearance and behavior is unacceptable to the community. You will be isolated and shunned.

It is important to note that the feeling of disgust can also be unreasonable—disconnected from actual disease threats—because disgust serves an "othering" function, creating a boundary between your own social group and outsiders. It is an emotion experienced by social groups who want to exclude certain types of people from their own group and to identify insiders from outsiders. For example, racists have often expressed disgust about the cultural practices of other societies (e.g., circumcision, female genital mutilation, the consumption of pork, or public displays of affection). Homophobes express disgust when confronted by public signs of homosexuality (e.g., seeing same-sex people holding hands and kissing in public or watching gay street parades). Don't forget that racist and homophobic policies have also been justified by misconceptions of the unhealthiness of these outsider groups (see the section on HIV/AIDS in Chap. 6 of this book). During the COVID-19 pandemic, anti-Asian hate crimes increased in Western countries due to misconceptions about the science of infectious disease and ethnicity. In the United States, for example, the US Department of Justice (2021) reported a 77% increase in anti-Asian hate crimes between 2019 and 2020. In summary, the emotion of disgust shows the complexity of the reason-biology dichotomy. While disgust may be an emotion that arose for its evolutionary advantages (namely, disease avoidance) and can therefore be understood scientifically, its secondary functions of social control, behavioral control, and "othering" serve a discriminatory social function.

Now, if you've ever been "disgusted with yourself," you are experiencing the emotion of shame or guilt. For the purposes of this discussion, disgust is other-directed not self-directed, like shame and guilt. But scholars also make an important distinction between shame and guilt: "In response to a moral transgression, a person experiencing shame would be likely to think 'I am a bad person' whereas someone experiencing guilt would be likely to think 'I did a bad thing'" (Terrizzi & Shook, 2020, pp. 1–2). So, the feeling of guilt encourages one to apologize or make amends for an individual wrong, but the feeling of shame is much stronger since it is focused back on one's own identity, one's personhood. For example, if you accidentally gave an elderly relative COVID, you probably experienced guilt; however, you probably did not necessarily conclude that you were a bad person at your core. The feeling of guilt encourages reconciliation and the righting of a wrong and serves the important social function of re-establishing harmony post-transgression. Perhaps after giving your grandma COVID, you became more cautious when interacting with the elderly. In this example, your guilt might have led you to change your behavior in order to establish future harmony.

(continued)

But what is the evolutionary function of shame? Here, things become much more complicated. Scientists point to a number of ideas wrapped up in the complex concept of shame. First, shame is a very powerful, negative emotion that strikes at the core of the individual's identity—it is self-directed. Second, shame leads to *both* psychological *and* behavioral responses. Besides the negative emotional response, shame leads to behavioral changes, which serve the powerful social function of regulating behavior within a group (Terrizzi & Shook, 2020, p. 2). These behavioral responses can be positive, but they are often negative. Take, for instance, eating disorders. If you feel ashamed of your body because the social norm is that you need to look a certain way, then you might adopt harmful behaviors to conform to a social norm. Furthermore, scholars suggest that the shame often causes the opposite of its supposed intent: to maintain social order and harmony (Terrizzi & Shook, 2020, p. 2). Instead, the shamed may opt-out of society or otherwise avoid interacting with the dominant society and otherwise continue to practice "behavioral avoidance" strategies. In homophobic societies, for example, homosexuals have been subjected to the humiliation of conversion therapy in the hopes that they might stop being gay. Alternatively, as has happened throughout history, they may continue to live as homosexuals in secret, while publically adopting heterosexual identities—avoiding the stigma of homosexuality in public life while maintaining it in private. Throughout history, religious minorities, from Jews and Christians to Muslims and Hindus, have either converted to the dominant faith in order to fit in or emigrated to countries where they could practice their faith in peace, without shame.

While public shaming can often come from a hate-filled perspective, it can also result from more positive public health impulses. Take, for example, the ongoing public health initiatives to reduce smoking rates. Fairly benign rules, such as the rule forcing smokers to smoke outside in defined spaces, have been highly effective at reducing smoking rates since the turn of the century. These minor social nudges have had remarkable results. Why? Eyal (2014) notes that human beings are social animals, "who are cued to react strongly to any signals of banishment. So the specter of even minor stigma prompts many smokers to smoke less or to quit" (para. 9). Even minor and mostly harmless regulations like those that discourage smoking, therefore, can have enormous benefits for personal and public health.

However, there is a fine line between lite nudging that is effective and public shaming that is both ineffective and also counterproductive. Take obesity, for example. Tomiyama and Mann (2013) note that there is a general trend to stigmatize overweight people as lacking self-control or being lazy. But they question the value of public shaming, arguing, "If stigmatizing fat people worked, it would have done so by now. Obese people are already the most openly stigmatized individuals in our society, with published data showing that weight stigma is more pervasive and intense than racism, sexism, and

(continued)

other forms of bias" (p. 4). Furthermore, Duong (2021) reports that shaming has clearly demonstrated negative consequences for public health issues besides obesity, namely, HIV and fetal alcohol syndrome.

Let us return to the question of COVID-shaming in China. These practices were meant to encourage the feeling of shame in the rule-breakers. The question, of course, is did they actually feel shame and change their behavior in order to align with social expectations, or did they continue to break the social norms while being more careful not to get caught. Regarding Macron's shaming of the unvaccinated in France, the question is did they get vaccinated or did they simply adopt more effective avoidance strategies and continue their resistance.

For the purposes of this discussion, it is important to emphasize the fact that shame can always lead to opposing outcomes. The evolutionary assumption is this: Dominant social groups feel disgust when confronted with transgressive behaviors; disgust causes feelings of shame in the transgressors; however, the transgressors might respond to the shame in contrary ways. They can modify their behavior in the way that society expects. Alternatively, they can adopt strategies of avoidance to carry on with their transgressive behavior. For example, people who oppose mandatory vaccination have become adept at forging immunization cards and finding other ways to avoid vaccination.

As a final note, it's important to realize that one evolutionary function of shame is to force people to be disgusted with themselves and their own identities. Self-disgust is a heavy emotional burden to bear. It is painful; it is emotionally traumatic. Throughout history, groups who have been shamed have found ways to avoid it. One method is submission to the dominant social order (e.g., religious conversion or renunciation of one's gender identity). But the other method is to seek social acceptance through creating safe places for that identity to be expressed without shame. Therefore, it should be no surprise that people who choose not be vaccinated have created social media groups and political organizations that reaffirm their identities as people who should not be shamed, who should not be objects of disgust. The desire to create safe, accepting communities is both rational and biological. In conclusion, public authorities—and indeed all of us—should think very carefully about the effectiveness of using public shaming in order to change behavior.

Discuss
- **Did you experience disgust or shame during the pandemic? Please describe your experiences.**
- **Next, do you think public shaming is an effective way to change behavior or is it counterproductive? Consider both the pandemic and nonpandemic examples discussed above: vaccination, masking, gender identity, race, religion, etc.**

(continued)

- How can the science of disgust and shame be used to encourage people to change their behavior voluntarily during a pandemic?
- The German government released a marketing campaign praising couch potatoes for being pandemic heroes because they stayed at home on their couches. This was considered to be an effective way to frame pandemic restrictions–namely, stay-at-home orders–in a positive way. Can you find additional examples of public health marketing campaigns that rely on positive messaging?

2.4 Alienation Versus Reconciliation

The last basic dichotomy to cover in this introductory chapter is that between alienation and reconciliation.[3] This dichotomy essentially addresses your vision of world history. Despite whatever stance you have taken in the previous points, how do you view the future? Are human beings—due to their egoism—doomed to have a future of perpetual alienation, a future of crisis after crisis, war after war, disaster after disaster? Or can something else—maybe absolute reason or universal religion or a single world government— be used to reconcile our differences in order to create a future without alienation?

Again, the evidence is mixed, and the COVID-19 pandemic complicated matters further. On the side of perpetual alienation, one can point to the persistence of ideologies that are meant to divide people from one another. Some of these were already addressed, such as Republican-Democrat, conservative-liberal, Shia-Sunni, Christian-Muslim, White-Black, etc. Each of these well-worn dichotomies stresses difference, and difference is alienation. History is full of the grim reality of intra-religious differences from the centuries of vicious wars between Protestants and Catholics in Europe to the present conflicts between Shiites and Sunnis. Beliefs in racial difference led to the slaughter of six million Jews and five million others by the Nazis during World War II. Also, the same belief in racial difference created the institution of slavery in the United States as well as profound alienation between the black community and white power structures that persist to this very day. Beliefs in class differences led to the rise of communism and the persistent division of the planet between so-called capitalist and so-called communist countries. Within both economic institutions, there still exists an abundance of alienation between workers and management, alienation which occasionally bubbles up in the form of Occupy Wall Street actions, general strikes, and other forms of proletarian protest. Even perceptions of gender differences have led to alienation between men and women, and sexual differences have prompted the ongoing disputes between gay-rights activists and religious conservatives. Environmentalists would add another difference to the list: the alienation between human beings and the natural world, an

---

[3] I would like to acknowledge Glenn Tinder's framing of this dichotomy in Chap. 2, "Estrangement and Unity," in *Political Thinking: The Perennial Questions* (2004).

alienation that has led to widespread exploitation and pollution of the environment and the extinction of innumerable species.

The COVID-19 pandemic further exposed these long-standing instances of alienation. Countries doubled-down on the most obvious symbol of perpetual alienation—national borders—which demarcate "us" and "them." During the pandemic, international travel became a bureaucratic nightmare with confusion over ever-changing rules and entry requirements. Even in the Schengen Zone (the free-travel area of the European Union), some countries erected border controls only to remove them before reinstating them once again. Countries hoarded medical supplies, and customs officials prevented shipments of PPE outside their own countries. The virus exacerbated racial alienation. Asian-Americans in the United States were subject to abuse for looking Chinese. Africans in China were subject to abuse for being suspected of carrying the virus. Black people in the United States feared shopping with masks, lest people think they were robbers. People all over the world avoided eating in Chinese restaurants. The virus inflamed political division. In the United States, Republicans accused Democrats of wanting people to die in order to discredit the previous president. Democrats accused Republicans of devaluing human life. Similar divisions erupted in Britain, Sweden, France, and Italy. Lastly, some maintain that COVID-19 exposed our fundamental alienation from the natural world, arguing that our continuing mistreatment of the environment is causing our own doom.

And, yet, numerous counterexamples can be set against the evidence that human beings are alienated in essence. While religious disputes flare up occasionally, the vast majority of people are tolerant of each other's religious beliefs. Protestants and Catholics are, for the most part, not openly at war with each other anymore. Racism persists in many forms, but slavery was abolished in the United States, and minorities are protected in many countries. Also, the Black Lives Matter movement has seen people of all races and ethnicities marching together to end systemic racism. Class differences persist, but workers and management, at least in Western democracies, coexist peacefully despite the occasional strike or protest. The creation of laws protecting women's rights and equality point to the reconciliation of sexes, and LGBTQIA+ rights are increasingly being seen as universal human rights. Despite the persistent consumption of fossil fuels and the depletion of natural resources, the environmental movement is beginning to shift our focus to environmental sustainability and protection. Organizations like the WHO are diligently working to coordinate global responses to future pandemics, and there is some hope that new treatments will be freely available to rich and poor alike. Maybe we have sown the seeds of global reconciliation.

There is plenty of evidence to support both views, but what difference would it make to take a side on alienation-reconciliation dispute? If you take the side of perpetual alienation, then you may not support global initiatives to secure world peace, eliminate poverty, control climate change, or guarantee universal human rights. The best you might hope for are moderate measures that would maintain the tense equilibrium of society both at home and abroad. In your private life, you may gravitate toward people who share the same social, economic, ethnic, religious, and political characteristics that you have because it is comfortable and maybe even "natural" (from an evolutionary perspective) to mingle with people who share your values and general outlook.

However, if you believe that human differences can and will be reconciled at some time in the future, the sky's the limit when it comes to plans to improve the world. You may support any initiative that seeks to break down social, economic, and political barriers between individuals, classes, communities, religions, and nation states. In your private life, you may actively seek out people who do not share your religious or ethnic background, you may actively get to know people from different socioeconomic backgrounds, and you might even attempt to befriend people of opposite political persuasions. In short, the perspective of reconciliation gives you space to hope for a better future.

To summarize the dichotomy between alienation and reconciliation, it seems once again that the evidence is mixed. One can either view the past, present, and future of our species and our planet in terms of overcoming alienation or in terms of perpetual alienation. The differences in outlook are great, but we have merely scratched the surface of similarity and otherness. This dichotomy will be central to each of the subsequent chapters.

Let us now explore the importance of the environment in our hopes for the future of our species and the planet. Perhaps no other contemporary issue reveals our fundamental view about the future more clearly than our feelings about climate change.

Box 2.3 Interdisciplinary Perspective #3: Climate Science

COVID-19 and Climate Change: A Future of Alienation or Reconciliation?
Before the emergence of COVID-19, we were already dealing with another looming threat: climate change. It is interesting to note that many environmentalists and scientists consider the pandemic to be part and parcel of the climate crisis, not a distinct and separate crisis. They ask us to see the creation of zoonotic diseases like SARS, MERS, avian flu, and swine flu, as yet another dire consequence of humanity's long-standing abuse of the natural world. The rise of new diseases is directly linked to specific human practices, such as our global logistics system, which transports diseases rapidly around the world; the hyper-development of natural land, which leads to closer interaction between human settlements and previously isolated animal species (Tollefson, 2020); industrialized farming of both plants and animals, which turns robust and biodiverse ecosystems into monocultures that are susceptible to disease (Greger, 2021); and the exotic animal trade, which helps to increase the chances of a disease jumping the species barrier (Gómez & Aguirre, 2008; Aguirre et al., 2020). Stewart M. Patrick (2021) of the Council on Foreign Relations notes that 75% of the roughly 400 new pathogens that have arisen in the last several decades are zoonotic diseases, which means that they originated in non-human animals and crossed over into humans; the global cost of

(continued)

managing these diseases is roughly $1 trillion per year, with the COVID-19 pandemic potentially costing as much as $28 trillion by 2025. He concludes, "It is tempting to treat pandemics as acts of God, but they are human-made, a function of our unsustainable exploitation of nature" (para. 3).

So how do your views about the environment connect to your belief about alienation and reconciliation? If you believe that perpetual alienation is our fate as a species, then you might never expect reconciliation between people and people or between human beings and the environment. Human beings will continue to be alienated both from each other and also from the natural world. Their estrangement from each other will lead to wars over natural resources and further environmental degradation. If this is the case, then "Drill, baby, drill!" may be your motto. On a geopolitical level, a forecast of perpetual alienation would mean that your nation should do its best to amass and protect its own resources in order to prepare for a future of rising sea levels, ferocious natural disasters, and competition for ever dwindling resources.

The US Department of Defense is now focused on the security challenges that climate change presents—and the strategists' outlook is one of continued alienation. Here is a sobering assessment from the 2014 Quadrennial Defense Review:

> Climate change poses another significant challenge for the United States and the world at large. As greenhouse gas emissions increase, sea levels are rising, average global temperatures are increasing, and severe weather patterns are accelerating. These changes, coupled with other global dynamics, including growing, urbanizing, more affluent populations, and substantial economic growth in India, China, Brazil, and other nations, will devastate homes, land, and infrastructure. Climate change may exacerbate water scarcity and lead to sharp increases in food costs. The pressures caused by climate change will influence resource competition while placing additional burdens on economies, societies, and governance institutions around the world. These effects are threat multipliers that will aggravate stressors abroad such as poverty, environmental degradation, political instability, and social tensions – conditions that can enable terrorist activity and other forms of violence. (p. 8)

This passage could have been written by a modern-day Hobbes with its focus on the role of resource competition as a perennial source of quarrel. It is also interesting to note that the DOD predicts that "more affluent populations" in developing economies will in part cause the devastation of "homes, land, and infrastructure." This is a curious comment given that political scientists and economists often insist that increased prosperity *reduces* the causes of quarrel. According to the DOD, prosperity and growth, which have been typically viewed as factors that reconcile human beings, will become factors that further divide us. Indeed, resource competition, saber rattling, and xenophobic attitudes among nations have increased significantly since the outbreak of COVID-19. On 8 May 2020, UN Secretary-General António Guterres cautioned that the pandemic was causing "a tsunami of hate and xenophobia,

(continued)

scapegoating and scare-mongering" to spread throughout the globe (as cited in the Atlantic Council, 2020). The outlook is grim even if you were a staunch optimist before the pandemic.

Despite these pessimistic assessments, you might still believe in the human capacity for reconciliation, in which case you might envisage a time when both our relationship to each other and also our relationship to the environment are harmonious. You may then believe that the climate catastrophe can be averted and that it will be averted as the other forms of alienation are reconciled. How is that to be achieved? Perhaps growing prosperity will actually lead to fewer conflicts and more responsible environmental behavior, or perhaps technological innovation will provide the key to solving the climate crisis. It may be too early to predict the unfolding of events, but one thing is certain: If we have managed to solve COVID-19, we may have a shot at solving the impending climate crisis as well as future global pandemics. If so, we will also have strong evidence to support the optimist's view that human beings are not doomed to a future of perpetual alienation.

Discuss
- **Does the emergence of COVID-19 and the global response to the pandemic provide evidence that we will be perpetually alienated or that we have the capacity for reconciliation? Provide examples to support your argument.**
- **Does climate change provide an opportunity for humanity to overcome its alienation, or do you see further alienation in our environmental future?**
- **What are some ways that climate science can be integrated more holistically into the disciplines of pandemic management and public health?**

2.5 Conclusion

Let us return to the framework with which I began the chapter, G. W. F. Hegel's concept from *The Philosophy of History* (1831): "To him who looks upon the world rationally, the world in its turn presents a rational aspect." It is a thought-provoking sentence that deserves careful consideration. Hegel explicitly argues that world history is rational and that a thinker can uncover the ultimate design of the world by utilizing his or her own reason to explain the rational basis of history, a rational basis that is hidden by faulty and limited thinking. When looking at the word rationally, one will see that history is moving toward a final reconciliation of differences, a reconciliation that reason will help us attain.

However, there are important ideas left unsaid in this passage. Indeed, what is most important in this quotation is what Hegel does *not* say explicitly but implies:

1. To the person who looks upon human history egoistically, human history will present its egoistical aspect.

2. To the person who looks upon the world irrationally, the world will present an irrational aspect.
3. To the person who looks upon fellow human beings in an alienated way, they will present their alienated aspect.

In short, Hegel implies that the world is complex and cunning enough to show each of us what we want it to reveal. If we choose to see discord, we can find it; if we choose to see harmony, we can find that too. If we choose to see viciousness, we can find it; if we choose to see virtue, we can find that too.

Hegel's important idea is this: The relationship between subject and object, between the self and the world, and between one's own reason and the Truth of the world is a *reciprocal relationship*. The historical evidence and examples listed throughout this chapter can lead one to draw perfectly rational and reasonable but perfectly contradictory and incompatible conclusions about human nature being good or bad, rational or irrational, alienated or reconciled. Hegel reminds us that the world will show us what we want it to show us. If Hegel is correct, then perhaps we can make the world reveal the development of the values we desire. If Hegel is correct, then each of us does play an active role in the future of our species and our planet. If Hegel is correct, then each of us has the responsibility to look the world in the face and force it to reveal the type of world we want it to be.

References

Aguirre, A. A., Catherina, R., Frye, H., & Shelley, L. (2020). Illicit wildlife trade, wet markets, and COVID-19: Preventing future pandemics. *World Medical and Health Policy, 12*(3), 265–265. https://doi.org/10.1002/wmh3.348

Aristotle. (350 BCE). *Politics* (W. Ellis, Trans.). Project Gutenberg. 2013. https://www.gutenberg.org/files/6762/6762-h/6762-h.htm#link2HCH0005

BBC. (2021, December 29). China: Public shaming returns amid Covid fears. *BBC.com.* https://www.bbc.com/news/world-asia-china-59818971. Accessed 10 June 2022.

CDC. (2022a, May 16). COVID-19 mortality overview. https://www.cdc.gov/nchs/covid19/mortality-overview.htm. Accessed 26 Aug 2022.

CDC. (2022b, August 11). Preventing getting sick. https://www.cdc.gov/coronavirus/2019-ncov/prevent-getting-sick/prevention.html. Accessed 5 July 2022.

Child and Adolescent Behavioral Health Foundation. (n.d.). Reckless youth attitude: I will not get COVID. https://www.childandadolescent.org/reckless-youth-attitude-i-will-not-get-covid-19/. Accessed 26 Aug 2022.

Chrisafis, A. (2022, January 5). Macron rebuke to unvaccinated citizens incurs anger in parliament. *The Guardian.* https://www.theguardian.com/world/2022/jan/05/macron-rebuke-to-unvaccinated-citizens-incurs-anger-in-parliament. Accessed 6 Jan 2022.

DOD. (2014). *Quadrennial defense review.* http://www.defense.gov/pubs/2014_Quadrennial_Defense_Review.pdf. Accessed 9 June 2022.

DOJ. (2021). 2020 FBI hate crime statistics. https://www.justice.gov/crs/highlights/2020-hate-crimes-statistics. Accessed 3 Mar 2022.

Duong, D. (2021). Does shaming have a place in public health? *Canadian Medical Association Journal, 11*(193), E59–E60. https://doi.org/10.1503/cmaj.1095910

Eyal, N. (2014). Nudging by shaming, shaming by nudging. *International Journal of Health Policy Management, 25*(3), 53–56. https://doi.org/10.15171/ijhpm.2014.68

Gómez, A., & Aguirre, A. A. (2008). Infectious diseases and the illegal wildlife trade. Animal biodiversity and emerging diseases prediction and prevention. *Annals of the New York Academy of Sciences, 1*, 16–19. https://doi.org/10.1196/annals.1428.046

Greger, M. (2021). Primary pandemic prevention. *American Journal of Lifestyle Medicine, 15*(5), 498–505. https://doi.org/10.1177/15598276211008134

Hegel, G. W. F. (1831). *The philosophy of history.* Marxists Internet Archive. https://www.marxists.org/reference/archive/hegel/works/hi/history3.htm#011

Hobbes, T. (1651). *Leviathan.* Project Gutenberg. 2021. https://www.gutenberg.org/files/3207/3207-h/3207-h.htm

Lewis, D. (2021). Long COVID and kids: Scientists race to find answers. *Nature, 595*, 482–483. https://doi.org/10.1038/d41586-021-01935-7

Machiavelli, N. (1517). *Discourses on the first ten books of Titus Livius* (N. H. Thomson, Trans.). Project Gutenberg. 2021. https://www.gutenberg.org/files/10827/10827-h/10827-h.htm

Oaten, M., Stevenson, R., & Case, T. (2009). Disgust as a disease-avoidance mechanism. *Psychological Bulletin, 135*, 303–321. https://doi.org/10.1037/a0014823

Oltermann, P. (2021, September 21). Petrol station worker killed in Germany after face mask row. *The Guardian.* https://www.theguardian.com/world/2021/sep/21/petrol-station-worker-killed-in-germany-after-face-mask-row. Accessed 1 Aug 2022.

Patrick, S. M. (2021, May 10). To prevent future pandemics, start by protecting nature. *World Politics Review.* https://www.worldpoliticsreview.com/articles/29637/under-threat-biodiversity-preservation-nature-protection-are-key-to-preventing-pandemics. Accessed 8 Aug 2022.

Rand, A. (1964). *The virtue of selfishness: A new concept of egoism.* Signet.

Schaller, M. (2006). Parasites, behavioral defenses and the social psychological mechanisms through which cultures are evoked. *Psychological Inquiry, 17*, 96–101. https://doi.org/10.1207/s15327965pli1702_2

Terrizzi, J. A., Jr., & Shook, N. J. (2020). On the origin of shame: Does shame emerge from an evolved disease-avoidance architecture? *Frontiers in Behavioral Neuropsychology, 18.* https://doi.org/10.3389/fnbeh.2020.00019

The Atlantic Council. (2020, May 8). US jobless rate worst since Great Depression, UN head decries 'tsunami of hate.' https://atlanticcouncil.org/blogs/coronavirus-alert/us-jobless-rate-worst-since-great-depression-un-head-decries-tsunami-of-hate/. Accessed 9 May 2020.

Tinder, G. (2004). *Political thinking: The perennial questions* (6th ed.). Pearson Longman.

Tollefson, J. (2020). Why deforestation and extinctions make pandemics more likely. *Nature, 584*, 175+. https://doi.org/10.1038/d41586-020-02341-1

Tomiyama, A. J., & Mann, T. (2013). If shaming reduced obesity, there would be no fat people. *The Hastings Center Report, 43*(3), 4–5.

Transparency International. (2021). Corruption perceptions index. https://www.transparency.org/en/cpi/2021. Accessed 8 July 2022.

Chapter 3
Kant and Deontology: Understanding Human Dignity

3.1 How Much Is a Human Life Worth?

So how much is a human life worth? Your answer to this question is important, but not as important as the justification of your answer and the consequences of that justification. Your thoughts will touch upon some of the most fundamental issues of morality, including universal human rights, the absolute value of human beings, and the inviolable dignity of every human being. If you were to ask strangers on the street if they believed in human rights, they would most likely say, "Yes!" However, if you were to ask them *why* human beings have inviolable rights, you might be met with a blank stare. This chapter focuses on the development of the concept of human dignity. Perhaps nothing is more important in ethics than developing a sound argument for the absolute value of human beings, a value beyond all price.

The concept of absolute and inviolable human rights is now widely accepted (although not universally accepted), but this was not always the case. The concept of the dignity of all human beings did not simply come out of thin air. Indeed, much of the tragedy that is human history can be explained by the *absence* of a prevailing notion of human dignity. Apartheid, slavery, ethnic conflict, sexism, homophobia, religious persecution, discrimination against people with disabilities, and war all rest on the premise that some people have less dignity than others, and many parts of our planet are still plagued with these divisions.

At the same time, in our everyday moral lives, most of us tend to have a robust notion of human dignity and an appropriate level of outrage when the dignity of others is violated. When women are groped or harassed by powerful men, we are outraged because their rights and dignity have been taken away. When senior citizens lose their life savings to scam artists who prey upon their loneliness and vulnerability, we are furious because their absolute worth has been undermined. When police brutalize innocent people, we are horrified that those entrusted with our safety have abused their power at the expense of the people they are supposed to be

A. Sola, *Ethics and Pandemics*, Springer Series in Public Health and Health
Policy Ethics, https://doi.org/10.1007/978-3-031-33207-4_3

protecting. When children are molested by pedophiles, we are shocked and demand justice because their priceless value has been despoiled. When innocent people are intentionally killed in terrorist attacks, we are saddened because precious human lives were taken, lives with absolute value.

During the COVID-19 pandemic, civilized society was justifiably appalled by stories of teenagers coughing on senior citizens (Halliday, 2020), government workers using their positions to start businesses that profit off of the PPE shortage (Davies & Goodley, 2020), and security guards getting killed for asking customers to wear masks (Kornfield, 2020). There seems to be some sense of human dignity that prevails throughout much of the world, some sense that every human being is deserving of respect, some sense that we should treat others the same way that we would like to be treated.

This chapter addresses one of the most important contributors to moral philosophy in the Western world, Immanuel Kant (1724–1804), the thinker who established a rational foundation for human dignity. Kant was born in Königsberg, East Prussia (now Kaliningrad, Russia), where he spent his entire life, first as a student and then as a lecturer at the local university. He followed the same rigid schedule every day— waking up, eating, reading, writing, teaching, walking, going to bed. Every activity happened exactly at the same time. His neighbors joked that they would set their clocks to the moment he appeared walking past their doors on his daily walk because he was more reliable than the old church clock. Kant spent most of his life trying to establish the rational foundation for moral rules, and he wrote three of the most influential and difficult-to-read philosophical treatises in the history of philosophy: *The Critique of Pure Reason* (1781), *The Critique of Practical Reason* (1786), and *Fundamental Principles of the Metaphysic of Morals* (1785).

3.2   The Origins of Morality

Where does morality come from? What is right and wrong, good and evil? Kant argues that morality derives from the fact that we are human beings who have the ability to reason. The ability to reason allows us to create values, an ability that no other creature has. Let's explore Kant's idea of value creation further, looking at the behavior of non-human animals. Beavers, for example, do not value their dams, nor bees their hives, nor ants their hills, in the same way that human beings value their homes. When his dam is destroyed, the beaver builds a new one. He doesn't cry about the mementos lost in his previous dam. He doesn't complain about the unfairness and injustice of existence. The dam fulfills only a natural purpose in his life. It is created out of instinct, but it lacks value. Humans, on the other hand, cry about their houses destroyed by flooding because houses are not just shelters, in general, but *homes*, for which there is no substitute.

Similarly, animals do not value beautiful sunsets. Only human beings have the ability to judge the beauty of a sunset. Only humans are able to create a value-based concept like beauty. Only humans can value nature. Without humans, nature is neutral. The beaver cannot value nature because he is a part of nature. We humans, Kant argues, are above it. (One might already sense that Kant's views have potentially harmful ramifications for the environment because he creates a sharp distinction between the human world and nature, and we will address those ramifications below.)

Since values cannot exist without humans, a coherent system of values—what we call *morality* or *ethics*—cannot exist without us either. Kant's conclusion is that morality does not exist without reason, which can only be found in human beings. Without humans, Kant (1790) says, nature is "without a final purpose" (p. 331). Kant effectively divides the world in two. On the one side is the realm of nature in which the laws of physics and causality reign. Nature does not decide that a wolf should or should not eat a lamb or that a virus should or should not transmit itself from bats to humans. Natural processes happen without agency or value. In this respect, nature lacks reason. It is the world of *what is the case*; it is free from *what should be the case* or *what ought to be the case*. On the other side is reason, which is the realm of *shoulds* and *oughts*. It is the realm of value-giving and evaluation, right and wrong. It is the world in which one says *thou shall not steal* and *thou shall not kill* and *thou shall not deliberately cough on old people* and *thou shall take appropriate safety measures to protect your community.*

Also note the means-end thinking that Kant sometimes employs in order to illustrate his point. As we saw above, the beaver does not value his dam for the purpose of preserving his memories. Humans, however, value their home for its value as a shelter *and* for its sentimental value. In a certain respect, then, the home (X) is a means to an end (Y). It exists for a variety of purposes set by the human owner. Kant believes that there is a point in thought whereby there is an end to ends, a point where it is impossible to say that X exists for the sake of Y. What then exists only for itself? What is an end-in-itself? Kant's answer is reason. Reason does not exist for the sake of anything else. It is the end, and its value is absolute and not contingent upon other values. The holders of reason, human beings, must also be ends-in-themselves, and Kant insists that we should never be used as a means to an end. Therefore, we may also not *use* other people as means to our own ends, for they are ends-in-themselves as well.

3.3 The Categorical Imperative

Once we understand Kant's claim that the moral universe is a consequence of reason, the next step is to recognize that we are members of a reasoning moral community. So, I might reason as follows:

> I know that I am special because I value things in my life. I know this is true because I am a thinking human being. At the same time, I must recognize that there are other creatures like me—other humans—who also value things because they think too. It is therefore *rationally consistent* for me to acknowledge that, just as I value things and am worthy of being valued myself, others are worthy of being valued as well.

In other words, morality only exists within a community of other rational beings who value things just like you do. Indeed, if COVID-19 had killed every single human being on the planet except for you, if you were the last human being to ever exist, could any of your decisions be said to be moral or immoral, right or wrong?

Now that we recognize that we are in a community of valuing, thinking, reasoning creatures, we have established Kant's bedrock for morality. So, how do we establish the specifics about right and wrong, moral and immoral behavior? Since reason is the basis of morality, there must be a rational method which allows us to test what the specific moral rules are. Kant developed a concept, the categorical imperative, which allows us to test the rationality of our moral judgments. Here it is, one of the most famous sentences in the history of philosophy: *Act only according to the maxim whereby you can, at the same time, will that it should become a universal law* (Kant, 1785, p. 30). Using this formula, we can begin to develop specific rules or universal laws and test them for their reasonableness. Some universal laws will clearly be shown to be rational, and others irrational. Table 3.1 provides some examples:

Kant argues that when you steal, you are creating a maxim: it is morally acceptable for me to steal. The maxim becomes a universal law because Kant insists that our moral decisions need to be consistently applied to all rational creatures. When you steal, you are saying that stealing is how *all* people should behave. When you murder someone, you are saying that murdering people is how *all* people should behave. When you lie, you are saying that lying to others is how *all* people should behave. When you mask or don't mask, you are saying that this is how *all* people should behave. This is how the maxim of our actions becomes a universal law in Kant's system.

Next, each specific universal law can be tested for its acceptability. If I decide to steal, I am creating a universal law from that fact. I am saying that everyone should steal. Kant then would ask us to imagine a world in which stealing is considered to

Table 3.1 Deriving universal laws from actions

Action	Maxim or universal law
I steal an apple from the grocery store	All people should steal
I pay for the apple	All people should pay
I lie to a friend about how bad his haircut looks	All people should lie
I tell the truth about it	All people should tell the truth
I commit suicide	All people should commit suicide
I do not commit suicide	All people should not commit suicide
I wear a mask during a pandemic	All people should wear masks
I don't wear a mask	All people should not wear masks
I get vaccinated during a pandemic	All people should get vaccinated
I do not get vaccinated	All people should not get vaccinated
I cough on people when I'm sick	All people should cough on people
I cover my mouth when I cough	All people should cover their mouths

be good behavior. Could we even live as a civilized, thinking, valuing species? Obviously, not, he thinks. We could neither commit time to develop complex projects nor engage in any activity with others, because we would expect them to steal from us and us from them. Such a world would be terrible. We would be thrust back into the *state of nature* which Hobbes envisioned, a world in which human life was nasty, brutish, and short. In the state of nature, morality ceases to exist. The same process can be applied for the prohibitions against murder, lying, and even suicide. (Kant insisted suicide is wrong because the universal law created from the act would lead to the end of humanity, hence the end of both reason and morality.) In short, stealing must be wrong because if it were right, the outcomes would be both catastrophic and self-contradictory. If I cough on someone intentionally, I am creating a universal coughing law. What would the world be like if everyone coughed on everyone else? Well, there would be massive pandemics and sickness at all times. Such a world, for Kant, would be chaotic and self-defeating. Therefore, we should not cough on others.

Kant's argument for the wrongness of these behaviors is perhaps convincing, but maybe you are not convinced that theft, murder, lying, and coughing are *always* wrong. After all, sometimes we might steal for the right reasons—to give to the poor or to save lives. We might tell a white lie in order to avoid making a friend feel bad about their new haircut. We might even occasionally allow the murder of innocents if doing so would help save many more innocent lives. And we might even deliberately cough on someone—say, Adolf Hitler—in order to cause infection and premature death, thereby preventing World War II and stopping the Holocaust.

However, Kant insists that these rules are *absolute moral rules*, and they are always wrong, no matter what good intentions one might have or what the beneficial consequences may be. This is called *deontology*—the idea that actions should be judged as being right or wrong based on the act itself, not on the consequences of the action. The categorical imperative demands that we always follow the moral rule, particularly when facing tough moral dilemmas that tempt us to grant exceptions. Indeed, the point of morality is to guide our actions when faced with the most difficult decisions. The categorical imperative does not allow us to exempt ourselves from moral rules, nor can we exempt others. Once we grant exceptions, the rules of right behavior collapse. Everyone then could exempt themselves from rules, and pretty soon we would always make excuses and justifications for immoral behavior. It is your duty to obey the moral law unequivocally, even when doing so is difficult and painful; as Kant (1788) says in his *Critique of Practical Reason*, "The majesty of duty has nothing to do with the enjoyment of life" (I, III, para. 34).

3.4   An Edge-Case: The Duty Not to Lie in Kant's System

Kant was faced with objections to his rigid categorical imperative during his own lifetime. In 1797, the French intellectual Henri Benjamin Constant de Rebecque challenged Kant's view of *always* abiding by strict moral rules with the famous thought experiment/edge-case known as the Inquiring Murderer. In this scenario, a murderer comes to your house and asks you if his next victim is hiding at home. You know exactly where the potential victim is, so the categorical imperative requires that you tell the Inquiring Murderer the truth in order not to violate the rule against lying. Still, many would lie in this situation because lying to the Inquiring Murderer in order to save your neighbor is a "common sense" moral decision.

Kant (1797) responded to this objection in the essay "On a Supposed Right to Tell Lies from Altruistic Motives," which I quote at length because the explanation deserves a full and careful reading:

> This benevolent lie, however, can become punishable under civil law through an accident (casus), and that which escapes liability to punishment only by accident can also be condemned as wrong even by external laws. For instance, if by telling a lie you have prevented murder, you have made yourself legally responsible for all the consequences; but if you have held rigorously to the truth, public justice can lay no hand on you, whatever the unforeseen consequences may be. After you have honestly answered the murderer's question as to whether this intended victim is at home, it may be that he has slipped out so that he does not come in the way of the murderer, and thus that the murder may not be committed. But if you had lied and said he was not at home when he had really gone out without your knowing it, and if the murderer had then met him as he went away and murdered him, you might justly be accused as the cause of his death. For if you had told the truth as far as you knew it, perhaps the murderer might have been apprehended by the neighbors while he searched the house and thus the deed might have been prevented. Therefore, whoever tells a lie, however well intentioned he might be, must answer for the consequences, however unforeseeable they were, and pay the penalty for them even in a civil tribunal. This is because truthfulness is a duty which must be regarded as the ground of all duties based on contract, and the laws of these duties would be rendered uncertain and useless if even the least exception to them were admitted.
>
> To be truthful (honest) in all declarations, therefore, is a sacred and absolutely commanding decree of reason, limited by no expediency. (p. 348)

Kant defends the absolute nature of the categorical imperative in this scenario in two ways. First, he asserts that we can never be held responsible for the consequences that arise from doing the right thing; we cannot be held morally (or legally) responsible for telling the truth. However, we can be held responsible for the consequences that arise from violating moral rules.

Second, Kant questions the faith we have in knowing the consequences of our actions. To what extent do we ever know the consequences of our actions? In this scenario, it may seem obvious that lying to the murderer will save an innocent life, but Kant cautions us about making such a presumption. We cannot ever know the full consequences of our actions as they ripple beyond the present and into the future. Therefore, we should not be tempted by our confidence in predicting the future. What we do know, however, is that certain actions are right or wrong, irrespective of the consequences. Lying is wrong, and honesty is right. Therefore, one should not lie to the Inquiring Murderer. Still, reasonable people might think that there should be exceptions to rules. We will explore a pandemic-related scenario now to evaluate Kant's absolutism.

Box 3.1 Interdisciplinary Perspective #4: Economics and Intellectual Property

Stealing Vaccine Technology for the Greater Good

The hope that the development of safe and effective vaccines against COVID-19 would lead to the swift end of the pandemic proved to be ill founded for several reasons.

First, technical problems with manufacturing, logistical challenges with distribution, and approval setbacks led to delays getting doses into the arms of everyone in the world. After all, it takes a long time to produce billions of doses, and some vaccine types are not easy to distribute safely everywhere on the planet. For example, the Pfizer/BioNTech vaccine must be kept at cold temperatures and shipped in temperature-controlled boxes with GPS sensors to ensure the doses are still viable upon arrival at their destination (Pfizer, 2022.). For hot and hard-to-reach places on the planet, safe distribution of this vaccine is a logistical challenge. On the other hand, the Oxford/AstraZeneca vaccine can be stored in normal refrigerators, making it much easier to preserve and distribute (UK Regulatory Agency, 2022). Despite these challenges, billions of doses were made and delivered into arms, primarily in rich countries, which received many, many more vaccine doses per capita than in developing countries—15 times more than in sub-Saharan Africa (UNICEF, 2021). Furthermore, many people in wealthy countries were able to receive even three or four doses, before people in developing countries received a single dose.

The second reason for the failure of vaccines to quell the pandemic was vaccine skepticism. Without very high levels of vaccination, the virus mutated into various forms—Delta and Omicron being the most well-known—that caused subsequent waves of infection. So, despite access to the vaccine, many people chose not to take it. Poor people in poor countries would certainly like to have had those doses that skeptics refused, but again distribution was a problem. Between March and September 2021, as many as 15 million doses in the United States were thrown out because they expired before they could be safely delivered to other countries that badly needed them (Eaton & Murphy, 2021). A common sense solution would be to allow vaccines to be produced where they are needed. But they are not. Why?

Let's focus here on the third reason that vaccines were not as widely manufactured and distributed as hoped: intellectual property law (Siripurapu, 2021). One of the fundamental features of international trade and capitalism is intellectual property protection, basically the right of inventors to profit from their inventions. The World Trade Organization enshrines this concept in the Trade-Related Aspects of Intellectual Property Rights Agreement (TRIPS). Of course, medicines, medical devices, vaccines, and vaccine manufacturing technologies all fall into this category of protected intellectual property.

(continued)

The argument in favor of keeping intellectual property protection on vaccines is straightforward: Companies will not invest in research and development unless they stand to make a profit from their investments through intellectual property protection. In most circumstances, this argument is widely accepted. Kant would agree: Theft of intellectual property is a type of stealing, and stealing is always wrong.

However, many argue that in extreme circumstances, such as a global public health emergency like COVID-19, these protections should be waived. There should be exceptions to the rule, and indeed there is an exemption for public health reasons in the WTO documents, a so-called intellectual property waiver which allows the WTO to suspend parts of the TRIPS agreement during a public health emergency. As early as October 2020, a number of developing countries led by India and South Africa asked the WTO (2020) to provide a waiver for COVID vaccines and technology. Discussions were held, and additional drafts of the proposed waiver were written, disseminated, studied, and re-written. However, no agreement was made mainly due to opposition from the EU and the United States (although in the meantime, the Biden administration reversed the Trump administration's opposition to the waiver). It is worth reviewing the exact text provided by developing countries in September 2021 to justify using the waiver:

> The extent of the current health crisis posed by COVID-19 is as undeniable as the current global response is untenable. Given the ongoing absence of sufficient engagement by the pharmaceutical industry to voluntarily and openly allow the use of their intellectual property rights, data and know-how with all possible manufacturers, to address the pandemic, mechanisms are needed to remove existing and potential legal barriers to scale up manufacturing and diversify sources of supply.
>
> The WTO needs to act now to arrest the rising human toll and economic strain from the COVID-19 pandemic. Global solidarity is required to ramp up and diversify global production of vaccines, therapeutics and diagnostics to effectively deal with the spread of the COVID-19 virus and to leverage the under-utilized manufacturing capacity in developing countries. Sustainable global economic recovery will only be possible when we end the health crisis. Ending the pandemic in a timely manner should be the overarching priority for the WTO. There is an overwhelming ethical, epidemiological, and economic case for urgent collective action and hence the motivation for the TRIPS waiver proposal. (WTO, 2021)

The arguments for a waiver seem to be clear; developing countries cite clear ethical, epidemiological, and economic grounds for it. However, opposition remains. Some counter-arguments are as follows:

- A waiver would lead to a reduction in safety and quality of vaccines and other technology, leading to further harm and even more vaccine skepticism.
- COVAX, the program to distribute vaccines from wealthy to developing countries through donation, adequately solves the problem. See WHO (2022) and UNICEF (2022) for additional information on COVAX initiatives.

(continued)

- Voluntary sharing of research is still possible through various government programs.
- And, again, future innovation will be discouraged if intellectual property protections are waived (Human Rights Watch, 2021).

These objections to revising TRIPS are not unreasonable. However, as we prepare for the next inevitable global pandemic, we should remember that there will be unused manufacturing and distribution capacity available around the world, a capacity that will be squandered due to TRIPS. Lives will be lost. We are faced with a Kantian dilemma. If intellectual property theft is always wrong, then during the next pandemic, developing countries will simply have to wait for legally manufactured and donated vaccines to arrive before lives can be saved. But what if Kant is wrong and a little bit of theft is okay?

Discuss
- **Let's say a new, terrible global pandemic has begun. A new vaccine has been developed and approved for emergency use, but it is protected by TRIPS. You operate a vaccine manufacturing facility in a developing country. You've tried to get licenses to produce the vaccine legally, but you've been denied. One day, you receive an anonymous letter and a USB-stick in the mail. The letter is from a disgruntled scientist at a major pharmaceutical company. She helped to develop the vaccine and believes that the vaccine specifications should be open-source and free to use during the pandemic. She says it is a violation of human dignity to put profits ahead of people. The enclosed USB-stick has all of the technical information you need to manufacture the vaccine at your facility. What would Kant do? What would you do? Why?**
- **From a wider public health perspective, how should TRIPS be modified so it can more effectively deal with global pandemics in the future?**

3.5 Human Dignity

Kant established two fundamental moral concepts: (1) Morality is derived from reason, and (2) moral rules must be followed absolutely, without exception. There is yet another reason why both murder and stealing are wrong. Murder is wrong because it destroys the only thing that has reason and creates value. Kant said that human beings have dignity precisely because they can value things. We have human rights, and we must respect other people's human rights because without the mutual recognition of rights, the entire moral universe would be destroyed. (Not surprisingly, he also argued that animals do not have rights because they lack reason.) Theft is always wrong because it involves using another person as a means to our own ends. Murder is wrong because the annihilation of a person attacks the very foundation of morality. Murdering an innocent person is the worst of crimes, and Kant insisted it must be punished with death.[1]

Kant (1785) created a second version of the categorical imperative to account for the absolute dignity of human beings: "Act in such a way that you treat humanity, whether in your own person or in the person of another, always at the same time as an end and never simply as a means" (p. 36). What does this mean? Essentially, Kant argues that we must realize that our own dignity rests on acknowledging the same dignity in others. We must constantly respect their rights, just like we demand others respect ours. When you steal from another, you are trampling on the dignity of another person, who is just like you. By destroying the dignity of another, you destroy the *whole* concept of morality. By destroying another value-giving creature, you by extension obliterate your own dignity as a human being as well.

Kant's insistence on the absolute worth of individuals is important because it puts your own absolute worth into perspective. No one wants to be killed, tortured, robbed, harmed, or deceived. And Kant helps us to explain why. If you do not want these bad things to happen to you, Kant reminds us that you should not want these bad things to happen to other people. And yet, we often excuse the violation of other people's absolute dignity. On a large scale, consider the dropping of the atom bombs on Hiroshima and Nagasaki, which led to the death of tens of thousands of innocent human beings: infants, women, senior citizens, and people with disabilities. On a smaller scale, think of the deaths of innocents—collateral damage—when drone strikes kill terrorist leaders in Afghanistan, Yemen, Syria, or the tribal regions in Pakistan.[2] Kant reminds us that once we grant exceptions for the killing of innocents in certain circumstances, we open the door to the violation of the dignity of all innocent human beings.

And this is precisely the problem that many political leaders faced during the pandemic after the first wave passed through the world in 2020. They faced pressure to loosen up restrictions on social distancing and also to allow businesses to open again despite the fact that the virus was still spreading and killing people. For some politicians, the arguments in favor of opening the economy were convincing if and only if you set a monetary value on human life. Kant would align with the strict approach to human dignity and strongly disagree with the temptation to weigh economic consequences against human life. The dignity of even a single human being is absolute, and the worth is priceless.

---

[1] Kant's opinion here seems to be contradictory. However, he makes a distinction between murder (the unlawful killing of an innocent person, performed by a private citizen) and execution (the lawful killing of a convicted murderer, performed by the embodied moral and legal community).

[2] The author is well aware of the complex rules and procedures that govern the legal selection of legitimate targets in war. Just War Theory, the Laws of Armed Conflict, and the Geneva Conventions all seek to create standards to judge the legal culpability of soldiers who kill innocent civilians, intentionally or unintentionally, during war. I simply wish to highlight here the moral objection that Kant would make. He would say that killing of innocent people is *always* and *absolutely* morally wrong despite any legal framework that may excuse it.

When we speak of absolute moral rules, like the rule not to kill innocent human beings, Kant means that these rules are indeed absolute. They must never be violated. If they are, then what is to stop someone else from saying that you—or your mom, dad, grandmother, or lover—*ought to be* sacrificed for the greater good?

COVID-19 put significant pressure on the concept of human dignity. For example, whenever a patient is removed from a life support system to make way for a patient with a higher chance of survival, a little bit of the principle of dignity slips away. This concept of triage will be discussed in Chap. 7, but let us now turn to a specific historical case of a real human being whose priceless dignity, some argue, was stripped away for the "greater good."

Box 3.2 Interdisciplinary Perspective #5: History

Typhoid Mary: A Question of Human Dignity

Typhoid fever (also known as enteric fever) is a disease caused by the bacterium, *Salmonella typhi*, and it is typically spread through contaminated food and water, the so-called oral-fecal route. In other words, human excrement carries the disease. In places with poor sewage and water treatment infrastructure, typhoid can spread rapidly. Also, washing one's hands is extremely important to prevent infection (provided that you have access to clean water, which many do not). Although there are both highly effective vaccines and antibiotics that should reduce the prevalence and mortality of typhoid, the disease persists primarily in poor areas with poor sanitation, primarily in sub-Saharan Africa and South-East Asia. The WHO (2018a) reports that there are somewhere between 11 and 21 million cases per year, accounting for about 130,000–160,000 deaths. However, before the discovery of the bacillus in 1879, the development of immunization in 1911, and then the production of antibiotics to treat salmonella in 1948, typhoid was far more dangerous. Indeed, the mortality rate without treatment, even today, is between 10% and 30%; however, with modern care, the mortality rate can be reduced to between 1% and 4% (WHO, 2018b, p. 156). (The reasons these figures vary so widely is because it is difficult to diagnose typhoid in areas of the world without labs that can process stool samples; hence, the true number of cases is difficult to ascertain.) Suffice it to say that typhoid was much more deadly 100 years ago than it is today. Currently, typhoid fever when treated appropriately is roughly as deadly as COVID-19 is (as of January 2022).

Enter Mary Mallon, aka Typhoid Mary, an Irish immigrant living in New York City at the end of the nineteenth century and the start of the twentieth. Mary worked as a cook for wealthy families, and everywhere she worked, people would contract typhus. However, typhus was common enough so no one suspected that Mary was the carrier, and Mary—a God-fearing, honest, and hard-working woman—did not suspect herself as the cause of the outbreaks. Why? She was an asymptomatic carrier of typhus before the concept of *asymptomatic carrier* was clearly understood.

(continued)

After one outbreak in a wealthy household that led to the death of a child, the father hired a private investigator to seek out the source of the infection. He traced the working history of the staff and discovered that seven out of eight of Mary's previous households had experienced outbreaks of typhus. The investigator tracked her down, and the authorities forcibly quarantined her because she refused to accept the fact that she was the cause of other people's deaths. How could she? She had never had any symptoms, so how could she infect people for years and years and years? As Janet Brooks (1996) wrote for the *Canadian Medical Association Journal*, Mary "denied that she was responsible for anyone's sickness or death and refused to recognize the authority of science or government to label her a menace to society" (p. 916).

After nearly 3 years of enforced quarantine—or was it imprisonment?—Mary was released under the condition that she not work as a cook. She returned to New York City and took a job as a washerwoman, but it paid much less than a cook, so she changed her name and became a cook once more. Additional outbreaks of typhus followed her wherever she went. Thinking back to the subject of public shaming in Chap. 2, it is understandable that a person who truly does not believe herself to be a public health menace would, first, reject the intense personal pain of public shaming and, second, adopt avoidance strategies—like changing one's name—in order to return to normal social life and reestablish her personal dignity and her status as a member of the human community. This is exactly what Mary did, and her story should serve as a cautionary tale for those who wish to use shame to change people's behavior.

For the next several years, Mary changed jobs often enough that it was difficult to identify her as the source of new infections. Eventually, the same investigator found her yet again and called the police. Mary was forcibly quarantined—this time for nearly 25 years—and she died in isolation on North Brother Island. She never accepted the fact that she was an asymptomatic carrier nor that she was the cause of so much suffering and death—how could she without causing herself the trauma of self-directed shame and disgust? The press didn't help matters, dubbing her Typhoid Mary. For the rest of her life, she believed she had been unjustly imprisoned. She said, "I never had typhoid in my life, and have always been healthy [...] Why should I be banished like a leper and compelled to live in solitary confinement with only a dog for a companion?" (as cited in Brooks, 1996, p. 916). Mary's case raises a number of ethical and legal questions with no easy answers.

- **The Right to Work**
  One issue is related to the relationship between one's profession and disease status. For example, Mary was forbidden to be a cook for fear of infection. During the height of the HIV/AIDS pandemic, people were banned from a variety of professions, including sports, the military, schools, and medicine, because they were HIV positive. Indeed, the NHS

(continued)

in the United Kingdom only lifted its ban on HIV-positive doctors and dentists from doing invasive operations in 2013 (Mahony, 2013), and the US military still bars HIV-positive people from enlisting (Congressional Research Service, 2019). Would it be appropriate to bar those who have chosen not to be vaccinated against COVID-19 from certain professions? We don't know much about long-COVID, but could that be disqualifying for certain professions?

- **Mandatory Quarantines: Sacrificing Individuals for the Greater Good** Was Mary's human dignity violated by effectively imprisoning her for decades? Is enforced quarantine the right thing to do? If it was right in Mary's case, would it be right with other people and other diseases? What about people with STDs like HIV/AIDS? Enforced quarantines (albeit for shorter periods of time) have been instituted across the globe in order to contain COVID-19. Is the benefit of quarantine for the community worth the loss of an individual's freedom?

Discuss
- How would Kant approach the case of Typhoid Mary? What universal rules can you apply in this situation? Which rules can you apply to Mary? Which rules can you apply to the government's response? Are there reasons why Mary should be considered an exception to a rule?
- Evaluate the two cases above: the right to work and mandatory quarantines. What powers should public authorities have in these scenarios? How do specific facts about disease transmission—for example, through respiratory droplets, sexual activity, or the oral-fecal route—change these calculations?

3.6 Conclusion

This book is about balancing different perspectives and integrating viewpoints that help solidify your own system of ethics. Whether or not you agree with Kant, his ideas demand consideration. Kant provides a convincing argument for the importance of absolute moral rules that uphold the dignity of all human beings. Our capacity to reason demands that we never steal, never lie, and never murder, no matter how tempting it might be to make exceptions to these rules. Indeed, Kant (1785) notes that we don't really need his long arguments to prove what is right and wrong: "We do not need science and philosophy to know what we should do to be honest and good, yea, even wise and virtuous" (I, para. 19). We should just know it is wrong because we all have enough common sense and sufficient imagination to acknowledge that since we do not want to be mistreated, we should not mistreat others because they do not want to be mistreated either.

Kant formalized the basic concepts of reciprocity, mutual respect, and human dignity. However, it is important to recognize these concepts are also implicit in a number of non-philosophical traditions. The concept of reciprocity resonates with diverse religious traditions that command us to treat others as we would like to be treated ourselves. But this lesson was also taught to us by our parents when we were toddlers and by our teachers in kindergarten. So important is this basic sense of moral right that we cannot ignore it or pretend not to understand it. Indeed, Kant (1781) wrote in the introduction to the *Critique of Pure Reason*, "Deficiency in judgment is just what is ordinarily called stupidity, and for that failing there is no remedy" (II, para. 2).

Despite the strength of the arguments in favor of reciprocity, mutual respect, and human dignity, Kant's way of thinking is not universal. Indeed, many would argue that an honest response to the Inquiring Murderer is what is ordinarily called stupid, despite Kant's long-winded and technical defense. Perhaps you still think that one ought to lie to him. Also, you might think the economy should *remain* open during a pandemic because there are unintended consequences when we shut the economy to halt the spread of a disease. After all, when people are forced to stay inside, domestic abuse cases increase, stress-levels increase, people become distressed and even suicidal, obesity increases, people lose their jobs, families starve, and nearly everyone loses money—lockdowns cause death and unhappiness too. So shouldn't we weigh *all* the short- and long-term costs when making a decision to shut down public life?

If you are not entirely convinced by Kant's arguments, you are perhaps a utilitarian, someone who believes that a moral rule may be broken if the consequences of breaking the rule would benefit the greatest number of people. For a utilitarian, lying to the Inquiring Murder would be a justifiable action because it would most likely increase happiness and decrease suffering. Imprisoning Mary Mallon would also be justifiable on the grounds that her suffering is less important than the harm she caused. The dispute between Kant and the utilitarians is rich, complex, and profound. It is perhaps the most fundamental dispute in ethics. The next chapter examines the strengths and weaknesses of the utilitarian mode of thought. Your position in this debate between Kant and the utilitarians has wide-ranging ramifications about how you choose to live your life during global pandemics.

Box 3.3 Criteria for Evaluating Ethical Theories: Part 1
At the end of this chapter and the next four chapters, you will be introduced to a variety of criteria for evaluating the five main ethical theories: Kantian deontology, utilitarianism, social contract theory, ethical egoism, and virtue ethics. The aim of this exercise is to identify both the strengths and weaknesses of each theory by selecting important evaluation criteria that you think ought to be included in a strong ethical theory. The long-term goal is to provide you with a solid foundation for constructing your own ideal personal ethical theory as well as your own ideal pandemic management theory when you complete the book. The instructions for this activity can be found in Sects. 8.4 and 8.5 of the final chapter.

(continued)

Kant's deontology raises a number of broad questions about what factors are most important in ethics in general. These evaluation criteria are useful when you think about the strengths and weaknesses of each of the five ethical theories discussed in this book. Furthermore, these criteria help you to determine your own values.

No theory is perfect, but each theory has some clear strengths and weaknesses depending on your own perspective. Let's look at three evaluation criteria raised by Kantian deontology.

1. Does the theory have an appropriate scope for who belongs in our moral community?

This is one of the most important questions we can ask ourselves. Who should be allowed in the moral community? Who should be excluded? Who is worthy of moral consideration?

Animals

Kant is quite clear that only rational human beings belong in the moral community. Animals do not belong because they lack reason. However, do you think animals should belong in the moral universe? Do you find Kant's theory inadequate because he restricts their inclusion? What type of rights should animals be given?

The Environment

Taking environmentalism a bit further, is the natural world as a whole worthy of moral consideration? Why or why not? If the natural world does indeed have rights, how do we resolve conflicts of interest between human rights and the rights of the environment?

Humans Lacking Reason

As we have seen, Kant insists that the ability to reason is the key element for moral consideration. What are the consequences of his view on people with disabilities or people with severe dementia? Do they lack reason, and are they, therefore, more like animals than like reasoning human beings? Should they be excluded from the moral community? During a pandemic when resources are scarce, is it appropriate to deny treatment to people with mental disabilities?

Future Generations

Lastly, what about future generations? Do they have any status in the moral community? How can one give rights to people who do not yet exist?

2. Does the theory exhibit an appropriate degree of rational consistency?

Rational consistency is one of Kant's hallmarks. He believed that we should treat others as we expect ourselves to be treated—this is a rule that can be applied consistently and universally. I don't want to infect you with COVID-19, so I wear a mask; therefore, you should wear a mask to avoid

(continued)

infecting me. I don't want you to steal my bicycle, so it is reasonable and consistent to expect me not to steal yours.

But what if you have ten bicycles and I only have one broken bicycle. Surely, I could steal your bicycle and it wouldn't be so bad. Kant, we know, disagreed with any exceptions to rules. However, maybe a suitable moral theory should allow for exceptions.

Even if you think an ethical theory should allow for exceptions to rules, then maybe some form of rational consistency should still apply. After all, if a theory does not adequately explain why exceptions should or should not be allowed, then it would still be rationally inconsistent or *arbitrary*. So the second question here is this: If an ethical theory allows exceptions to rules, should there be a consistent set of rules to determine exceptions?

3. Does the theory align with "common sense"?

   Kant said, "We do not need science and philosophy to know what we should do to be honest and good, yea, even wise and virtuous." Despite his life-long study of ethics, even Kant admitted that common sense was sufficient to tell us how to be good people. Much is made of common sense, despite the fact that it is difficult to define. Still, when it comes to common sense ethics, most people believe they have an abundance of it while others totally lack it. Indeed, most people have a high opinion of themselves and are in the habit of claiming to know, beyond the shadow of a doubt, what is right and what is wrong.

   Taking a step back, it might be worthwhile to acknowledge these facts. After all, if moral problems were so obviously solved and if it were so easy to know what the right thing to do is, then the world would not be faced with any problems at all.

   We will see that there are some fairly extreme aspects of ethical theories that may not align with common sense. Indeed, Kant's insistence that we never allow exceptions for rules seems to be one such extreme. So should a good ethical theory align with common sense, or would you rather leave any concept of common sense out of your ideal theory because the concept itself is impossible to define?

References

Brooks, J. (1996). The sad and tragic life of Typhoid Mary. *Canadian Medical Association Journal, 154*(6), 915–916.

Congressional Research Service. (2019, May 31). HIV/AIDS in the US military. https://sgp.fas.org/crs/natsec/IF11238.pdf. Accessed 27 Aug 2022.

Davies, H., & Goodley, S. (2020, May 1). Revealed: NHS procurement official privately selling PPE amid Covid-19 outbreak. *The Guardian*. https://www.theguardian.com/society/2020/may/01/revealed-nhs-procurement-official-privately-selling-ppe. Accessed 1 May 2020.

Eaton, J., & Murphy, J. (2021, September 1). America has wasted at least 15 million Covid vaccine doses. *NBC News.* https://www.nbcnews.com/news/us-news/america-has-wasted-least-15-million-covid-vaccine-doses-march-n1278211. Accessed 2 Sept 2021.

Halliday, J. (2020, March 23). Three teenagers held for allegedly coughing at elderly couple in Hertfordshire. *The Guardian.* https://www.theguardian.com/uk-news/2020/mar/23/three-teenagers-held-for-allegedly-coughing-at-elderly-couple-hertfordshire. Accessed 23 March 2020.

Human Rights Watch. (2021, June 3). Seven reasons the EU is wrong to oppose the TRIPS waiver. https://www.hrw.org/news/2021/06/03/seven-reasons-eu-wrong-oppose-trips-waiver. Accessed 5 June 2021.

Kant, I. (1781). *Critique of pure reason* (J. M. D. Meiklejohn, Trans.). Project Gutenberg. 2021. https://www.gutenberg.org/files/4280/4280-h/4280-h.htm

Kant, I. (1785). *Fundamental principles of the metaphysic of morals* (T. K. Abbot, Trans.). 2018. https://www.gutenberg.org/files/5682/5682-h/5682-h.htm

Kant, I. (1788). *Critique of practical reason* (T. K. Abbott, Trans.). Project Gutenberg. 2018. https://www.gutenberg.org/files/5683/5683-h/5683-h.htm

Kant, I. (1790). *Critique of judgement* (W. S. Pluhar, Trans.). Hackett. 1987.

Kant, I. (1797). On a supposed right to tell lies from altruistic motives. In *Immanuel Kant: Critique of practical reason and other writings in moral philosophy* (L. W. Beck, Trans.). University of Chicago Press. 1949.

Kornfield, M. (2020, May 6). Three people charged in killing of Family Dollar security guard over mask policy. *The Washington Post.* https://www.washingtonpost.com/nation/2020/05/04/security-guards-death-might-have-been-because-he-wouldnt-let-woman-store-without-mask/. Accessed 6 May 2020.

Mahony, C. (2013). Ban on healthcare workers with HIV performing certain procedures is lifted. *British Medical Journal, 347.* https://doi.org/10.1136/bmj.f5162

Pfizer. (2022, April). COVID-19 vaccine U.S. distribution fact sheet. https://cdn.pfizer.com/pfizercom/Pfizer_PGS_COVID-19_Factsheet_071122.pdf. Accessed 23 Aug 2022.

Siripurapu, A. (2021, May 26). *The debate over a patent waiver for COVID-19 vaccines: What to know.* Council on Foreign Relations. https://www.cfr.org/in-brief/debate-over-patent-waiver-covid-19-vaccines-what-know. Accessed 26 May 2021.

UK Regulatory Agency. (2022, January 26). Package leaflet: Information for the recipient the AstraZeneca vaccine. https://www.gov.uk/government/publications/regulatory-approval-of-covid-19-vaccine-astrazeneca/information-for-uk-recipients-on-covid-19-vaccine-astrazeneca. Accessed 23 Aug 2022.

UNICEF. (2021, October 27). *G20 members have received 15 times more COVID-19 vaccine doses per capita than sub-Saharan African countries.* Press Release. https://www.unicef.org/press-releases/g20-members-have-received-15-times-more-covid-19-vaccine-doses-capita-sub-saharan. Accessed 30 Oct 2021.

UNICEF. (2022). COVID market dashboard. https://www.unicef.org/supply/covid-19-vaccine-market-dashboard. Accessed 27 Aug 2022.

WHO. (2018a, January 31). Typhoid. https://www.who.int/news-room/fact-sheets/detail/typhoid. Accessed on 23 Aug 2022.

WHO. (2018b, March 30). Typhoid vaccines: WHO position paper. *Weekly Epidemiological Record, 93,* 153–172. https://apps.who.int/iris/bitstream/handle/10665/272272/WER9313.pdf?ua=1. Accessed 27 Aug 2022.

WHO. (2022). COVAX Act. https://www.who.int/initiatives/act-accelerator/covax. Accessed 27 Aug 2022.

WTO. (2020, October 2). IP/C/W/669. Waiver from certain provisions of the TRIPS agreement for the prevention, containment and treatment of COVID-19. Doc #: 20-6725. https://docs.wto.org/. Accessed 28 Aug 2022.

WTO. (2021, September 30). IP/C/W/684. Council for Trade-Related Aspects of Intellectual Property Rights – Waiver from certain provisions of the TRIPS agreement for the prevention, containment and treatment of COVID-19. Doc #: 21-7337. Available at https://docs.wto.org/. Accessed 28 Aug 2022.

Chapter 4
Utilitarianism and Consequentialist Ethics: Framing the Greater Good

4.1 Consequentialism

On 23 March 2020, during the first wave of the COVID-19 pandemic, then President Donald J. Trump tweeted in all caps: "WE CANNOT LET THE CURE BE WORSE THAN THE PROBLEM ITSELF." What did this cryptic tweet mean? Presumably, he was arguing that the cure to the pandemic (shutting down the economy) should not be worse than the problems posed by the pandemic (overflowing hospitals, rationing of ICUs and ventilators, and people dying from the rapid spread of the virus); he was making a point that an influential strand of philosophers would agree with. Shuttering the economy leads to many bad outcomes—increases in substance abuse, obesity, mental illness, domestic abuse; the loss of jobs; and unfortunately loss of life through all of the above. If we had a system to calculate which approach to pandemic management would increase happiness and decrease pain in the long run, surely we should choose the option that would have the best long-term consequences. In plain terms, if shutting the economy leads to two million deaths in the long term, but letting the virus run its course leads to one million deaths in the short term, then clearly one should choose the policy that reduces the pain and increases the happiness of the greatest number. If the cure is worse than the problem itself, it is reasonable to argue for ending the cure.

Such a thought process is called utilitarian or consequentialist. Utilitarians believe that an action is right or wrong based on the consequences of the action. They characterize good and bad actions as follows: *An action is right if it increases the overall happiness of those affected by the action, and an action is wrong if it does the opposite.* Furthermore, utilitarians believe that people have a moral obligation—they are morally required—to act in such a way. As the most famous living utilitarian philosopher Peter Singer (2000) argues, "We are responsible not only for what we do but also for what we could have prevented [...] We should consider the consequences both of what we do and of what we decide not to do" (p. xiv). In other

A. Sola, *Ethics and Pandemics*, Springer Series in Public Health and Health
Policy Ethics, https://doi.org/10.1007/978-3-031-33207-4_4

words, if we can prevent the suffering of others without causing a similar amount of suffering to ourselves or anyone else, we are obligated to do so. For Singer, actions should be judged by their consequences; furthermore, choosing not to act should also be judged by the consequences of inaction.

We often make decisions based on the likely consequence of the action, and we often follow utilitarian rules of behavior in everyday ethical decision-making. For example, if you choose to let a stressed-out mom with an infant and a toddler cut in front of you in the security queue at the airport so they can catch their flight, you are being a good utilitarian. The pain caused to you by losing one place in the queue is far less than the pain that would result from the family missing their flight. Therefore, allowing them to cut the queue is a moral obligation for utilitarians. You could, of course, take an absolute Kantian position and refuse to allow the mother to cut the queue: "Sorry, lady. If you cut in, you would be creating a universal law that queue-cutting is OK. However, you should know that there can be no exceptions to moral rules. If you cut in the queue, you would be violating the dignity of all of the people ahead of you, which pretty much means you are destroying the whole moral universe, at least according to Kant." Nevertheless, utilitarians would insist that you should always think about the consequences of your actions, so letting this poor mother cut in would be required. Indeed, it is *obligatory*. (Also note that there would be no utilitarian obligation to allow her to cut the queue if she were simply being impatient.)

Similarly, charitable donations can be seen through a utilitarian lens. Donating $20 to a food bank or $5 to a COVID-19 vaccination program may be a small sacrifice for you, but your donation would reduce the suffering and increase the happiness of the beneficiary considerably. For utilitarians donating to charity is a moral obligation for everyone with excess wealth (Singer, 1999). Not donating excess wealth to charity makes you something of a moral monster for many strict utilitarians. They also advocate telling lies when appropriate. For example, if your spouse asks you if a new outfit or a new hairstyle looks good, you might respond with a little white lie. If it really does not look good, you might say it does because lying will create more happiness than telling the truth, which will lead to embarrassment and pain for both parties. Utilitarianism, unlike Kantianism, would *require* you to lie in such circumstances. A final example: If wearing a face mask or a condom were to prevent you from spreading any illness to even one other person, you are morally obligated to do so. Whatever discomforts these preventative measures may cause you are insignificant compared to the pain and suffering created if you transmit a disease to another person. By not wearing a mask or a condom, you are making a choice of inaction that may cause suffering. This too, for a utilitarian, is morally wrong.

As much as utilitarianism influences small ethical decisions made in the private sphere, it is also arguably the most powerful factor that influences decisions made at the highest levels of economic, social, political, and public health policy. Indeed, the utilitarian approach to ethics attempts to come to terms with some of the central problems of civilized life: How do leaders weigh the good of the community against the good of the individual? The good of a community against the good of the nation?

The good of a nation against the good of the world? The good of shareholders against the good of other stakeholders? The good of an endangered species against the good of the human community? The good of the environment against the good of the economy? The good of the economy against the good of public health?

Unfortunately, for important decisions that change people's lives, a clear ethical path that satisfies all parties rarely presents itself. Instead, most decisions lead to some people feeling aggrieved and others feeling satisfied. One side claims the decision is unjust, and the other claims it is just. Utilitarianism provides a useful tool to weigh those difficult decisions. The utilitarian always asks: What action will lead to the best outcome for all parties affected by the decision?

In this chapter, we will discuss the origins of utilitarian thinking as well as the strengths and weaknesses of the theory. Also, we will look at the only pandemic disease that we human beings have eradicated through our own initiative: smallpox. The smallpox vaccine raises some important questions about forcing people to be vaccinated for the common good. At the end of the chapter, you may agree or disagree with utilitarian thinking. In either case, you will understand that it is a powerful force when making difficult ethical decisions about pandemic management.

4.2   Jeremy Bentham and the Hedonic Calculus

Utilitarianism was created by Jeremy Bentham (1748–1832) in Great Britain in the late eighteenth century and early nineteenth century, partly as a response to the Industrial Revolution and the sharp increase in misery for the working poor, who labored long hours in dangerous factories while earning low wages and living in filthy slums. Bentham believed that the role of the government and policy makers was *not* to make it easier for the rich and powerful to make their fellow human beings more miserable, but instead to create the conditions whereby as many people as possible could live happy lives with the minimum amount of suffering. Furthermore, Bentham was an ardent proponent of the equality of all people— equality defined as the ability to feel both pleasure and pain, a definition which also made him an early proponent of animal welfare. As he wrote in *An Introduction into the Principles of Morals and Legislation* (1789), "Nature has placed mankind under the governance of two sovereign masters, pain and pleasure. It is for them alone to point out what we ought to do" (I, Sect. 1).

Bentham was also influenced by the scientific method and empirical inquiry. He noted that morality and ethics had been discussed for thousands of years without providing any definitive answers. Perhaps, he thought, morality could be pinned down once and for all with a clear, scientific system of identifying right and wrong behavior. To this end, he developed the Hedonic Calculus (also referred to as the Felicific Calculus), which provides seven criteria for making decisions, all based on calculations about the pain and pleasure that result from an action:

(1) Intensity: How powerful will the pain or pleasure be?
(2) Duration: How long will the pain or pleasure last?

(3) Propinquity: How soon will the pain or pleasure occur?
(4) Certainty: How likely is it that the pain or pleasure will actually occur?
(5) Fecundity: Will the action produce even more pain or pleasure?
(6) Purity: Will any additional pain or pleasure accompany the action?
(7) Extent: How many people will be affected by the action? (Bentham, 1789,
    IV, Sect. 2–3)

Many consider these factors when making decisions without actually thinking about them, and the seven factors provide a useful way to begin to analyze the pleasure and pain that are the result of our decisions. Still, the Hedonic Calculus may seem incomplete, particularly because it is difficult to evaluate which pleasures are "better" than others. Is junk food better than healthy food because French fries taste better than cooked carrots? Is intense training for a triathlon "bad" because it causes pain? Is lying better than telling the truth because telling the truth may cause pain? Is spending one's free time writing a symphony better than spending that time building shelters for the homeless? Is donating money to vaccine research better than donating money for the protection of endangered species? It seems that this calculus is much too confusing and complex to guide our decision-making process.

4.3   John Stuart Mill and a Revised Definition of Pleasure

John Stuart Mill (1806–1873) is without question the most famous utilitarian thinker in history. His father, James, was a friend and disciple of Bentham. Together they set out to raise John Stuart as a calculating utilitarian machine, well-versed in the art of applying the Hedonic Calculus to all questions great and small; he was to be the perfect human accountant of pains and pleasures. He did become such a man, but only at great cost to his emotional development. His education was so strict that he never developed a sense of empathy or love until later in life after he recovered from a depressive episode at the age of 20. In his *Autobiography* (1873), he remembers asking himself:

> "Suppose that all your objects in life were realized; that all the changes in institutions and opinions which you are looking forward to, could be completely effected at this very instant: would this be a great joy and happiness to you?" And an irrepressible self-consciousness distinctly answered, "No!" At this my heart sank within me: the whole foundation on which my life was constructed fell down. All my happiness was to be found in the continual pursuit of this end. The end had ceased to charm, and how could there ever again be any interest in the means? I seemed to have nothing left to live for. (V, para. 2)

The utilitarian calculator had lost his own personal sense of happiness. "I became persuaded that my love of mankind, and of excellence for its own sake, had worn itself out" (V, para. 4). He felt that he was alone, "with a well-equipped ship and rudder, but no sail; without any real desire for the ends which I had been so carefully fitted out to work for; no delight in virtue or the general good, but also just as little in anything else" (V, para. 5). Like many disaffected youth, he began to question the meaning of life, which had been dictated by those who forced upon him a value system that he had not chosen for himself. As a result, he began to develop his own philosophical system. Eventually he recovered from depression and developed a less calculating, more caring utilitarian philosophy, partly through the help of his wife, Harriet Taylor, the women's rights activist, about whom he wrote, "What was abstract and purely scientific was generally mine; the properly human element came from her" (VII, para. 14).

As Mill rediscovered his human element, he turned his sights on developing a more nuanced view of utilitarianism, one that did not simply calculate units of pleasure and units of pain. After all, pleasures cannot be added up like numbers—there is a *qualitative* aspect of pleasure, in addition to a quantitative one. He notes in his seminal text, *Utilitarianism* (1863), "It is better to be a human being dissatisfied than a pig satisfied; better to be Socrates dissatisfied than a fool satisfied. And if the fool, or the pig, is of a different opinion, it is because they only know their own side of the question. The other party to the comparison knows both sides" (II, para. 6).

So Mill revised Bentham by suggesting that there are "higher" and "lower" pleasures. Higher pleasures would include learning a foreign language, educating oneself, mastering an artistic skill, playing an instrument, developing long-term relationships, etc. Lower pleasures would include various types of immediate sensual pleasures, such as drug and alcohol use, sex, and gluttony. (Critics have suggested that Mill's ranking of pleasures is elitist, arguing that the "higher" pleasures are only available to the wealthy and not even remotely attainable by the great mass of society.) Mill also suggests that the development of higher pleasures is a critical part of a just and civilized society. Developing those pleasures requires that people be given the time and freedom to cultivate them. A good society promotes the happiness of all people equally, and in such a society people will naturally develop a sense of brotherhood and kinship with others.

Although John Stuart Mill turned Bentham's utilitarianism into a more nuanced system by refining the concept of pleasure, the broad outlines of the theory remain mostly unchanged to this day. Utilitarianism still requires that we always choose the action that leads to more pleasure and less suffering for all those affected by the action.

4.4 Peter Singer: The Modern Utilitarian Champion

One of the most famous living philosophers, Peter Singer (b. 1946), is the undisputed modern champion of utilitarian thinking. Among his contributions to ethics are books on animal rights (*Animal Liberation: A New Ethics for our Treatment of Animals,* 1975) as well as poverty reduction (*The Life You Can Save: Acting Now to End World Poverty,* 2009). Never one to shy away from controversy, Singer likes to provoke the public and expose our moral hypocrisy. Although many consider his views to be extreme, his ideas proceed clearly and rationally from four core utilitarian principles, which he outlines in the Introduction to *Writings on an Ethical Life*

(2000). His first core principle restates the traditional utilitarian view of pain and pleasure: "Pain is bad, and similar amounts of pain are equally bad...Conversely, pleasure and happiness are good" (para. 5). Of course, he is careful to remind us of the nuance of these positions. He notes that going to the dentist might cause short-term pain, but it still may be the right action because it leads to less pain in the future. Similarly, he notes that some people might take pleasure from harming others, but harming others might still be wrong for the pain it causes the victim. Still, the overall goal of this principle is to maximize pleasure and minimize pain for as many "beings" as possible.

His second principle explicitly states that "beings" must include non-human animals: "Human beings are not the only beings capable of feeling pain or suffering" (para. 6). Since non-human animals also feel pain, we should consider that fact when deciding how to treat them. This principle forms the bedrock of his view on the moral status of animals in utilitarian philosophy. Animals are worthy of moral consideration—indeed, we must give them equal consideration—since they too feel pain, just like we humans do.

His third principle touches on the controversial subjects of suicide and euthanasia: "When we consider how serious it is to take a life, we should look [...] at the characteristics of the individual being killed, for example, its own desires about continuing to live, or the kind of life it is capable of leading" (para. 7). It should not be surprising that Singer is in favor of euthanasia, particularly in cases where the creature does not wish to continue living a life full of pain. This view, which was highly controversial in the past, is beginning to gain acceptance.

Singer's fourth and most damning principle touches upon one of the most basic human behaviors—we value our own selfish pleasure so much more than the real suffering of others that we refuse to accept the moral imperative that we should sacrifice our own luxuries in order to help those who are suffering. He writes:

> We are responsible not only for what we do but also for what we could have prevented. We would never kill a stranger, but we may know that our intervention will save the lives of many strangers in a distant country, and yet do nothing. We do not then think ourselves in any way responsible for the deaths of these strangers. This is a mistake. (para. 8)

Here he points out what he believes to be the fundamental hypocrisy of modern life. Most people claim to care about the suffering of the poor, and yet they still spend money on frivolous luxuries rather than donating their money to those in great need.

To put Singer's argument into concrete terms, the UN (2021) estimates that roughly 750 million live in extreme poverty, defined as living on under $1.90 a day. Furthermore, the World Bank (2018) notes that 3.4 billion people "struggle to meet basic needs," defined as $3.20 a day in lower-middle income countries and $5.50 in upper-middle income countries. It may be painful for us to even comprehend life in extreme poverty, but billions of people face its challenges every single day. Singer's forceful argument is this: Since we know we can do immense good by sacrificing some of our luxuries for the global poor, we must do so. Secondly, it is wrong to claim that we are not responsible for their pain and suffering.

Before you accuse Singer of hypocrisy, it is important to note that Singer himself donates a considerable percentage of his income to charity. In 2021, he won the Berggruen Prize which comes with one million dollars, all of which he donated to charity (Schuessler, 2021). Still, his ideas are controversial for a number of reasons. People have very emotional reactions to his arguments, since most of us believe that we are good people, and Singer reminds us that we are not. Here are some standard objections:

- If I give all my money to the poor, then I will be no better off than the poorest people. How does that increase the overall happiness?
- Giving money to the poor does not teach them how to be self-sufficient, and learning self-sufficiency would actually increase their happiness in the long run.
- I know there are starving children far away, but my children are here with me. Why should I deprive my own children of a good education and Christmas presents in order to support children on the other side of the planet?
- I'm a comedian, and I spend all of my time and energy on making people laugh—and I'm good at it. Maybe it would be a better use of my time to care for the poor, but making people laugh causes happiness.
- Resources are scarce. There isn't ever enough to go around. No matter how much money anyone gives, we will never be able to solve the problem of global poverty.

These objections are reasonable and worthy of further consideration; they will be discussed at greater length below, but now let us turn to utilitarian principles and vaccine inequality: How can we distribute vaccines in a fair and equitable way in order to increase the greatest happiness for the greatest number?

Box 4.1 Interdisciplinary Perspective #6: Global Public Health and Health Economics

Vaccine Equity, Boosters, and the Fair Priority Model for Vaccine Distribution

As mentioned in the previous chapter, the WTO's intellectual property protection rules have prevented developing countries from producing vaccines and other technologies (illegally, so to speak) that would increase supplies where they are needed. One of the work-arounds is the COVAX program, which collects donated vaccines from wealthy countries and redistributes them to developing countries. The WHO (2021) is quite direct about the rationale for this program:

> By the end of September [2021], almost 6-and-a-half billion doses had already been administered worldwide. With global vaccine production now at nearly 1.5 billion doses per month, there is enough supply to achieve our targets, provided they are distributed equitably. This is not a supply problem; it's an allocation problem.

Equitable distribution is the central ethical concept here. Vaccine equity is closely connected to utilitarian principles of equitable distribution of all types

(continued)

of resources, including money, food, energy, livesaving medicines, and other resources that are in abundant supply in one place and deficient in another. Peter Singer reminds us that if we have excess resources, we should always donate our excess to those who can benefit the most from them. However, one need not follow utilitarianism to claim that throwing away vaccine doses is bad policy; indeed, most conscientious people would agree that wasting resources is wrong.

But there is a more subtle problem here. Many conscientious people in the developed world also felt guilt about receiving a third COVID booster before poor people in developing countries received their first dose. Was the booster dose a Western "luxury" that we should have refused in order to consider ourselves good people? Nancy S. Jecker (2021), a bioethicist at the University of Washington, weighed in on the topic. She suggests that booster shots might have violated the principle of "health equity," the idea that we should use our resources to help those most in need. Second, she cites the principle of "diminishing marginal utility," noting that the first dose of the COVID vaccine provided far more benefits across the board than the third dose. On the other hand, she recognizes that many politicians felt that it was their solemn duty to protect their own people first (which led to vaccine hoarding, also known as vaccine nationalism) before it was appropriate to help others. Also, she suggests the word-choice of "booster" dose might have led to unnecessary guilty feelings, whereas a word like "final" dose would have sounded less controversial.

From a wider perspective, the guilt felt when getting a booster may be similar to the guilt felt when wasting food. You know that there are starving people around the world who would gladly eat your leftovers, so you feel a twinge of guilt when you chuck it in the trash. However, if you make too much food for dinner and waste some, that excess food will not magically end up on the plate of a starving child on the other side of the world. Similarly, if you decline a booster that is available at your local health center, your dose will not magically appear in an under-vaccinated country. In some ways then, there is a confusion of personal responsibility and systemic inequality here. Individual citizens with limited resources can't simply project their excess to the farthest corner of the globe. We need big and complex institutions to do so. What would utilitarians think? They might suggest that it is your moral duty not to waste the booster available to you while simultaneously providing financial support to the institutions that have the expertise to distribute vaccines to developing countries.

Given the presence of systemic inequality in global public health, what can powerful institutions like national governments and NGOs do about it? How can we create a new system that reduces vaccine inequality? A group of 18 ethicists around the world has created the Fair Priority Model for Vaccine Distribution (Emanuel et al., 2020). The model rests on three core values. It

(continued)

(1) benefits people while limiting harm, (2) prioritizes those who are "disadvantaged," and (3) upholds the principle of equal moral concern (p. 2). The first value is traditional across most ethical theories. Whenever possible, we should try to help others and not hurt them. The second value is slightly more problematic. Utilitarians argue that the disadvantaged and underprivileged deserve more concern than those who already have excess resources. However, not everyone would agree with this approach. For example, we will see in the next chapter on the social contract that many philosophers argue that our own community, our own society, and our own nation deserve more attention than outside groups—this is the justification for vaccine nationalism. The third value follows from the second: "Equal moral concern requires treating similar individuals similarly and not discriminating on the basis of morally irrelevant differences, such as sex, race, and religion" (Emanuel et al., 2020, p. 2). Note that neither nationality nor wealth is on this list.

In short, the Fair Distribution Model sees everyone on the planet as having an equal right to vaccine access, but since wealthy nations are able to take care of their citizens more effectively and efficiently, an equitable model needs to cut through the economic disparity and prioritize the disadvantaged. The authors then propose complex metrics that allow public health bodies to determine where vaccines ought to be distributed. One metric is SEYLL (standard expected years of life lost), which determines how many more years of life will be preserved with high levels of vaccinations. Further, they use the metric of GNI (gross national income), which determines how the income of a nation will increase per dose provided. The calculations reveal a three-stage system with accompanying priorities:

Phase 1 Goal: Reduce Premature Deaths
   Priority: Countries that "reduce more SEYLL per dose"

Phase 2 Goal: Reduce Serious Economic and Social Deprivations
   Priority: Countries that "reduce more poverty, avert more loss of GNI, and avert more SEYLL per dose"

Phase 3 Goal: Return to Full Functioning
   Priority: Countries "with higher transmission rates" (Emanuel et al., 2020, pp. 2–3)

The Fair Priority Model for Vaccine Distribution is indeed fair and equitable. It is also set up to maximize vaccine distribution for the greatest good. Furthermore, it provides calculations that prove its streamlined utility. No problems here then.

But wait one second. Let's say you are in Country A, which has lower transmission rates compared to Country B. Should you be denied a vaccine for the greater good of those living in Country B? Utilitarians like Peter Singer say *yes*. Human worth should be compared in order to determine the most

(continued)

effective means of allocating limited resources. And this is the critical difference between the utilitarian approach to human dignity and Kant's. While utilitarians take a quantitative approach to enhancing the greatest good for the greatest number of people, Kant focuses on the more fundamental and absolutist point that each human life is priceless.

The Fair Priority Model, if implemented, would certainly help to decrease vaccine inequality. However, it also shows that we do live in a utilitarian world in which *the value of every individual human life is* constantly being calculated and, perhaps, even devalued.

Discuss

- **Despite the problems of systemic inequality around the world, Peter Singer reminds us that we can still make personal choices to do good. Furthermore, he argues that we cannot call ourselves good people while at the same time doing nothing to prevent pain and suffering among the world's poor. The global charity GAVI, the Global Alliance for Vaccines and Immunization, provides low-cost vaccines to children in low-income countries. A single $28 donation provides full immunization for a child in a developing country (as opposed to $1300 in the United States). You can donate to GAVI right now with one click of your smartphone and save the life of a child. Will you donate? Why or why not? See https://www.gavi.org/donate-gavi-routine-immunisation.**
- **Evaluate the fair priority model. Does it effectively deal with the issue of vaccine inequality?**
- **Should wealthy nations always prioritize equitable distribution of resources to other countries, even if it comes at the expense of their own citizens?**

4.5 The *Telos* of Morality

Perhaps the strongest argument in favor of the utilitarian way of thinking is that, unlike other systems of ethics, it answers an important question which other theories either fail to address or only address obliquely: What is the *telos* of morality? (*Telos* is an ancient Greek word that means the aim, final goal, or ultimate purpose of something.)

For example, religious people might believe that the point of morality is to go to Heaven or to follow God's commands. Kantians believe that the point of morality is to behave according to the inviolable laws of reason. Cultural relativists believe that there is no point to morality at all because morality is simply a descriptive term that means behaving according to the traditions of one's culture. Ethical egoists believe that the point of morality is to follow one's self-interest and to live one's own life to the fullest (even at the expense of other people's happiness). Social contract theorists believe that the point is to live according to the rules that will guarantee the frictionless running of a civilized society. However, only the utilitarian thinkers say explicitly what the goal of all this discussion about morality really should be: more happiness and less suffering—on this planet, in the present and in the future, for as many creatures as possible.

Their point is a good one: Why do we have moral rules if not to ensure the greatest possible happiness and the least amount of suffering for as many creatures as possible? Why are religious people focusing on being happy in Heaven when life on earth is miserable? Why does Kant focus on following absolute moral rules when doing so often leads to pain? In short, utilitarians believe that the real and ever-present happiness and suffering of humans and non-human animals living now on this planet is much more important for ethical decision-making than any other consideration.

We have seen that utilitarianism anchors morality in a universal sense of moral good—more happiness, less suffering. What could possibly be wrong about such an idea? Let's examine this uncomfortable topic by calculating the monetary value of your own precious life.

Box 4.2 Interdisciplinary Perspective #7: Healthcare Economics

How Much Is Your Life Really Worth?

Resource scarcity is a fact of life, especially when it comes to healthcare. Even if there are enough resources to go around, there are always new drugs, new treatments, and new medical devices that are constantly in development. During the height of the COVID-19 pandemic, resource scarcity was the norm. Hospitals around the world faced shortages of swabs, tests, reagents, PPE, ventilators, ICU beds, nurses, doctors, lab technicians, and so on. Faced with resource scarcity, what is an ethical way to determine who should get scarce resources?

Policy makers have always faced intense pressure to determine fair ways of distributing finite resources. Some have taken a Kantian position, refusing to put a value on human life. They suggest, "No matter what the cost, my policies are centered on preserving the absolute dignity of every human life." Other policy makers are guided by the utilitarian approach: Since we have limited resources, what policy will create the greatest good for the most people? The devil, of course, is in the details. What is fair? How does one define "the greatest good"? How does one allocate those resources?

The most important point is this: For policy makers, there is a precise value one can put on human life. Indeed, one important role of the government is to create rules and regulations to safeguard public health. For example, food producers are required to comply with food safety regulations in order to prevent the spread of food-borne illnesses. Pharmaceutical companies are required to comply with drug regulations in order to prevent the misuse and

(continued)

abuse of medicine. A variety of industries are required to comply with regulations to prevent the contamination of air, water, and soil. Financial institutions are required to comply with rules to prevent people from being defrauded. The car industry is regulated to prevent deaths due to inadequate safety measures. Of course, these regulations cost money, and the key question for regulators and policy makers is if a regulation is cost-effective. In other words, is the cost of implementing the regulation less than the benefit of no regulation? In order to make that calculation, the price of a human life must be quantified.

Some statistics help to put these questions in perspective. The US Environmental Protection Agency (2022) insists that it "does not place a dollar value on individual lives" (para. 1); however, when weighing regulatory actions and performing cost-benefit analysis, it does admit to having precisely such a value, which is called the value of a statistical life (VSL). This value is currently set at $7.4 million. The US Department of Transportation (2021) puts the VSL at $11.8 million for 2021, a $200,000 increase from 2020. These valuations help government regulators determine whether or not safety regulations should be placed upon businesses (e.g., the requirement to install seat belts and airbags in automobiles).

Turning to healthcare, there are serious issues connected to resource scarcity and cost-effectiveness in both wealthy and poor countries. In wealthy countries with national health systems, doctors, administrators, and policy makers constantly attempt to determine which treatments can be delivered to the most patients at the lowest cost. (The de facto rationing of care happens in wealthy countries like the United States in which the uninsured are untreated or undertreated due to the lack of the ability to pay.) Unfortunately, not everyone can receive the most expensive and revolutionary treatments all the time. This is due to a number of metrics, the most important of which is the quality-adjusted life year (QALY), which is used to determine if a treatment is cost-effective or not.

To further explain the QALY calculation, let's say you have cancer and there's a treatment that will increase your life span by 10 years with a fairly high quality of life (0.8) during those additional years. The QALY would be 10×0.8 or 8 QALYs. Next, we must put a price on a QALY to determine if your treatment is cost-effective. In the United States, a QALY is priced at about $50,000 (Neumann et al., 2014). In your case, 8 QALYs times $50,000 = $400,000. If your cancer treatment costs more than $400,000, it would not be cost-effective. Sorry! One consequence of this formula is that it is usually more cost-effective to provide expensive treatments to young people who generally have a longer life span. Older people, obviously, have a shorter potential life span, so their treatment necessarily becomes less cost-effective as they age. Furthermore, since older people use more healthcare resources, a utilitarian might question why we spend more money on the elderly who, despite the high cost of their treatment, will not have many "quality" years to enjoy the benefits of the treatment.

(continued)

Another example of this number-based approach to health is the National Health Service (NHS) in the United Kingdom. The NHS suggests a variety of different economic analyses to use when determining the effectiveness of health treatments: cost-consequence analysis, cost-effectiveness analysis, cost-utility analysis, and cost-benefit analysis (UK Health Security Agency, 2021). Each is worth exploring if you are interested in the mathematical complexities of healthcare economics. However, to provide a concrete example about treating a patient with a new medicine, the NHS only allows treatment if it costs less than 30,000 GBP per QALY (Gandjour, 2020). In other words, the medicine will not be reimbursed if it is too expensive according to the formula. If the price is right, your life might be saved.

These formulae should give us pause for thought. Kant would object to the entire premise of the discussion. The exercise of determining the price of a human life violates our dignity—the exercise itself forecasts the obliteration of the moral universe. If human life is not sacred, then there is no longer such a thing as right and wrong. On the other hand, resource scarcity is a fact of life. We can't stick our heads in the sand and ignore the grim reality of the world. At least utilitarians confront the problem openly and have a methodology for creating a "fair and equitable" solution.

Even if we understand the utility of understanding the economics of healthcare, would you really be OK if someone said your grandmother doesn't merit expensive, lifesaving treatment because the quality-adjusted life year calculation doesn't add up?

Discuss
- **Does it comfort you to know that a decision about your own access to lifesaving medical treatment can be reduced to a monetary value?**
- **Can Kant's concept of human dignity ever be reconciled with the real problem of resource scarcity?**

4.6   Objections to Utilitarianism

We have seen that utilitarianism provides a clear set of parameters for decision-making: Weigh the likely consequences of the action and the choices should be clear. Many thinkers have had profound objections to the utilitarian idea. Let's explore five of these now.

1. **The Future Is Unknowable**

Utilitarians believe that the consequences of our actions can be reasonably forecast. However, others argue that we never truly know the consequences of our actions. We simply cannot foresee the future. (Indeed, one of Kant's central objections to the Inquiring Murderer case was that we do not know the consequences of our actions; therefore, we should follow the rule that we know is right and tell him the truth.) Other philosophers such as David Hume (1748) make a similar epistemological point about the limits of knowledge. As much as we like to think that we can foresee the consequences of our actions, we never actually know the consequences until they occur.

Let's take a hypothetical COVID-19 case. President Y of country Z is facing a difficult decision to open up businesses despite the continuing spread of the virus. She knows that senior citizens, people with pre-existing medical conditions, obese people, and asthmatics are all highly susceptible to the virus, much more so than fit people. After much utilitarian calculation, President Y decides that the benefits of opening the country outweigh the risk of increasing the spread of the disease. She is a caring leader, and she also realizes that people with compromised immune systems should remain in isolation until a vaccine is discovered. Still, she believes the rest of the country should be allowed to reopen. Epidemiologists tell her that they predict a small increase in deaths for the at-risk population due to the rest of society reopening, but the projected death figures are deemed to be minimal: about 100 additional people may die. So President Y changes the policy, and the country reopens. Parks, bars, cafes, and restaurants open. People return to work. There are some increases in cases in nursing homes, but, for the most part, the policy seems to be a success.

However, 1 month after reopening, scientists secure approval of a vaccine that can be mass produced immediately. It's great news, but President Y is facing criticism because she allowed some people to die unnecessarily due to her impatience. They argue that she put the economy ahead of people's lives. Indeed, 100 elderly people died in nursing homes between reopening and the discovery of the vaccine. President Y feels miserable. At the time, she didn't know that if she had just waited another month, the vaccine would have been ready. In effect, she allowed some people to die for some bars and restaurants to open. She couldn't foresee the future. She could have saved them if she had only waited a little longer.

Is President Y a moral leper or did she do the right thing? Well, Kant would remind President Y that since we never know the consequences of our actions because we can never know the future, we should never sacrifice the sanctity of human life for any hypothetical benefit. We may be tempted to think we are doing the right thing because we have confidence in our abilities to predict consequences. In reality, however, we never can.

2. Amusement Parks, Libraries, or Vaccine Labs?

Despite Bentham's Hedonic Calculus and despite John Stuart Mill's more nuanced and qualitative definition of "pleasure," utilitarianism still fails to provide clear guidance for most decisions. Let's say you have 100 million dollars that you, as a good utilitarian, want to donate to charity. Would you build amusement parks or libraries or vaccine labs? All would increase pleasure immensely, but which investment is the moral one? It's difficult to say. Libraries would create "higher" pleasures but for fewer people; amusement parks would create "lower" pleasures but for more people; and vaccine labs may or may not produce a safe and effective vaccine and might not lead to any happiness at all.

At this point some would argue that these are false choices. If you have 100 million dollars, you should donate it to the World Food Program because saving people from starvation would lead to more happiness than building amusement parks, libraries, or labs.[1] Others might argue that saving starving people would decrease happiness in the long run because the planet is overcrowded as it is. The money should be spent on protecting the environment for the happiness of future generations.

In short, despite its claim to moral clarity, many critics of utilitarianism argue that the theory actually raises more questions than it answers. Also note that Kant's theory would not consider this dilemma to be problematic at all because the action of donating to any charity is morally good,[2] whatever the consequences may be.

This objection to utilitarianism is typically countered with the concept of effective altruism, a social movement that believes people can and should use their own unique talents in individual ways to enhance the greater good. Therefore, there would be no contradiction if investment bankers were to pursue their talents at making enormous amounts of money with the specific goal of donating that money back to charitable causes. The same would be true for comedians, Hollywood celebrities, or rock stars. (See effectivealtruism.org for additional information on this social movement.) While effective altruism allows for personal choice in our life paths, a strict utilitarian would still claim that the comedian's efforts to make starving people laugh would be better spent on feeding them.

3. **Justice, Rights, and Human Dignity**

Another forceful critique of utilitarianism is this: The theory allows for and even demands the violation of individual human rights if the consequences of the violation yield more happiness (McCloskey, 1965). Let's say we're in the city of Springfield during the COVID-19 pandemic. A man described as having neck tattoos has been seen intentionally coughing at senior citizens throughout the city. There are lots of men with neck tattoos, but the police can't find which specific man is doing it. Some senior citizens end up dying from COVID. People in the community are angry and demand justice. They form lynch mobs and threaten to hang any man they find with a neck tattoo. The police chief wants to end the rioting, but she needs to find the perpetrator. The longer she waits, the more innocent tattooed men will be assaulted and maybe even killed.

She eventually rounds up a group of men with neck tattoos, and one of them, Tom, tests positive for COVID-19. Is he the culprit? Maybe, but Tom has a solid alibi. The police chief is certain that Tom didn't do the coughing. What now? In the

[1] Peter Singer has consistently argued that people in wealthy countries should donate their money to the poorest places on this planet since a dollar goes much further in, say, alleviating hunger in a developing nation than it does in a wealthy nation.

[2] When you donate to charity, the universal law you are creating would be as follows: "All people should donate to charity."

meantime, other tattooed men are being hunted down and several are beaten so badly they end up in the hospital. The chief decides that she might be able to frame Tom in order to stop the violence. Of course, Tom would be unjustly convicted, but this doesn't matter for the utilitarian police chief. If framing Tom for a crime he didn't commit leads to less violence and harm for the whole community, then that action would be justified.

We have already seen in the previous chapter that Immanuel Kant presents some strong objections to this way of thinking. His most simple objection is that many people falsely believe that they can accurately predict the consequences of their actions. In the scenario above, why would the police chief be certain that framing the innocent man would really lead to less violence? There are other potential consequences. Maybe the violence would not end if the innocent man were framed. Maybe the real perpetrator would confess. In short, Kant argues, we cannot predict the future with certainty. What we *do* know, Kant would insist, is that framing innocent people is always wrong. It violates basic human rights, and we must never violate the rights of innocent people no matter what the positive consequences may be.

Let's look at other problematic examples. What is wrong in the utilitarian worldview if you violate someone's privacy without them knowing it (Rachels & Rachels, 2012, pp. 113–14)? For example, what is wrong with hacking into a stranger's webcam in order to spy on them? In a utilitarian system, nothing. If Jack chooses to spy on Jill for his own arousal, he could not be blamed (if and only if she never discovers the spyware—the knowledge might cause her pain). After all, Jack is increasing his happiness, and Jill is not even aware of the violation of her privacy. Critics of strict utilitarianism argue that the right to privacy is one that we all should have whether or not we are aware that right is being violated.

Furthermore, in utilitarian theory, one person counts only for one unit of happiness, but the community counts for much more than one; therefore, an individual's rights can be violated for the good of the community. Eminent domain laws, which require individuals to give up their land in order to make way for railroads, airports, pipelines, or highways, are utilitarian devices that take away people's rights to property. One healthy person has enough blood, tissue, and organs to save the lives of 20 people. A utilitarian might conclude that the healthy person can be sacrificed— against her own will—for the benefit of the others.

In short, the inviolable and priceless dignity of each and every human being—the dignity that Immanuel Kant took great pains to establish—is completely lost in the utilitarian system. And to put this point more plainly, if you are inclined toward utilitarian thinking, would you also agree to allow yourself, your spouse, your child, your father, or your grandmother to be sacrificed for the greater good?

4. The Problem of Pleasure as the Only End of Morality

Despite John Stuart Mill's attempt to revise Bentham's notion of hedonistic pleasure, there are other important ends in the world besides pleasure. We have seen that Kant would argue that upholding justice, preserving rights, and respecting human dignity are much more important than maximizing pleasure. St. Thomas Aquinas, Mohammed, Gandhi, Buddha, St. Teresa of Avila, and many other religious people would argue that following God's commands is more important than achieving pleasure. The ancient Stoic philosophers would argue that being a virtuous person is much more important than achieving pleasure. And parents might argue that taking care of their children, despite the stress and sleepless nights, is more important than maximizing pleasure. Children might argue that taking care of their aging parents is more important than maximizing their own pleasure. In short, many would argue that focusing on achieving pleasure ignores many other important goals in life.

5. **Ignoring the Past**

A final problem with utilitarianism is that its exclusive focus on the consequences of actions means that the theory ignores obligations derived from the past. Let's say you promised to go for a walk in the park with a friend, but you don't feel like going anymore. One reason to still go, despite your change in attitude, is because *you promised to do so in the past*. However, a utilitarian would ignore your past promises when making a decision because all that matters is the consequences of your current decision. Obligations derived in that past are wiped away. You could justify canceling the walk because whatever pain you would cause by not going would be outweighed by the pleasure achieved by doing whatever else you chose to do instead of going. Of course, a utilitarian would also allow you to break your promise if you tested positive for COVID-19 and felt that it would be safer to quarantine at home—for the benefit of all. In this instance, breaking your promise would also be justified.

Let's look at another example: You are a cancer doctor, and your favorite patient is a kind, gentle old man named Winston. You've developed a relationship of mutual support over the years, and you rely on each other for advice and assistance. One day after his wife passed away in the early stages of the COVID-19 pandemic, you promised Winston that you would always look after him and give him special attention if he was worried about his cancer returning. But now the pandemic has added additional stress to your life, and you are exhausted and overworked. One day, Winston calls you and asks for an unscheduled check-up after hours to see if his cancer has returned. You've already worked a 70-h week and really don't want to give anyone any special favors. What do you do? Well, your past relationship and your promise might be good reasons for you to continue to be supportive. However, a utilitarian might argue that neither your past relationship nor your promise to always help is a reason to continue to spend time and resources on him. Indeed, if you feel that your time and resources could be better spent helping others or even yourself, a utilitarian would allow you to deny Winston's request.

And this is the final important criticism of utilitarianism: Its exclusive focus on future consequences ignores many other important factors in ethical decision-making, namely, obligations, duties, and promises made in the past.

We have seen that utilitarianism is an influential and powerful ethical theory, but it is not completely free of serious flaws. In the section below, we will analyze an important historical case that reveals its strengths and weaknesses.

Box 4.3 Interdisciplinary Perspective #8: History

Smallpox: A Utilitarian Justification for Involuntary Medical Testing and Compulsory Vaccination

Vaccination—whether voluntary or involuntary—became an increasingly hot political topic during the COVID-19 pandemic, so it is worthwhile to provide a very brief history of vaccination in order to understand the wider historical and ethical context. Here, I would like to note that the book *Epidemics and Society* by Frank M. Snowden (2019) provides the definitive introduction to the history of the fight against smallpox as well as other diseases.

Vaccination comes from the Latin *vaccinus*, meaning coming from cows. Edward Jenner (1749–1823), who discovered the first vaccine for smallpox, chose the word because he used the cowpox virus to vaccinate people against smallpox. Jenner's technique was successful because cowpox is closely related to smallpox, and cowpox antibodies provide immunity to smallpox as well. Crucially, humans usually don't get cowpox, because it is a disease that affects cows, as the name suggests. However, occasionally, like with COVID-19, a virus is able to jump the species barrier from animals to humans, and in rare instances people did catch cowpox.

Jenner was able to discover vaccination through making a simple, straightforward observation that was arguably the most decisive in the history of medicine. A country doctor, Jenner noticed that milkmaids would sometimes contract cowpox, which is a fairly mild disease; however, he also observed that they would never contract smallpox afterward. Why did this happen? He reckoned that somehow cowpox could protect people from smallpox as well. If he infected people with cowpox intentionally, then they should become immune to smallpox. And so he did.

His first subject in 1796 was his gardener's 8-year-old son, who was inoculated with cowpox and then intentionally infected with smallpox. Kant would most certainly have disapproved of this action since it required using an innocent human being as a means to an end. However, the experiment was successful, and 15 more subjects—this time volunteers—were given cowpox and then smallpox. The vaccination process was a success. It took another 200 years to secure total victory over smallpox, but through the tireless dedication of public health experts and the support of governments around the world, smallpox was finally eradicated in 1980.

It is frankly impossible to contest the benefit of eradicating smallpox. The best estimates suggest that 30–40% of those infected perished (Snowden, 2019, p. 95). It often led to blindness and insanity in those it did not kill. Enduring the disease itself was torture, with patients needing to be tied down so they didn't scratch themselves to death. Smallpox created permanent scars on the face, the scalp, and all over the body, and those who survived faced lifelong mental health problems. Furthermore, it caused what we would now call PTSD in its tens of millions of victims, many of whom never recovered emotionally from the gruesome infection. However, it also terrified those who

(continued)

never contracted it because the mere thought of being exposed led to mass stress and public hysteria. Given all of the suffering smallpox caused, would it not be appropriate to compel everyone to be vaccinated in order to eradicate the disease forever?

A utilitarian thinker approaches the problem of compulsory vaccination by analyzing the happiness and unhappiness that result from an action. In the case of the smallpox vaccine, it is, as noted, uncontestable that the eradication of the virus has led to more pleasure and less pain. Even if the vaccine were not perfectly safe, it would still be right to compel vaccination for the greater good.

The next step of this line of reasoning is to consider seriously the utility of using human beings as involuntary test subjects for potentially lifesaving treatments. Let's say the son of Jenner's gardener perished in the first experiment, but Jenner eventually developed a successful vaccine later, due to the lessons learned from the first one. Would that child be an acceptable utilitarian sacrifice for the infinite amount of good that resulted from his death?

Discuss
- **Although humanity has triumphed over smallpox, can the same utilitarian analysis be used to justify involuntary vaccination against other diseases, such as measles, mumps, rubella, the common flu, and, of course, COVID-19 or future pathogens? Why or why not?**
- **Do you think Edward Jenner and the father of the child were morally reprehensible for using an 8-year-old as the first involuntary test subject for the vaccine? Why or why not?**
- **Would you be angry if you were forced to be a test subject for a vaccine against a new, deadly illness? Why?**

4.7 Conclusion

In this chapter, we have outlined the theory of utilitarianism and discussed both its strengths and weaknesses. We have also seen that there is a profound disagreement between utilitarian and Kantian ways of thinking. Utilitarians are consequentialists—they assess the rightness or wrongness of an action based on the consequences of the action. Kantians are deontologists—they do not consider consequences when assessing the rightness or wrongness of an action; instead, they consider only the conformity of the action to absolute moral rules.

Now you need to make a decision. Do your values lean toward utilitarianism or Kantianism, consequentialism or deontology? The implications of your decision are profound. Would you violate intellectual property laws and steal the specifications of a new, groundbreaking vaccine in order to achieve a greater good? Would you frame the innocent man with neck tattoos to save the lives of others? Would you advocate opening up a nation's businesses during a pandemic for the greater good? Would you force people to get vaccinated against their wishes? Would you test medicines on unwilling subjects?

Maybe you believe that none of these options is satisfactory. You may feel that neither philosophical system offers sufficient guidance for moral decisions. So, is there another path to resolving these issues? Fortunately, the great philosophers offer us another route to explore—social contract theory, which is the subject of the next chapter.

Box 4.4 Criteria for Evaluating Ethical Theories: Part 2
In the previous chapter, we discussed three key criteria for evaluating ethical theories. Use this opportunity to evaluate the strengths and weaknesses of utilitarianism according to those criteria before learning about the next two criteria.

1. Does the theory have an appropriate scope for who belongs in our moral community?
2. Does the theory exhibit an appropriate degree of rational consistency?
3. Does the theory align with "common sense"?
4. Does the theory adequately explain issues about moral distance?

If we insist that a theory ought to treat everyone the same, how do we explain some facts about human behavior? Is it not normal for a mother to care more for her own children than other children? Is it not normal for people to care more about their own neighbors than for strangers on the other side of the planet? Is it not normal to care for people living in the present more than for those yet to be born?

Also, it is important to look back to Criteria #3 about common sense. Isn't it just common sense to accept the fact that we care more about our own families, friends, pets, communities, and nations than strangers halfway around the world? Is utilitarianism not aligned with these criteria because it insists that emotional distance is irrelevant when making ethical decisions?

Emotional Distance
An ethical theory like Kant's insists that all people in the moral community deserve the same rights and treatment. However, the reality of human behavior is much different. Indeed, if your best friend's parent dies, you will likely be sad. However, if your own parent dies, you will likely be even sadder. If you have children, you certainly treat your best friend's children with care and affection; however, you likely treat your own children with additional care and affection. The problem of emotional distance is that we do care about our own inner circle of family and friends more than we care about others—and

(continued)

we treat them differently, often better, than others. Utilitarians reject the idea that emotional distance should be used to determine who is worthy of our time, energy, and charitable assistance. Everyone's happiness counts the same, whether or not they are part of your emotional community.

Geographical Distance
Emotional distance is strongly linked to geographical distance. It is worthwhile to note that pets in the developed world live fuller lives than many impoverished human beings in developing countries. A quick Google search reveals that one session of LED light therapy for your pet in Brooklyn, NYC, will cost $120. A pet photo shoot will set you back 99 GBP in London. Compare that figure with poverty statistics from the World Bank, which I cited earlier in the chapter: The UN estimates that roughly 750 million live in extreme poverty, defined as living on under $1.90 a day. Furthermore, the World Bank notes that 3.4 billion people "struggle to meet basic needs," defined as $3.20 a day in lower-middle-income countries and $5.50 in upper-middle-income countries.

Peter Singer insists that if we are serious about our values, we should donate our excess wealth to alleviate poverty—a clear problem that is fairly easy to rectify through charitable giving. Furthermore, geographic distance should not be used as an excuse to absolve ourselves from the fact that we do not live up to our own professed values about caring for the impoverished.

Temporal Distance
The last type of distance is temporal. Should a suitable ethical theory explicitly account for our obligations to future generations? Are we required to think about their needs? A significant aspect of environmental ethics is the understanding that we do indeed have obligations to future generations. How would utilitarians approach the issue of future generations? And what about Kant?

5. Does the theory have an appropriate *telos* or ultimate goal?
What should the ultimate goal of an ethical theory be? A happy planet? Obedience to the laws of God? The triumph of Reason and Truth? World peace and stable societies? The preservation of human rights and dignity? Furthermore, should a theory articulate that goal clearly and provide an explanation of the means required to attain that goal?

Different theories approach these questions in different ways. Utilitarianism has a forthright *telos*: maximizing the happiness of all human and non-human animals. It also attempts to articulate the ways in which the goal can be achieved, and we've seen that dubious means can be used to achieve the noble end.

But what about Kant's theory? What is the ultimate goal of the theory? If it is to live one's life according to Reason, that is an admirable goal. However, he does not explicitly argue that the goal is happiness (although he did chart a path to world peace in his 1795 work *Perpetual Peace: A Philosophical Sketch*). Also, Kant did not believe that dubious means could be used to achieve any noble end.

(continued)

Utilitarians might respond to Kant by asking him, "What is the point of following rules, when doing so makes people miserable? If I tell my friend, he looks fat in that shirt, how is that helpful? If I tell the Inquiring Murderer the truth about where my neighbor is and he kills my neighbor, what good have I done?" In short, what's the point of Kant's system if it only rests upon blind rule-following with no positive outcomes?

So think about your own values now. First, is it important for an ethical theory to have a clearly articulated *telos*? Second, should a path to that goal be clearly explained?

References

Bentham, J. (1789). *An introduction to the principles of morals and legislation*. Econlib. 2018. https://www.econlib.org/library/Bentham/bnthPML.html

DOT. (2021, March 23). Departmental guidance on valuation of a statistical life in economic analysis. https://www.transportation.gov/office-policy/transportation-policy/revised-departmental-guidance-on-valuation-of-a-statistical-life-in-economic-analysis. Accessed 1 Sept 2022.

Emanuel, E. J., et al. (2020). An ethical framework for global vaccine allocation. *Science* 10.1126. https://philpapers.org/archive/EMAAEF-2.pdf

EPA. (2022, March 30). Mortality risk valuation. https://www.epa.gov/environmental-economics/mortality-risk-valuation. Accessed 1 Sept 2022.

Gandjour, A. (2020). Willingness to pay for new medicines: A step towards narrowing the gap between NICE and IQWiG. *BMC Health Services Research, 20*, 343. https://doi.org/10.1186/s12913-020-5050-9

Hume, D. (1748). *An enquiry concerning human understanding*. Project Gutenberg. 2011. https://www.gutenberg.org/files/9662/9662-h/9662-h.htm

Jecker, N. S. (2021, September 17). Are COVID-19 boosters ethical, with half the world waiting for a first shot? A bioethicist weighs in. *The Conversation*. https://theconversation.com/are-covid-19-boosters-ethical-with-half-the-world-waiting-for-a-first-shot-a-bioethicist-weighs-in-167606. Accessed 18 Oct 2021.

Kant, I. (1795). *Perpetual peace: A philosophical sketch*. Project Gutenberg. 2016. https://www.gutenberg.org/files/50922/50922-h/50922-h.htm

McCloskey, H. J. (1965). A non-utilitarian approach to punishment. *Inquiry, 8*, 239–255.

Mill, J. S. (1863). *Utilitarianism*. Project Gutenberg. 2004. https://www.gutenberg.org/files/11224/11224-h/11224-h.htm

Mill, J. S. (1873). *Autobiography*. Project Gutenberg. 2018. https://www.gutenberg.org/files/10378/10378-h/10378-h.htm

Neumann, P. J., Cohen, J. T., & Weinstein, M. C. (2014). Updating cost-effectiveness—The curious resilience of the $50,000-per-QALY threshold. *New England Journal of Medicine, 371*, 796–797. https://doi.org/10.1056/NEJMp1405158

Rachels, J., & Rachels, S. (2012). *The elements of moral philosophy* (7th ed.). McGraw-Hill.

Schuessler, J. (2021, September 11). Peter Singer wins $1 million Berggruen Prize. *The New York Times*. https://www.nytimes.com/2021/09/07/arts/peter-singer-berggruen-prize.html. Accessed on 11 Sept 2021.

Singer, P. (1975). *Animal liberation: A new ethics for our treatment of animals*. Harper Collins.

Singer, P. (1999, September 5). The singer solution to world poverty. *New York Times Magazine.* https://www.nytimes.com/1999/09/05/magazine/the-singer-solution-to-world-poverty.html. Accessed 28 Aug 2022.

Singer, P. (2000). *Writings on ethical life.* Harper Collins.

Singer, P. (2009). *The life you can save: Acting now to end world poverty.* Random House.

Snowden, F. M. (2019). *Epidemics and society: From the black death to the present.* Yale UP.

UK Health Security Agency. (2021, May 19). Economic evaluation: Health economic studies. https://www.gov.uk/guidance/economic-evaluation-health-economic-studies. Accessed 10 Sept 2022.

UN. (2021). No poverty: End poverty in all its forms everywhere. https://unstats.un.org/sdgs/report/2021/goal-01/. Accessed 28 Aug 2022.

WHO. (2021). Vaccine equity campaign. https://www.who.int/campaigns/vaccine-equity. Accessed 28 Aug 2022.

World Bank. (2018, October 17). Press Release. Nearly half the world lives on less than $5.50 a day. https://www.worldbank.org/en/news/press-release/2018/10/17/nearly-half-the-world-lives-on-less-than-550-a-day. Accessed 5 Dec 2021.

Chapter 5
The Social Contract: Exploring the Concept of Freedom During Pandemics

5.1 An Introduction to the Social Contract

One illustrious group of philosophers—Thomas Hobbes, John Locke, and Jean-Jacques Rousseau—has influenced the development of the modern world more than any other. The key themes that they explored—freedom, equality, reason, morality, self-interest, property, government, democracy, power, order, virtue, justice, and the good life—form the bedrock of the world in which we live, for they created the concept of the *social contract*, which is the voluntary agreement of individuals to join forces in order to secure the mutual protection and welfare of both the individual and society. They established the political, economic, legal, and ethical frameworks that explain the social structures in which we are born, live, play, work, suffer, and die. In short, they defined what it means to live in a free society.

It is crucial to note here that each of these philosophers also survived outbreaks of the Black Death. Consider this: Is it possible that our modern understanding of free societies is intertwined with and inseparable from our history of combatting pandemic disease? This chapter argues that they are, indeed, fundamentally connected.

What it means to be free became a deeply problematic and divisive concept during the COVID-19 pandemic especially in liberal, democratic countries. Enforced closures of businesses, stay-at-home orders, and the cancellation of religious services effectively curtailed some of the most cherished freedoms of liberal societies: the freedom of commerce, the freedom of movement, and the freedom of assembly. Even the freedom to practice religion was curtailed through restrictions banning family funerals, for example. These emergency measures were bound to lead to a backlash, and countries around the world experienced protests against what many saw as government overreach. Of course, the protestors were not a monolithic bunch, and among them were those who believed that power-hungry politicians were attempting to enforce unconstitutional social controls over their citizens, those

A. Sola, *Ethics and Pandemics*, Springer Series in Public Health and Health Policy Ethics, https://doi.org/10.1007/978-3-031-33207-4_5

who believed that government rests on the *consent* of the people, and those who believed that when the government no longer has their consent, then it is the duty of a free citizenry to disobey. Despite the diversity of protestors, the one thread that tied them together was their belief that the measures taken to slow the spread of the virus violated their personal freedom.

But what does it mean to be a free person in a free society? *Freedom* is a concept that most people, wherever they might live, champion. The precise definition of freedom, however, is anything but clear. We will attempt to define the different facets of freedom in the course of this chapter, and we will also challenge its elevated status by asking another set of questions. Is ensuring personal freedom the single and most important goal of government? Or are there other equally important or more important goals, such as establishing justice, promoting equality, or ensuring community health and well-being?

In order to explore these questions, you will be presented with an overview of the three important social contract thinkers: Thomas Hobbes, John Locke, and Jean-Jacques Rousseau. Within each section, we will explore a set of important ideas that affect our own pandemic lives.

5.2   Thomas Hobbes and Leviathan

Thomas Hobbes was born in England in 1588. The son of a vicar, he studied at private schools before attending Oxford, where he graduated in 1608. After university, he worked as a tutor to young noblemen and toured Europe. He spent much time in Paris, where he wrote his masterpiece on social and political philosophy, *Leviathan*, a fascinating treatise written partly in response to his observation of the English Civil War, which lasted from 1642 to 1651. His book argues forcefully that a strong central government is needed in order to maintain the benefits of stability and to avoid the scourge of war.

5.2.1   Egoism and Equality in the State of Nature

We have already learned a little about Hobbes in Chap. 2 in connection to our first question about human nature: Are human beings egotistical or altruistic creatures? Hobbes believed firmly in human egoism. Human beings are chaotic, spiteful, mean, greedy, vicious, power-hungry, and suspicious. However, Hobbes insisted we also possess reason, which might be our only saving grace. Our reason helps us realize that we are, in fact, better off living in an orderly society than in a chaotic one.

While Hobbes insisted humans are fundamentally selfish, he also was a staunch advocate of human equality. Some of us might be stronger or wiser than others, but we are all equal in four important respects.

First, Hobbes (1651) notes that death is the great equalizer; it is the most important fact of life from which no living being, no matter how powerful, can escape
(XIII, para 1). We will all die.

The second equality is that of ability. No matter how strong or wise one man is,
he is not strong or wise enough to defend himself from assassination or from a
group of people who join together in order to overthrow him. As Hobbes writes,
"For as to the strength of the body, the weakest has strength enough to kill the strongest, either by secret machination, or by confederacy with others" (XIII, para. 1).[1]
Hobbes also thinks that while some people might in reality be wiser than others,
most people think they are just as smart or indeed even smarter than everyone else.
He writes, "For such is the nature of men, that howsoever they may acknowledge
many others to be more witty, or more eloquent, or more learned, yet they will
hardly believe there be many so wise as themselves; for they see their own wit at
hand, and other men's at a distance" (XIII, para. 2). This is an important insight that
helps to explain, for example, the total self-confidence of extremists of all
persuasions.

Humans are fundamentally equal in a third respect, namely, there is an equality
of *need*, which means that we all require the same basic necessities in order to survive: food, water, shelter, etc. Unfortunately, there are not enough resources for
everyone. In Hobbes' view, the world is not a place of abundance, but of scarcity
(XIII, para. 13).

This leads to the fourth equality, "the equality of hope in the attaining of our
ends" (XIII, para. 3), which means that we are equally competitive. Everyone
believes that we can secure what we need in order to preserve our lives from competitors. Hobbes writes, "If any two men desire the same thing, which nevertheless
they cannot both enjoy, they become enemies; and in the way to their end…endeavor
to destroy, or subdue one another" (XIII, para. 3). According to Hobbes, everyone
thinks this way: *I value my own money, power, and possessions; therefore, others
must value them too; they lust after them and desire to possess them by force or by
deceit. In light of this fact, I must defend my own possessions, but I also have to
ensure that no one else is strong enough to dispossess me. Therefore, I must undermine others' power in case they undermine mine.* Hobbes thinks that there may be
those who are satisfied with their own modest possessions and who are not in competition with anyone else, but they are fools: "If others, that otherwise would be glad
to be at ease within modest bounds, should not by invasion increase their power,
they would not be able [for a] long time, by standing only on their defense, to sub-
sist" (XIII, para. 4).

For Hobbes, the consequence of these basic equalities is that men always have
three reasons to wage war against each other: (1) competition for scarce resources;
(2) lack of confidence in one's ability to defend one's own possessions, which he
calls *diffidence*; and (3) social status or *glory*. Of these three reasons for war,
Hobbes writes:

---

[1] I have modernized Hobbes' spelling and punctuation for the purpose of clarity.

The first maketh men invade for gain; the second, for safety; and the third, for reputation. The first use violence to make themselves masters of other men's persons, wives, children, and cattle; the second, to defend them; the third, for trifles, as a word, a smile, a different opinion, and any other sign of undervalue, either direct in their persons, or by reflection in their kindred, their friends, their nation, their profession, or their name. (XIII, para. 7)

Hobbes paints a bleak picture of human nature. With so many forces impelling human beings to distrust one another, it might be impossible to create a stable society. What Hobbes describes here is *the state of nature*. This is the default state of human history. Only when a strong central government is in place to check our violent urges can peace reign. All other times are war, either open war or immanent war—a simmering cauldron of hatred and suspicion of others threatening to explode at any moment. He writes, "Hereby it is manifest that during the time men live without a common power to keep them all in awe, they are in that condition which is called war; and such a war as if of every man against every man" (XIII, para. 8).

5.2.2   *Justice and Morality*

Most importantly for Hobbes, in the state of nature, there is no such thing as morality, ethics, virtue, right or wrong, good or evil: "To this war of every man against every man, this is also consequent: *that nothing can be unjust*" (XIII, para. 13). Justice and morality only arise after human beings join together in stable, peaceful, and law-abiding societies—right and wrong do not exist in the state of nature. "The notions of right and wrong, justice and injustice, have there no place. Where there is no common power, there is no law; where no law, no injustice. Force and fraud are in war the two cardinal virtues" (XIII, para. 13). Indeed, the basic right of nature, or *jus naturale*, is the right of self-preservation. All human beings have this right and, therefore, can use any and all means to maintain their own lives. This is our natural liberty, the freedom to do what we need to do in order to survive, which might mean taking the women, children, or cattle of others—or their lives.

5.2.3   *Reason and Self-Interest*

For Hobbes, the situation is almost hopeless. But all is not lost. Fortunately, there are "passions that incline men to peace," namely, the "fear of death, desire of such things as are necessary to commodious living, and a hope by their industry to obtain them" (XIII, para. 14). In other words, living in the state of nature makes it obvious that we need to establish security and stability in order to invest our resources and energy on projects that will improve the lives of our friends, our families, and ourselves. Of course, it is fruitless to invest in such projects if, at any moment, a powerful neighbor can strip us of our possessions and freedom.

Furthermore, human beings possess reason, and reason gives us a way out of this miserable state of nature, where no perks of civilized life can exist—no arts, no culture, no grand buildings, no infrastructure, no trade, no contracts, and no commerce. So, Hobbes writes, "Reason suggests convenient articles of peace, upon which men may be drawn to agreement" (XIII, para. 14). These articles of peace form *the social contract*.

Based on these preliminary facts, Hobbes constructs two rules:

(1) *Every man ought to endeavor peace, as far as he has hope of obtaining it; and when he cannot obtain it, that he may seek and use all help and advantages of war.* (XIV, para. 5)

In other words, we should pursue peace, because the alternative—war or perpetual fear and insecurity—is intolerable. If peace is unattainable, then war is the justified remedy. However, since peace is possible, Hobbes presents us with a second rule:

(2) *A man [must] be willing, when others are so too, as far as for peace and defense of himself he shall think it necessary, to lay down this right to all things; and be contented with so much liberty against other men, as he would allow other men against himself.* (XIV, para. 6)

The curious phrase, "this right to all things," is important. As Hobbes stated earlier, in the state of nature, we have the right to do everything and to possess anything, by force or fraud, in order to secure our own lives. The social contract is, therefore, based upon the idea of a *loss* of rights—a loss of natural liberty in exchange for another type of liberty, the liberty that comes from living in a society with rules against theft, deceit, and murder.

Curiously—and this is the great paradox of social contract theory—*it is in our own self-interest to give away our natural rights*. This is a significant claim that we will return to again in this chapter: Renouncing some specific natural freedoms enhances our overall civil freedoms. In the state of nature, it would never be in our self-interest to renounce our right to use force or fraud. Being a good person in the state of nature only leads to enslavement or a bloody death. But reason helps us to distinguish between our short-term and long-term interests. Reason tells us that the state of nature is intolerable and that the social contract will be better. And so, we renounce our natural liberty for the promise of a *good* outcome, a society in which peace reigns and commodious living is attainable. In short, reason tells us that our long-term self-interest is secured by ignoring our short-term interest. (We will explore this paradox further in our discussion of Rousseau below.)

Regarding the voluntary renunciation of natural rights, Hobbes describes the creation of the social contract not so much as a renunciation of rights, but as a transferal. The right to kill another, to take property from another, and to seek vengeance for another's crimes is transferred to a *common power*—a single person or a group of people who ensure the peace and safety of all. The social contract, therefore, is a system whereby all people say to all of the other people around them: "I authorize and give up my right of governing myself to this man, or to this assembly of men, on this condition, that you give up your right to him, and authorize all his actions in like manner" (XV, para. 13). After everyone agrees, a society, a commonwealth, or a *Leviathan* is created—and law, justice, and morality are born with it.

Box 5.1 Interdisciplinary Perspective #9: Political Philosophy

The COVID-19 Pandemic: Evidence for Hobbes' Sources of Order or Disorder?

COVID-19 exposed the fragility of civilized society in many ways, so it is worthwhile to apply Hobbes' first principles to the pandemic.

Hobbes begins his analysis with his list of the four equalities: the equality of death, ability, need, and competitiveness. First, the pandemic confirmed the undeniable truth of the great equalizer: death. A virus has no preconceived notions and expresses no intrinsic bias (although, due to various systemic inequalities in healthcare, different groups of people did experience different medical outcomes). At the end of the day, no matter how rich or famous you were, you could still contract the virus and be killed by it. And even if you survived a bout of COVID-19, you will die eventually, as will we all. There is no escaping this fact. Regarding the second equality—ability—Hobbes would remind everyone not to overestimate their own strength or intelligence because a group of people will always be stronger than any individual. Therefore, it would not be wise to believe that one could, for example, hoard all the food while everyone else is starving. At any moment, an angry mob could band together to take it all from you. Human behavior during COVID-19 also confirmed Hobbes' third thesis about the equality of need. If two people want the same thing which they cannot both enjoy, then conflict is inevitable. Resource scarcity is a fact of life. The fierce competition for PPE during the early stages of COVID-19 confirmed that when order breaks down, bad things happen and our nasty, brutish nature is confirmed. The COVID-19 pandemic also confirmed the fourth and final equality—the hope of attaining our ends. Despite the other equalities, Hobbes argues that we all believe we can secure our own safety and resources through offensive and defensive action, through being crafty competitors. Hence, many people stockpiled toilet paper, food, water, PPE, medicine, and even weapons, because there was a realization that the resources that they desired were also coveted equally by their neighbors.

Hobbes' four equalities are readily confirmed, but he also helps us understand both the stability and chaos of the world—the sources of order as well as the sources of disorder.

Let's start with Hobbes' three sources of disorder: resource competition, lack of confidence in one's ability to protect one's own resources, and status. First, resource competition is one of the hallmarks of any crisis, and the COVID-19 pandemic was no different. The desire to acquire PPE, food, medicine, and medical equipment was a strong force of disorder both within nations and between them (Sheikh, 2020). Second, the lack of confidence was revealed in the hoarding of these scant resources—and conflicts arose due to fears about being able to protect one's own self and one's own community (Robbins et al., 2022). Lastly, the desire for status or glory caused additional disorder. Those who had extra resources to distribute used their abundance as

(continued)

leverage to increase their power and status over those who experienced scarcity (Bittner, 2020). These power plays happened both within nations and between them.

Fortunately, Hobbes also identified three factors that are sources of order, factors that "incline men to peace": the fear of death, the desire for commodious living, and the hope to attain the things they need to live well through their own industry and effort. Since people fear death, many citizens chose to comply with business closures, quarantine orders, social distancing, and other hygiene rules. They did this not only to avoid death but also to increase their chances of living comfortable lives in a civilized and pandemic-free future society. Lastly, despite the hopelessness of seeing increasing death tolls, many people believed that through obeying the rules, they would be able to return to work eventually and carry on with their lives as normal.

So if Hobbes were a talking head on television today, how might he analyze the COVID-19 pandemic? His first important point would be to remind everyone that we are all better off living in an orderly society than in a chaotic one. Second, he would remind us that the promise of peace and safety is the main reason for which people renounce their natural liberty. The state is justified in demanding both our allegiance and obedience to its rules because it provides safety and security—it preserves our lives.[2] When assessing stay-at-home orders that are meant to preserve our lives, it might seem unreasonable to protest them since the goal is clear and aligns with the justification of state power.

Furthermore, Hobbes would argue that it is rational to give up our natural freedoms—the freedom to lie, kill, and steal, as well as the freedom of movement, assembly, and commerce as well as the freedom not to wear a mask—provided that others do so as well because it is in our long-term self-interest to do so. In effect, the social contract requires that we all follow the same rules, not merely for the benefit of society, but for our own self-interest as well. A pandemic highlights life's dangers like few other events, and Hobbes would remind us that banding together and subjecting ourselves to the same rules of behavior will be better for us in the long run.

(continued)

---

[2] This would explain why, for example, people living in New Orleans during the chaotic aftermath of Hurricane Katrina or those currently living in many areas of Afghanistan resort to violence. When the common power ceases to secure peace and safety of the people, everyone is returned to the state of nature, where morality ceases to exist as well—and the life of man is "solitary, poor, nasty, brutish, and short." Peace eventually returned to New Orleans after the Leviathan (the US government) reestablished its power. Will peace eventually come to Afghanistan? Time will tell. If peace does comes, Hobbes would argue that it will only happen because people have determined that their current state is intolerable and that they all will be better off if they transfer their rights to a new Leviathan who will maintain order and dispense justice.

However, if the state cannot live up to its end of the bargain, then the people can and will reclaim their natural liberty. Indeed, the people are entitled to reclaim their natural liberty if the state ceases to preserve our lives—this is, after all, its primary responsibility. Therefore, a nation that proves incapable of halting the spread of a pandemic would lose its legitimacy. The citizens would be thrust back into the state of nature, and they would then be left with the natural right to form a new government and a new constitution—in other words, a new social contract—or they could choose to live in perpetual chaos with no rules, no laws, and no justice.

Discuss
- **Reevaluate your stance on human nature from Chap. 2. Does the COVID-19 pandemic provide additional evidence for Hobbes' various claims about human nature?**
- **From a public health perspective, consider Hobbes' insistence that everyone must be compelled to follow the same rules of behavior. Is such a sweeping rule appropriate for pandemic management? Should exceptions be made for certain people? If exceptions are made, what is to prevent people from exploiting them and causing further harm?**

5.3   John Locke and *Two Treatises of Government*

Turning now from Hobbes to Locke, we will explore social contract theory from the perspective of a thinker who did not believe that all human beings are naturally selfish, violent, and greedy. Locke believed, to the contrary, that human beings might be partially altruistic because, like Kant, he thought that humans are reasoning creatures. Whereas Hobbes viewed reason as a sharp and aggressive mental tool used to maximize our self-interest at the expense of others, Locke viewed it as a civilizing tool. It is certainly used to secure our property and life aspirations, but not always at the expense of others because when we use our own reason, we are forced to recognize that others use it as well. For Locke, reason signifies reciprocity and imagination, the ability to put oneself in another's shoes. Reason, therefore, is both an *intellectual* capacity and a *moral* one.

John Locke was born near Bristol, England, in 1632. He attended Oxford University, where he studied philosophy and medicine. He eventually became a physician, but he is not famous for any medical books; he is famous for one book on epistemology, *An Essay Concerning Human Understanding* (1690), and another on political philosophy, *Two Treatises of Government* (1689). The latter book is a classic of political thought; it is considered to be the founding text of modern liberalism, the belief that human beings are free and equal, and endowed with fundamental and inalienable rights. It heavily influenced the framers of the US Constitution. In it, Locke argues quite forcefully that humans are not by nature subject to either a monarch or any other form of political rule. We can only be subject to the power of another *through our own consent*. This one simple idea changed the world—it spelled the end of absolute monarchy, led to the creation of both the United States of America and the French Republic, and is still used both to legitimize and delegitimize governments all over the world, from South Africa to Russia and from China to Greece.

5.3.1   *Reason, Morality, and Justice in the State of Nature*

In the second of the *Two Treatises*, Locke describes the origin and extent of government. Like Hobbes, he describes the state of nature, where men live in "a state of perfect freedom to order their action and dispose of their possessions and persons as they see fit…without asking leave, or depending upon the will of any other man" (sect. 4). Also, following Hobbes, Locke argues that the primary characteristic of the state of nature is "equality, wherein all the power and jurisdiction is reciprocal, no one having more than another" (sect. 4).

Unlike Hobbes, however, Locke insists that reason adds a moral dimension to the state of nature—it is not a completely amoral world. This insight marks an important shift in the development of Locke's version of the social contract. It reveals his belief that there might be some level of altruism in human beings. Locke writes, "The state of nature has a law of nature to govern it, which obliges everyone: and reason, which is that law, teaches all mankind who will but consult it, that, being all equal and independent, no one ought to harm another in his life, health, liberty, or possessions" (sect. 6). Locke advocates reason as a source of order and stability, and he insists that such a view is compatible with the religious view that we were created by "an omnipotent and infinitely wise Maker" (sect. 6).[3] Locke veers even further away from Hobbes by implying that the state of nature is not necessarily a time of total war among everyone. Indeed, he indicates that the state of nature does not always require competition for resources, although we still have the responsibility to preserve our own lives:

> Everyone, as he is bound to preserve himself, and not to quit his station willfully, so, by the like reason, when his own preservation comes not in competition, ought he, as much as he can, to preserve the rest of mankind, and not, unless it be to do justice on an offender, take away or impair the life, or what tends to the preservation of the life, the liberty, health, limb, or goods of another. (sect. 6)

Again, the differences between Hobbes and Locke are clear. Hobbes assumed that there is no time in the state of nature when people are not in competition. During a period of apparent peace, people must build up their own offensive and defensive capabilities because the next competitor may appear over the horizon to plunder and

---

[3] I will avoid any religious discussions, but it is important to note, first, that there is a strong Judeo-Christian tone in Locke's writings and, second, that Locke scholars have differing views about the strength and extent of Locke's religious beliefs.

pillage at any moment. Locke disagrees. There are times of peace in the state of nature, so it is not necessarily the fear of perpetual war that brings people together in organized societies.

Another unfortunate reality drives people to band together for mutual protection—the presence of evil and irrational people. Locke thinks that if everyone were good and reasonable, there would be a sufficient amount of stability for people to remain in the state of nature and not band together in a commonwealth. However, this is not the case. He writes, "And were it not for the corruption and viciousness of degenerate men there would be no need of any other, no necessity that men should separate from this great and natural community [the state of nature], and associate into lesser combinations [individual states]" (sect. 128). While reason is a profound source of order, it is not spread around adequately to ensure that it and it alone will keep the peace.

Hobbes and Locke also differ on the presence of justice in the state of nature. Hobbes insisted that justice does not exist in the state of nature, but Locke argues otherwise. Justice does exist, but it is an imperfect form of justice. In the state of nature, every man is judge, jury, and executioner; "everyone has the executive power" (sect. 13) to judge and punish transgressions as they see fit. Of course, in a system where individuals decide for themselves what the laws are and what punishments are appropriate, there will be miscarriages of justice. After all, Locke says, people are hypocrites: " 'Tis easy to be imagined that he who was so unjust as to do his brother an injury, will scarce be so just as to condemn himself for it" (sect. 13). Civil government and an orderly judicial system, therefore, are two areas in which the inconveniences of the state of nature can be remedied.

5.3.2   Critique of Absolute Power

We recall that Hobbes insists that individuals transfer to the sovereign, the Leviathan, their natural rights, so he becomes the common power above all—particularly in matters of justice and punishment. The sovereign has the responsibility of maintaining peace and has absolute authority. Here is another area in which Locke thinks differently. We quote Locke at length in order to explain his strong opposition to endowing a monarch with absolute power:

> Absolute monarchs are but men, and if government is to be the remedy of those evils which necessarily follow from men's being judges in their own cases, and the state of nature is therefore not to be endured, I desire to know what kind of government that is, and how much better it is than the state of nature, where one man commanding a multitude, has the liberty to judge in his own case, and may do to all his subjects whatever he pleases, without the least question or control of those who execute his pleasure; and in whatsoever he doth, whether led by reason, mistake, or passion, must be submitted to? (sect. 13)

In short, Locke argues that absolute monarchy might be no better than the state of nature. In absolute monarchy, people transfer their rights to someone who is just as prone to error as the rest of us. Miscarriages of justice are just as likely to occur in this system as in the state of nature. If Hobbes prizes order and stability above war,

Locke prizes justice. The only reason for people to renounce their natural rights or to transfer their natural liberties to someone else must be to secure justice—and also to secure peace and their possessions. And people eventually think that coming together in a society presents many benefits, so they form a social contract:

> Men being, as has been said, by nature all free, equal, and independent, no one can be put out of this estate, and subjected to the political power of another, without his own consent, which is done by agreeing with other men to join and unite into a community for their comfortable, safe, and peaceable living one amongst another, in a secure enjoyment of their properties, and a greater security against any that are not of it. (sect. 95)

Perhaps the most revolutionary concept here is that of *consent*. Locke insists that the consent of the individual is the only legitimate justification of political power.

5.3.3   Property

Property is another central theme of Locke's work. His defense of personal property is one of the most influential theories for capitalists, libertarians, and laissez-faire econo-mists. As the *Second Treatise* develops, the subject of property rights becomes more and more central to the argument. Having argued that peace and justice are the key reasons for men to join into societies, he begins to argue that the security of personal property is as important, perhaps even more important, than the others. He says, "The great and chief end, therefore, of men's uniting into commonwealths, and putting themselves under government, is the preservation of their property" (sect. 124). This sentence has convinced many people in the past and in the present that the role of government should be limited to this single end and this end alone. Any additional aim of government—e.g., to redistribute individual wealth in the form of taxation, corporate subsidies, social services, or welfare payments—goes beyond the appropriate scope of legitimate politi-cal power. For strict libertarians, any additional governmental authority is tyranny. I do not wish to wade into this debate at the present, but it is important to review the entirety of Locke's theory, not simply this single statement about the preservation of property.

Here is Locke's argument in full. People are driven from the state of nature because of three deficiencies therein:

(1) The Absence of Law—While morality and justice do exist in the state of nature (as a consequence of our reason), there is no set standard of right and wrong, no publicly known laws, and no consensus on the meaning of justice. The social contract, on the contrary, provides formalized rules of appropriate behavior—*laws*.

(2) The Absence of Judges—Since there are no laws in the state of nature, there are no judges. In the state of nature, everyone may act as their own judge. Since Locke believes people cannot be unbiased when critiquing their own decisions, judges who are trained in disinterestedness provide another advantage.

(3) The Absence of Law Enforcement Officers—Lastly, in the state of nature, individuals must act as their own police officer, judge, jailer, and execu-

tioner. Of course, it is impossible in the state of nature to punish those who merit punishment. In fact, in the state of nature, it would be unwise to punish those who have harmed you, because they will not submit to your authority. Therefore, a social contract is preferable to the state of nature because it enables punishment and the *restoration* of order and justice.

While we secure our property rights by joining the social contract—and this is an important benefit—we transfer other rights to the commonwealth: the right to create our own laws, the right to judge others, and the right to punish those who deserve it. These rights, which are tainted in the state of nature, are purified in the social contract.

Locke was not only interested in the protection of property; his theory is focused on the establishment of a fair and functional judiciary. While a system of justice protects our property, the protection of property is not necessarily the only end of power.

5.3.4 Other Ends of Power

Some conservative thinkers argue that the preservation of property is Locke's primary concern, but he is equally forceful in his support of justice and the rule of law. Securing our property rights might be the selfish and egotistical goal for consenting to join a social contract; however, establishing a transparent and orderly judicial system—that is unbiased and even altruistic in its protection of all citizens—is an equally important goal of the government.

Locke defines the ends of government, the ends of political power, in Book IX of the *Treatise* as follows:

> And so whoever has the legislative or supreme power of any commonwealth is bound to govern by established standing laws, promulgated and known to the people, and not by extemporary decrees; by indifferent and upright judges, who are to decide controversies by those laws; and to employ the force of the community at home only in the execution of such laws, or abroad, to prevent or redress foreign injuries, and secure the community from inroads and invasion. And all this to be directed to no other end but the peace, safety, and public good of the people. (sect. 131)

First, one notes that the government must be open and transparent. Laws must be publicly advertised. They cannot be created and applied retroactively to punish offenses. Legal disputes must be resolved by responsible judges. Force can only be used to maintain the law internally (or to protect the community from external threats). Lastly, all of this is done for the public good—after all, this is why people consent to the social contract in the first place.

In sum, Locke is an ardent proponent of reason, justice, transparency, and limitations on governmental power. No ruler, no sovereign, no Leviathan, has an absolute right to rule:

> The end of government is the good of mankind, and [what] is best for mankind, that the people should be always exposed to the boundless will of tyranny, or that the rulers should be sometimes liable to be opposed when they grow exorbitant in the use of their power, and employ it for the destruction and not the preservation of the properties of their people? (sect. 229)

All people, therefore, have the right to disobey those in power. We do not merely give our consent to the government one single time and then accept its power over us forever. For Locke, consent is a continuous act.

5.3.5   *Consent and Rebellion*

Another contribution from Locke in the field of political philosophy involves the tricky concept of consent. Locke's argument about the movement from the state of nature to a commonwealth implies that real people actually come together and give their consent to form a community. Critics have asked if people have ever actually done this. They suggest, to the contrary, that people have only very rarely come together to form a social contract. For the most part, people find themselves living in a state with laws and government already established. Most of us reading this, for example, possess citizenship in a specific state through the accident of birth, not because we decided one day to voluntarily give our consent to join the social contract of the United States, Mexico, Great Britain, Germany, India, Saudi Arabia, Turkey, China, or Japan.

Locke answers this objection by offering two alternatives: proactive consent and tacit consent. First, there is a "perfect member" (sect. 119) of society who does give open consent. In contemporary terms, a perfect member would be one who renounces their citizenship of one country and swears an oath of allegiance to another. This person thereby openly and voluntarily gives their consent—submits—to the laws, rules, and customs of the state that they have freely chosen to join. Unfortunately, these perfect members of society are as few in number in the twenty-first century as they were in the seventeenth. We should note here that immigrants who choose to become citizens in a new country by their active consent are, in many respects, more "perfect" citizens than those native-born citizens who only become citizens by accident of birth and tacit consent.[4]

The second alternative is tacit consent, which is a complicated concept that even Locke has trouble pinning down:

> The difficulty is, what ought to be looked upon as a tacit consent, and how far it binds, i.e., how far anyone shall be looked on to have consented, and thereby submitted to any government, where he has made no expressions of it at all. And to this I say that every man that hath any possessions or enjoyment of any part of the dominions of government doth thereby give his tacit consent, and is as far forth obliged to obedience to the laws of that government during such enjoyment as anyone under it; whether this his possession be of land to him and his heirs forever, or a lodging only for a week; or whether it be barely travelling freely on the highway; and in effect it reaches as far as the very being of anyone within the territories of that government. (sect. 119)

Many scholars have argued that Locke overreaches in this passage. Tacit consent might be derived from continuous presence in a country or from long-term

---

[4] We might imagine a world in which all people, upon reaching adulthood, are required to give their active consent in order to join the social contract of a specific nation state.

possession of property, but how can tacit consent be derived from one's mere physical presence in a country? In Locke's epoch, when large swathes of the planet were still not organized into nation states, it was possible for a group of people to withdraw their consent, leave their country, and create a new social contract on another continent. The Pilgrims represent one such group. Today, however, when every habitable tract of land is possessed by a nation, when every child is born with citizenship to a nation, with membership in a social contract, it is not easy simply to decide to found one's own state or to change citizenship (oftentimes because the nation you want to join may *not* want you).

The definition of tacit consent has been debated for centuries, and there is little agreement on what it actually means. Two thousand years before Locke, Socrates weighed in on the subject of consent when he was on trial for corrupting the youth of Athens, for which he was convicted. As punishment, he could have chosen either death or banishment, but he famously chose death. Socrates argued that he was required to accept the death sentence because he had *tacitly consented* to the government of Athens for his entire life. In this passage, Socrates is talking to his friend, Crito, who is urging him to escape prison and banish himself rather than accept the death sentence. Socrates speaks, here, from the perspective of the personified "Laws of Athens" and describes how the Laws might respond to his escape:

> He who has experience of the manner in which we order justice and administer the state, and still remains, has entered into an implied contract that he will do as we command him. And he who disobeys us is, as we maintain, thrice wrong; first, because in disobeying us he is disobeying his parents; secondly, because we are the authors of his education; thirdly, because he has made an agreement with us that he will duly obey our commands [...]
>
> You, Socrates, are breaking the covenants and agreements which you made with us at your leisure, not in any haste or under any compulsion or deception, but having had seventy years to think of them, during which time you were at liberty to leave the city, if we were not to your mind, or if our covenants appeared to you to be unfair. (Plato, 360 BCE, para. 92–5)

Socrates' friend Crito eventually agrees with this analysis, albeit with sadness. Crito understands that Socrates cannot avoid punishment because he has tacitly consented to the Laws of Athens throughout his entire life. To flee would be to behave as a "miserable slave" because he "agreed to be governed according to [the Laws of Athens] in deed, and not in word only" (para. 92). And so Socrates drank the hemlock—an act of active consent that reaffirmed the tacit consent he showed throughout his entire life, an act that purified his status as the perfect citizen of Athens.

5.3.6   Disobedience and the Dissolution of Government

Socrates' trial and death raise important issues about consent, but some of you might be wondering if Crito was not right all along. Surely, if a government uses its power unjustly, citizens may consider the social contract to be broken, and they may no longer be required to obey the authorities. If Socrates' trial were unjust, would he not be entitled to reject his punishment as well?

This query raises the specter of disobedience. Under what circumstances can people be justified in disobeying the reigning political power? Locke provides several reasons, all of which involve some abuse of power by the government. First, Locke (1689) insists that the people who join a social contract do so only because they choose the rules of the society in which they will live. Therefore, laws cannot be made by those who have not been chosen to make them:

> When any one or more shall take upon them to make the laws, whom the people have not appointed so to do, they make laws without authority, which the people are not therefore bound to obey; by which means they come again to be out of subjection, and may constitute to themselves a new legislative, as they think best, being in full liberty to resist the force of those who without authority would impose anything upon them. (sect. 212)

A second reason the social contract might be dissolved is if anarchy reigns because the system of justice has broken down. The primary functions of government are to preserve property, protect the people, and punish offenders. If a government can no longer do this, then the contract is broken, and the people reacquire the absolute liberty that they had in the state of nature. The third reason that justifies the dissolution of government is when the rulers violate the property rights of the people. The reason people joined the social contract in the first place was to secure their property; if, then, the rulers take their property, "they put themselves into a state of war with the people, who are thereupon absolved from any further obedience" (sect. 222). He continues:

> Whensoever, therefore, the legislative shall transgress this fundamental rule of society, and either by ambition, fear, folly, or corruption, endeavor to grasp themselves or put into the hands of any other an absolute power over the lives, liberties, and estates of the people, by this breach of trust they forfeit the power the people had put into their hands, for quite contrary ends, and it devolves to the people, who have a right to resume their original liberty, and the establishment of the new legislative (such as they shall think fit) provide for their own safety and security, which is the end for which they are in society. (sect. 222)

In short, there are a number of reasons that justify rebellion against a power that has lost its legitimacy to govern. The most important concept to remember about the social contract is that it is a contract. Both sides have duties and obligations. Yes, citizens must obey the laws. However, those in power only are in power if they uphold the laws to which the people have consented.

We can see now that Socrates was perhaps correct in insisting that he must obey the rules of Athens and submit to punishment. The authorities were not abusing their power by putting him on trial. Indeed, the authorities were obeying the law, and Socrates, through his tacit consent throughout his life, knew that he was obliged to obey the law. While it might have been in his own self-interest to escape, doing so would undermine Athens as a commonwealth—and therefore would not really be in his own self-interest. Socrates was wise because he could clearly see his own interests and those of society. He understood what Rousseau called the difference between the *general will* and the *particular will*, a dichotomy we will explore in the section on Rousseau below. But first let's explore some examples of strict COVID-era policies in order to see if they might provide legitimate justifications for rebellion against the government.

Box 5.2 Interdisciplinary Perspective #10: Political Philosophy and Public Health

Strict Zero-COVID Policies: Reasons to Rebel or Obey?

How can Locke help us to understand the challenges nations faced during COVID-19? Under what circumstances would Locke think that it is appropriate for people to continue to obey or start to rebel? Let's perform a short analysis from Locke's perspective.

First, Locke argues that the social contract is needed to protect society from "degenerate men." Unlike Hobbes, Locke insists that human beings are not naughty by nature. Indeed, right and wrong exist in the state of nature because human beings possess reason. Even in the state of nature, there is a rule not to harm others, even though the rule is unenforceable. If everyone were nice, then governments would not need to be created. However, there are always degenerates who ruin life for everyone else. According to Locke, the government exists in order to protect us from these degenerates. During the COVID-19 pandemic, governments did not act perfectly, but most attempted to protect their people from illness, fraud, scarcity, and the degenerates who would do further harm. Protection from evildoers is the most obvious reason for people to obey.

Second, Locke mentions that another advantage of government—another reason to obey— is that it protects us from outsiders. He writes that people "unite into a community for their comfortable, safe, and peaceable living one amongst another, in a secure enjoyment of their properties, and a greater security against any that are not of it." It is the government's role to prevent harm from external threats as well as internal ones. All of the COVID-era restrictions on international travel, the securing of borders, and even enforced testing and quarantining of outsiders would not violate any of Locke's principles. One might disapprove of Locke's strict delineation of those within the social contract and those outside of it, but the conclusion follows from the premise. During COVID-19, most nations implemented varying pandemic travel policies to control non-citizen arrivals (Holpuch, 2022). However, those policies changed as often as the virus mutated. Most countries required, at various times, evidence of a negative test or full vaccination to enter, and some banned outsiders outright (Lefton, 2021). Still, Locke's concept of the social contract does not give all human beings the same rights; those within the social contract are given special status, and unequal treatment of foreigners is built into the fabric of the contract. In this view, foreigners must obey the laws of their country of arrival since they have no legal or moral standing to rebel against a government that is not their own.

Although most countries implemented policies that were stricter against non-citizens, some countries imposed strict rules on their own citizens. Australia, for example, temporarily banned its own citizens from returning to

(continued)

their own homeland if they had been in India 14 days prior to arrival, prompting serious backlash (Pillai, 2021). Furthermore, the Australian government banned its own citizens from *leaving* the country, except in exceptional circumstances, using its biosecurity powers. The leaving-ban was upheld by the courts despite challenges from civil rights groups, who argued that the right to leave one's own country is a fundamental right; however, the court insisted that the right to leave is not an absolute right and can indeed be suspended during emergencies (McGuirk, 2021). Still, one might question the entire foundation of Australia's social contract if even its own citizens lose the right to enter or leave.

So when, for Locke, is the violation of a basic right a reason to rebel? He outlines three reasons that justify rebellion: (1) when laws are made by those without the authority to do so; (2) when anarchy reigns because the justice system has collapsed; and (3) when the government exerts unwarranted authority over "the lives, liberties, and estates of the people." Furthermore, when power is used to destroy rather than preserve property, people can choose to dissolve society and return to their original liberty in the state of nature. For reason (1), in countries where new pandemic laws were made through the duly elected legislators, there would be no cause to rebel. For reason (2), in countries where the justice system still functioned, there would also be no cause. The tricky point is with (3). What exactly is unwarranted authority? Was the ban on Australian citizens entering or leaving their own country unwarranted at all times, or is it warranted only in emergency situations, such as during war or pandemic? It is certainly a question worth exploring.

During the pandemic in many other countries around the world, there were serious protests against the closure of businesses. Locke would define businesses as "the estates of the people." While the protestors were a diverse bunch (and there were always some extremists present), let's assume that they were all protesting in good faith as honest and reasonable citizens. When they argued that they were protesting because they were not allowed to work and could not earn money and, therefore, could not feed themselves or their families, they were expressing reasonable frustration because they were not receiving the advantages that living in a social contract was meant to provide. After all, the entire point of government is that it is better to live in an orderly society than in the state of nature. If a government, in Locke's words, grows exorbitant in its use of power and uses it to destroy not preserve the livelihoods of the people, then the government has lost its legitimacy as the guarantor of people's livelihoods. After the first wave of COVID passed, most governments eased economic lockdowns precisely because they recognized that strict measures were harming the "estates of the people."

Let us look at a final example that Locke's ideas help illuminate: China's zero-COVID policy. I mentioned above that Australia, a developed liberal

(continued)

democracy, banned international travel in order to slow international transmission of the virus, raising difficult questions about the government's devotion to its own social contract. China, a developing nation with single-party rule, also adopted strict measures, encapsulated in the government's desire both to prevent the virus from arriving from outside its borders and also to eliminate transmission of the virus within (Wang, 2021). One such defense measure was the lockdown of entire cities.[5] For example, Xi'an, a city of 13 million people, was completely locked down in December 2021 after the discovery of local transmission (Yuan, 2022). Furthermore, partial lockdowns affected millions of additional residents in Shenzhen, Dalian, and Guangzhou as recently as August 2022 (Farrer, 2022). Lockdown was meant quite literally in China—citizens were forbidden from leaving their homes even to go shopping for food. Some of the consequences of the lockdown were reported by the *New York Times* in January 2022: A man died of a heart attack after hospital workers refused to admit him because he was supposed to be in lockdown; a woman had a miscarriage because she was refused admittance because her COVID test had expired; people were unable to procure food and medicine because they could not leave their homes, but the government failed to provide them with these necessities (Yuan, 2022).

Locke argues that the purpose of government is to provide for the safety and security of the people. If the government does not provide these benefits, "it devolves to the people, who have a right to resume their original liberty, and the establishment of the new legislative (such as they shall think fit) provide for their own safety and security, which is the end for which they are in society." Do the above examples justify rebellion against the government?

Perhaps there were reasons to rebel, but there were always powerful reasons to obey—to obey even the onerous rules of pandemics. Locke argues that we have all given either our active or tacit consent to obey the government. You cannot argue that you like some laws and you don't like others precisely because you have shown throughout your entire life—through your choice to live in a country—that you have tacitly consented to the laws of the land. As Socrates suggested, only hypocrites would argue that certain laws do not apply to them despite the fact that they showed throughout their entire lives that they consented to obey the laws, pandemic laws included.

Discuss
- **Evaluate Australia's ban on allowing its own citizens to enter and leave the country. Should the right to travel be an absolute right for citizens?**
- **Evaluate China's zero-COVID policy. Does the goal to eradicate the virus outweigh any and all hardship suffered by citizens?**

---

[5] Note that in December 2022, China did finally soften many aspects of its strict zero-COVID measures, partly due to the public protest of its citizens.

5.4 Rousseau's *Social Contract*

Jean-Jacques Rousseau was one of the most brilliant and eccentric thinkers of eighteenth-century Europe. Born in Geneva in 1712, he had an unsettled childhood. His mother died shortly after his birth, and he was raised and educated by his father, a watchmaker. At 16, he moved to Turin and converted to Catholicism. He dabbled in a number of professions—servant, monk, musician—but never really settled into a stable career. Finally, in 1749, he wrote an essay for a competition sponsored by the Academy of Dijon. Rousseau's *Discourse on the Sciences and Arts* won first prize and gave him his first taste of philosophical acclaim. Throughout the rest of his life, he wrote about a variety of subjects from education to ethics, but his main concern was the reconciliation between the individual and society, between personal liberty and political power. In fact, the third dichotomy between alienation and reconciliation, which was presented in Chap. 2, is very much influenced by Rousseau's lifelong interest in the theme.

In 1762, he published *The Social Contract*, which represents his deepest exploration of political philosophy. It begins with the famous quotation: "Man is born free; and everywhere he is in chains" (I, I, para. 1). Immediately the reader might think that this comment will lead to a tirade about why tyranny is bad and why people should throw off their chains and become free again. However, this is not the case. The "chains" about which Rousseau speaks are not necessarily evil, nor is absolute "freedom" necessarily good. Through understanding the paradoxical meaning of this quotation, we will be able to understand some of the trickiest and most profound ideas about our political existence.

5.4.1 The State of Nature

Like both Hobbes and Locke, Rousseau begins *The Social Contract* (1762) by painting a picture of the state of nature, from which key political concepts emerge. In Rousseau's state, there is "common liberty" for all, and the most important rule for each man to follow is the rule of "self-preservation." People only give up their natural freedoms in order to achieve something better; they "all, being born free and equal, alienate their liberty only for their own advantage" (I, II, para. 3)—ideas echoed in the works of Hobbes and Locke.

Of course, our natural freedoms can be taken away by force, but Rousseau suspects that societies founded through enforced obedience cannot last. He writes, "The strongest is never strong enough to be always the master, unless he transforms strength into right, and obedience into duty" (I, III, para. 1). In this passage, we hear echoes of Hobbes' belief in the equality of power in the state of nature. But Rousseau disagrees with Hobbes with respect to the role of power in an existing commonwealth. Hobbes gives to the Leviathan absolute power to maintain peace, but Rousseau insists that the power of the sovereign is as precarious as the power individual men have in the state of nature. If people are forced to obey, then they will naturally cease to obey as soon as they can. Rousseau concludes, "Force does not create right," and "we are obliged to obey only legitimate powers" (I, III, para. 4). At best, submitting to force is prudent or it might even be a temporary necessity; however, commanding obedience through force will never be a long-term solution because obedience dissipates as soon as force disappears. Already one can see that Rousseau—like Locke—will construct his political argument around *legitimate* power.

5.4.2   The Founding of the Social Contract

Following both Hobbes and Locke, Rousseau imagines a time when people realize that they can neither preserve their own lives nor protect their property on their own. They must find a solution:

> The problem is to find a form of association which will defend and protect with the whole common force the person and goods of each associate, and in which each, while uniting himself with all, may still obey himself alone, and remain as free as before. (I, VI, para. 4)

The answer, of course, is the social contract. Rousseau sums up his basic definition of the social contract as follows: "Each of us puts his person and all his power in common under the supreme direction of the general will, and, in our corporate capacity, we receive each member as an indivisible part of the whole" (I, VI, para. 9).

5.4.3   Justice and Morality; Freedom and Obedience

Like Hobbes and Locke, the movement from the state of nature to the social contract involves both a renunciation of the natural liberty that we have in the state of nature and also the transfer of our natural rights to the collective. Rousseau further describes the improved human being as follows: "What man loses by the social contract in his natural liberty and an unlimited right to everything he tries to get and succeeds in getting; what he gains is civil liberty and the proprietorship of all he possesses" (I, VIII, para. 2). Crucially for Rousseau, individuals do not give themselves to any single person or special-interest group, but to the whole. The whole, therefore, grows in force as each individual adds their rights and liberties to it. Furthermore, once united in a collective, any attack on an individual represents an attack on all. Victims of crime do not need to punish the attacker alone or seek private vengeance, for they have the force of the whole to do so on their behalf.

    With the creation of a collective, we see the rise of morality—and the first glimpses of true freedom: "The passage from the state of nature to the civil state produces a very remarkable change in man, by substituting justice, for instinct in his conduct, and giving his actions the morality they had formerly lacked" (I, VIII, para.

1). Here, Rousseau aligns himself with Hobbes and against Locke. In the state of nature, morality does not exist because there are no rules except the rules of war, a state in which force and fraud are virtues. Locke would suggest that reason would establish moral values even in the state of nature. But Rousseau insists that proper moral freedom arises with the creation of the social contract. A person "acquires in the civil state, moral liberty, which alone makes him truly master of himself; for the mere impulse of appetite is slavery, while obedience to a law which we prescribe to ourselves is liberty" (I, VIII, para. 2). This is a confusing and paradoxical statement. Rousseau seems to be changing the common meanings of words. However, if we follow the line of his reasoning, the comment makes sense. In the state of nature, we are slaves to all of the chaotic forces that crash against us—degenerate people, scarce resources, as well as the jealousy, suspicion, and hatred of the *other*. By creating a social contract, we free ourselves from these chaotic forces while, at the same time, renouncing the freedoms we enjoy in the state of nature. In doing so, we become *moral* creatures with a qualitatively different, more profound freedom. This new *civil* liberty rests upon obedience to the social contract—which is the moral system we have set for ourselves.

Recall that Rousseau begins *The Social Contract* with this sentence: "Man is born free, and yet we see him everywhere in chains." Perhaps those chains are a good thing. Perhaps freedom can only be found in obedience.

5.4.4 Equality Before the Law

Rousseau, like Hobbes, has a complex view on equality. Hobbes recognized that people were physically and mentally unequal. Some are stronger and wiser than others. Still, Hobbes maintained that there is sufficient equality in the state of nature that no man is strong enough or wise enough to prevail over others who band together to defeat him. Rousseau agrees to both the reality of physical and mental inequalities but argues that a more pure and qualitatively better equality is established through the creation of a social contract:

> Instead of destroying natural inequality, the [social contract] substitutes, for such physical inequality as nature may have set up between men, an equality that is moral and legitimate, and that men, who may be unequal in strength or intelligence, become every one equal by convention and legal right. (I, IX, para. 8)

And so Rousseau establishes the concept of equality before the law. In a just society, no one is above the law, and all are equal before it. This is one great advantage for living in an appropriately ordered society. Additionally, Rousseau sides with Locke and against Hobbes on the subject of absolute power. Hobbes thought that the sovereign was legitimately endowed with absolute power, but Rousseau differs. Both leaders and common citizens are equal before the law.

5.4.5 The Particular Will and the General Will

Yet another important theme of Rousseau's is that of egoism or self-interest. Rousseau says we should always follow our self-interest, and this egotistical command raises a variety of questions, the most important of which is this: How do we know what our own self-interest really and truly is?[6]

Rousseau provides an interesting and complex solution to this problem. It involves breaking apart self-interest into a two different concepts: (1) the particular will, which is each individual's own will and focused on the good of each particular individual, and (2) the general will, which is the will of society as a whole and focused on the good of society as a whole.

One great problem is that people are often mistaken when they think about their own particular wills because the particular will is often conceived of as being the same as one's narrow self-interest. We often fail to recognize that our own particular self-interest is always strengthened by doing what is best for society as a whole—the general will.

Rousseau does acknowledge the fact that there will exist in the social contract a number of particular wills. He writes:

> In fact, each individual, as a man, may have a particular will contrary or dissimilar to the general will which he has as a citizen. His particular interest may speak to him quite differently from the common interest [...]. He may wish to enjoy the rights of citizenship without being ready to fulfill the duties of a subject. (I, VII, para. 6)

Such is the position of an egoist or a free rider, one who desires the benefits of citizenship but who does not wish to perform the duties of a citizen. Rousseau says, "Whoever refuses to obey the general will shall be compelled to do so by the whole body. This means nothing less than that *he will be forced to be free*; for this is the condition which, by giving each citizen to his country, secures him against all personal dependence" (I, VII, para. 7).

For Rousseau, the end of power, the reason for the social contract in the first place, is the common good. There are two consequences of this fact: (1) the general will must be inalienable (it must be equivalent to the common good), and (2) the general will must be indivisible—it must represent each member equally. Regarding (1), Rousseau writes:

> For if the clashing of particular interests made the establishment of societies necessary, the agreement of these very interests made it possible. The common element in these different interests is what forms the social tie; and, were there no point of agreement between them all, no society could exist. It is solely on the basis of this common interest that every society should be governed. (II, I, para. 1)

Common interest, not self-interest, must be the bond that holds society together, and the general will is the pure expression of the common interest. Regarding (2), Rousseau says:

---

[6] We will explore this theme at great length in the next chapter on ethical egoism, when we explore Ayn Rand's view that people should follow their own self-interest at all times.

> For will either is, or is not, general; it is the will either of the body of the people, or only of a part of it. In the first case, the will, when declared, is an act of Sovereignty and constitutes [illegitimate] law: in the second, it is merely a particular will, or act of magistracy—at the most [an illegitimate] decree. (II, II, para. 1)

Here, we begin to see additional elements of Rousseau's theory on just and unjust laws. All laws must be aimed at the common good and the common interest in order to be legitimate; if a law favors a specific individual or group, it is by definition illegitimate and not a law at all.

Rousseau has presented two abstract theoretical points about the general will—it is inalienable and indivisible. However much we might accept these points in theory, it is often difficult to apply them in practice. How does anyone know what the general will really is, what the common interest really is, or what the common good of society really is? Are we not all more profoundly influenced by our own self-interest, by our own particular will? Rousseau concedes this point, with a caveat: "Our will is always for our own good, but we do not always see what that is; the people is never corrupted, but it is often deceived, and on such occasions only does it seem to will what is bad" (II, III, para. 1). If we could only perceive the general will as being our own self-interest, we could see through the lie that is our particular will. Sadly, we deceive ourselves and others deceive us, so we mistake our self-interest for our true interest. Rousseau states:

> The general will is always in the right, but the judgment which guides it is not always enlightened. It must be got to see objects as they are, and sometimes as they ought to appear to it; it must be shown the good road it is in search of, secured from the seductive influences of individual wills, taught to see times and spaces as a series, and made to weigh the attractions of present and sensible advantages against the danger of distant and hidden evils. The individuals see the good they reject; the public wills the good it does not see. (II, VI, para. 10)

The key to good government, therefore, is to cut through all of the lies that try to convince us that our self-interest is really what we desire. Once we can see the general will as our true, long-term self-interest, we can overcome the false self-interest created by our particular wills.

Rousseau envisages a process whereby we can strip away our self-interest in order to arrive at the common interest. As we think about our self-interests, we can compare them with other self-interests. We cancel out our interests that exclude others and add those that include others. After these calculations, the general will remains as the sum of the differences. This sum of differences should form the basis of all laws in society.

5.4.6 Consent and Submission to the Law

The next important point to discuss is that of consent and submission to the law. Rousseau considers the critical issue raised by Socrates' trial: Should one submit to punishment by the authorities even if the punishment is death? Socrates insisted that he must submit because he had given his tacit consent to the laws of Athens for 70 years. Locke would agree. Tacit consent places the individual at the mercy of the legitimate laws of society, and an individual must submit to their authority. Rousseau also agrees:

> The citizen is no longer the judge of the dangers to which the law desires him to expose himself; and when the prince says to him: "It is expedient for the State that you should die," he ought to die, because it is only on that condition that he has been living in security up to the present, and because his life is no longer a mere bounty of nature, but a gift made conditionally by the State.
>
> The death-penalty inflicted upon criminals may be looked on in much the same light: it is in order that we may not fall victims to an assassin that we consent to die if we ourselves turn assassins. (II, VII, para. 2–3)

Rousseau presents a strong case for submission to judicial punishment. His argument rests on the concept of consent. Security from violence is one gift that the social contract bestows upon its members, and so the gift can be withdrawn for legitimate reasons, forfeiting the life of a member. And so the death penalty is a just punishment for those who murder. In effect, when murderers kill, they have returned themselves to the state of nature—where there is no law or justice, no right to life—so the commonwealth has every right to execute them.[7]

5.4.7   Rousseau and Freedom

Rousseau and Locke are closely aligned in many respects, since both have strong beliefs in the creation and maintenance of *legitimate* political power, in the necessity of express or tacit consent, and in the ultimate end of political power, which is the common good of society as a whole. However, Rousseau is perhaps more eloquent than Locke in presenting the central paradox of civilized life—that man is everywhere in chains, but that this is not necessarily a bad thing. He says, "Force does not constitute right," and "obedience is only due to legitimate powers." He also says that "man must be forced to be free" and that "it is *slavery* to be under the impulse of mere appetite, and *freedom* to obey a law which we prescribe for ourselves." Freedom, Rousseau argues, comes in many forms, some of which are chaotic and primal, and others which are moral and civilized. Chains also come in many forms, some of which are created by illegitimate powers, others of which are created by ourselves, voluntarily, in order to secure our persons, our property, and "commodious living," as Hobbes would argue. The chains of the social contract are these good chains. Through restricting our natural freedoms, the chains create the civil liberty we need to exist as fully developed, moral, civilized creatures. In the state of nature we are animals; in the social contract we are human beings.

Of course, after creation of the social contract, new problems are bound to arise, and Rousseau paints a helpful picture of the confusions that lead to civil strife. The most important of these is self-interest, the human tendency to be egotistical. People

---

[7] There are echoes of Kant's categorical imperative here. When someone commits murder, they create a universal law from that action: All people should murder. Therefore, it is not a contradiction, at least according to Kant, to *respect* the choice of the murderer by taking their life.

are often deceived, encouraged by demagogues to follow their self-interest, but the particular will is often misaligned with the general will. It is the role of political leaders to remind citizens of their shared interests, not to inflame the differences of our ever-present particular wills. A moral political leader aligns those interests in a conception of the general will—the good of society.

In short, Rousseau creates an argument that, at its heart, rebuffs the ethical egoists, whom we will study in the next chapter. We will see that Ayn Rand (1964)—the twentieth-century philosopher and defender of the virtue of egoism—champions selfishness over altruism or the particular will over the general will, writing:

> The basic *social* principle of the Objectivist ethics is that just as life is an end in itself, so every living human being is an end in himself, not the means to the ends or the welfare of others—and, therefore, that man must live for his own sake, neither sacrificing himself to others nor sacrificing others to himself. To live for his own sake means that the achievement of his own happiness is man's highest moral purpose. (p. 23)

Rousseau would agree to a certain extent. Living for himself and following his own particular will is man's highest purpose—*but only in the state of nature*. However, there is a qualitative change in morality that arises upon creation of the social contract. In civilized society, the right to live "for himself" and to follow "his own self-interest" is transferred to society as a whole, and a person's highest purpose becomes living life in accordance with the general will (which is altruistic). In short, Rand desires *natural liberty* to remain in civil society, but Rousseau insists that it cannot because we renounce our natural liberty when we join society and acquire, as a result, all of the securities and protections that accompany the new state of civilized existence. In the social contract, we are no longer enslaved by our natural freedom, living for our own sake; we are instead freed by the chains with which we bind ourselves. One might wonder if compulsory vaccination is one of these chains that free us.

Box 5.3 Interdisciplinary Perspective #11: Political Philosophy and Public Health

Compulsory Vaccination: Should We Be Forced to Be Free?
Rousseau's great philosophical achievement, which resonates today more than ever, is his attempt to reconcile the two great forces that alienate people from each other and from society: self-interest and the common good. During a pandemic, it may be sometimes difficult to comply with hygiene orders like mask-wearing or social-distancing. However, it is perfectly just and rational to do so. All we need to do is remember that there is tension between our individual private will and the general will. If we focus on the common interest, not our own self-interest, it is much easier for us to submit to the law. At the same time, if we see injustice, if we see laws applied to some but not others, if we see an unbalanced social contract, we are also justified in our dissent—not because our own self-interest has been threatened, but because the common good is undermined. It is in this important distinction between

(continued)

self-interest and the common good that we can begin to understand the vaccination debates from a philosophical perspective.

Before beginning, let's point out an important distinction in how we use language. First, philosophers have often pointed to the important difference between *descriptive* and *normative* (or prescriptive) statements. Sometimes, we describe things and sometimes we prescribe them. "Jack likes chocolate ice cream" is a descriptive comment. "Jack should like chocolate ice cream" is a normative one. "Some people are fearful of vaccines" is a descriptive statement. "They should not be fearful of vaccines" is a normative one. When thinking about vaccination, it is important to keep this distinction in mind since it is not helpful to slip between the two types of statements. Typically, the language of ethics is normative language, e.g., thou shall not kill. However, it can also be descriptive; for example, different people have different opinions about abortion, the death penalty, or pandemic laws.

So, what is at the core of the debate about vaccination and how can Rousseau help us understand it better? Some people fear vaccines and some people do not. There seems to be no dispute over these descriptive statements. But there are two very real normative disputes. First, some believe that people *should* fear vaccines and others believe that people *should not* fear vaccines. Furthermore, some believe that people should not be forced to be vaccinated and others believe that people should be forced to be vaccinated (despite their objections). The first normative dispute is not really critical for the purposes of this discussion. Fear is an emotion, and one might fear snakes or spiders, but a government cannot prevent fear of spiders through legislation.

However, the second dispute is important, because it touches upon the key themes of this chapter: freedom, self-interest, the common good, obedience, force, the particular will, and the general will. Under what circumstances can a society force people to be quarantined or vaccinated? To use Rousseau's language, under what circumstances can people be forced to be free?

- **Natural Liberty Versus Civil Liberty:** Rousseau's first point is that the transition from the state of nature to civilized society involves the renunciation of natural liberties in return for the acquisition of civil liberties. Paradoxically, the renunciation of natural liberty actually increases our freedom—we are even freer in civilized society. Let's put this in plain terms: In the state of nature, we are free to die from highly contagious diseases because no one has the power to tell us what to do to protect ourselves and because we do not have the power to compel others to behave in such a way that would protect us. However, in civilized society, we should be free to live without the fear of pandemics because we—the "signers" of the social contract—are able to create the rules to prevent disease spread and because people can be compelled to obey the rules. The rules are those positive chains—they force us to be free by liberating us from the chaotic forces of nature. Quarantine orders, sanitary cordons, and indeed forced

(continued)

vaccinations may be some of these positive chains that liberate a society from the threat of pandemic disease.

- **The General Will and the Particular Will:** Rousseau recognizes the very real and ongoing tension between private self-interest and the common good. He writes, a citizen's "own private interest may dictate to him very differently from the common interest…He may wish to enjoy the rights of a citizen without being disposed to fulfill the duties of a subject." The primary reason that interests misalign is because people sometimes carve their own self-interest out of the general will. However, Rousseau insists that it is in our own long-term self-interest to align our interest with the common good. If citizens refuse to enjoy the benefits of civilized society without sacrificing their perceived self-interest, then they may be compelled to do so. Rousseau again: "Whoever refuses to obey the general will shall be compelled to it by the whole body: this in fact only forces him to be free; for this is the condition which […] guarantees his absolute personal independence." Quarantine orders, sanitary cordons, and even vaccinations should be followed in general because their goal is to enhance the common good. For Rousseau, people who resist should be compelled to comply because, unfortunately, sometimes people must be forced to be free—forced to enjoy the benefits of living in a disease-free society.
- **Unjust Public Health Laws:** Although it seems that Rousseau gives a blank check to the authorities to compel certain behaviors during a pandemic, this is not necessarily the case. Laws must be legitimate and apply to all. He writes, "For will either is, or is not, general; it is the will either of the body of the people, or only of a part of it. In the first case, the will, when declared, is an act of Sovereignty and constitutes [illegitimate] law: in the second, it is merely a particular will, or act of magistracy—at the most [an illegitimate] decree." Laws that exempt, for example, the rich or the powerful or the well-connected from complying with public health orders—for no reason other than their elevated status—would be illegitimate decrees. Still, public health orders created and enforced in order to comply with the general will are perfectly legitimate, according to Rousseau. Furthermore, the state can force citizens to comply with them.

Lastly, it may be worthwhile to remember here that citizens are *forced to be free* in a number of other ways, some of which are far less controversial than involuntary vaccination. Different countries compel citizens to do all sorts of things: to pay taxes, serve in the military, register businesses, comply with regulations, perform jury duty, apply for driver's licenses, wear seat belts, avoid drugs, possess a personal ID at all times, register a home address with the authorities, etc. One might argue that forced vaccination is a different category because people fear (rightly or wrongly) the harm that might come from the vaccine. However, there is no guarantee in social contract theory that a citizen must never face personal inconveniences or even personal danger.

(continued)

Indeed, many countries practice universal conscription or mandatory non-military public service (e.g., Israel, South Korea, and Switzerland). During times of war, most countries have the legal authority to institute compulsory conscription. Even conscientious objectors can be compelled to serve although they may not be forced to carry weapons or participate in combat. Instead, they may be required to perform other extremely dangerous military roles by serving as frontline medics or stretcher bearers. There is nothing in the social contract theory that says that a citizen should not face any risks or dangers at all. The only rule is that everyone should have the same duties and obligations in order to receive the same protections. Rousseau argues that one cannot reap the rewards of civil society while at the same time avoiding legitimate duties.

Discuss
- **Using Rousseau's philosophical principles discussed in this section, evaluate the legitimacy of a wide range of COVID-19 pandemic rules: enforced quarantines, travel restrictions, mandatory vaccination, social distancing, mask-wearing orders, closure of places of worship, closure of businesses, closure of schools and universities, and bans on funerals. What are the common principles that might help to create a unified position on these different rules?**
- **The next global pandemic will force governments to restrict freedoms, at least temporarily. There will also surely be public unrest and protests opposing those restrictions. As we prepare for an inevitable future crisis, how can we help the public better understand the complex relationship between individual freedom and the common good?**

5.5   The Social Contract as a Guide to Ethical Behavior: Public Versus Private Ethics

We have seen in previous chapters that some philosophers have viewed ethics as primarily a private matter. Kant focuses on the rational basis for private ethical decisions; J. S. Mill and the utilitarians, on the other hand, focus their morality on achieving the greatest possible happiness for the most creatures possible, thus creating an important link between private ethics and public life. Hobbes, Locke, and Rousseau provide further insights into the connection between personal and public ethics. Here are some lessons we can draw from them.

First, how can we justify rules of behavior? The social contract theory insists that we only join a society provided that everyone gives up the same rights as everyone else and that everyone follows the same laws as everyone else—but these laws are only those that facilitate peace and prosperity for all. Certain rules are, therefore, clearly justified. No one wants to be murdered, so we give up our natural right to kill. No one wants to be robbed, so we give up our natural right to steal. No one wants to be deceived, so we give up our natural right to defraud others. What about, then, rules against certain behaviors, like smoking, having an abortion, or engaging in homosexual activity? It is not clear that *everyone* wants to give up these rights nor is it clear that engaging in these behaviors undermines peaceful coexistence, so such rules might not be justified by social contract theory.

Second, social contract theory establishes clear bounds of acceptable behavior. To put it simply, you must obey the law. No other rules of behavior are necessary or justified. Religions might demand you pray daily, attend church weekly, and not eat meat on Fridays, but these are not rules that you or the rest of the community are obligated to follow. Other ethical systems might demand that you must be kind to strangers or donate money to the poor, but in social contract theory, you can ignore both strangers and keep your money for yourself—after all, the community needs to take care of them, not you as an individual. In short, the law sets the boundaries of your charity, generosity, and goodness. Individuals can choose to be even more kind and generous, but they are not required to be.

Third, why is obeying the law in our self-interest? Why is it good for each of us? One reason is because life is eminently better in civilized society than it is in the state of nature. The peace, prosperity, and power of our society advance our own self-interest immeasurably. Furthermore, since there are degenerate people out there who will violate our civil freedom, it is in our self-interest to have a functioning judicial system to punish them. In the state of nature, it is difficult to punish people because we, as individuals, lack the force necessary to do so. In the social contract, the whole body combines its force to create a judiciary, which punishes offenders and restores justice. A crime against an individual becomes a crime against the whole community, and the community takes upon itself the role of judge, jury, and jailor.

While the social contract provides strong explanations of right and wrong behavior, it might be incomplete in a number of respects. For example, the social contract explains why stealing is wrong. However, if you have an illegal stash of heroin in your house and a thief steals it, you do not have legal recourse. In this case, is stealing wrong? And would taking the law into your own hands be wrong? Unfortunately, the social contract theory cannot adequately deal with this case, while Kant would have no trouble arguing that the theft of your heroin is wrong.

Another example of incompleteness is that the theory seems to neglect the basic rights of non-citizens, such as asylum seekers, refugees, and immigrants. Indeed, to what extent do outsiders have any rights at all? Social contract theory is at its heart exclusionary. It creates a boundary between one's own society and the rest of humanity. Of course, a society can choose to allow foreigners to enter—in order to travel, to work, or to become full citizens—but it can also choose to seal its borders. There is no compelling reason within the parameters of social contract theory to require a nation to care for refugees and asylum seekers or to grant any foreigner any rights whatsoever. The debate about illegal immigration in both the United States and the European Union centers on this fundamental incompleteness in the theory. Some argue that illegal immigrants have broken the law, are criminals, and have no rights; others insist that illegal immigrants do possess universal human rights, that they should not be treated as criminals for wanting to be part of another nation's social contract, and that they ought to be treated humanely. Since social contract theory is constructed on exclusivity, it has great difficulties explaining our responsibilities to the rest of the world.

Another example of incompleteness is the problem of one generation's obligation to future generations. According to a strict interpretation of the theory, the social contract is an agreement between members of society who are living concurrently. There are no explicit obligations to future generations. After all, those living in the future cannot benefit us in the present, nor can they agree to a contract—either expressly or tacitly—when they have yet to be born. Our descendants are no different from foreigners. In social contract theory, the interests of the present members are all that matter. So, why not go into massive debt, extract as many resources from the earth as possible, hunt species to extinction, and pollute the air and water? Future problems are for future generations to solve with their own social contract.

Yet another example of the incomplete nature of the theory is that many people believe being a good person requires doing more than simply following the law. Actions that go beyond the established standard are called *supererogatory* actions. So in the United States, there are laws against fraud, but there are no laws against having an illicit affair. What makes deceiving a business partner worse than deceiving a spouse or lover? Also in the United States, there are no positive laws (so-called Good Samaritan laws) that require assistance be given to fellow human beings in need. Some countries, such as Germany, do have laws that require you to help others, for example, if you are the first person to witness a car accident; those who do not render aid can be punished in criminal court. Americans are not required to stop on a highway to render assistance if they are the first to witness an accident, but German drivers are legally obligated to do so. Perhaps many Americans do stop to offer help, but those who do not stop are not violating a law. Are they bad people? Well, the US social contract does not think so, but many ethical theories (and some social contracts) require us to provide assistance. Both Kant and Mill would offer compelling reasons for helping others; they would further argue that people who do not help others are indeed bad people. Social contract theory does not have a solution to this problem.

Here's a final example of the incompleteness of the theory: Businesspeople who are being investigated for fraud and wealthy people who are being investigated for tax evasion often use similar arguments to defend themselves. "We have complied with all of the regulations that the law requires" and "I have paid every cent of tax that the law requires" are common defenses for behavior that the public condemns as being selfish and greedy—behavior that the law might actually promote. In short, the social contract sets a minimum standard for right behavior, and many people will make decisions right at the boundary of that behavior in order to maximize their profit and preserve their wealth and further their self-interest.

The preceding discussion helps us to realize the importance of a profound moral question: What does being a good person mean? There are at least three potential answers that social contract theory suggests. Being good might mean:

1. Civil compliance: simply complying with the law
2. Civil compliance + virtuous living: complying with the law *and* being good in other ways that the law does not require
3. Civil compliance + civil disobedience + virtuous living: complying with just laws *and* disobeying unjust laws *and* being good in other ways

How you answer this question determines to a great extent the rigor of your personal ethics and the defining characteristics of your ethical choices. It is important to remember that there is no right answer. You can summon plenty of evidence and philosophical support to justify any of the positions. Option (1) means that you can be a good public citizen but also not so virtuous in your private life, (2) means that you must be both a good public citizen and a virtuous person, and (3) means that you should be a good public citizen while also actively striving to improve the overall good of society (even if that means disobeying unjust laws) while also being a virtuous person.

In conclusion, the laws of living in civil society are implemented and enforced by the government, but citizens still have plenty of flexibility within a social contract to make their own decisions in many aspects of everyday life. Hobbes, Locke, and Rousseau articulated the contours of government in social contract theory, and their ideas profoundly influenced the development of the modern states in which we live. The modern state is really the child of these great thinkers, and, curiously enough, all three lived while Europe was being ravaged by the mother of all pandemics, the Black Death.

Box 5.4 Interdisciplinary Perspective #12: History

The Black Death and the Development of the Modern Nation State
No pandemic in history has generated as much fear and hysteria as the Black Death. Partly as a response to the plague, the modern nation state was born. As the medical historian Frank M. Snowden (2019) suggests, "The campaign against the plague marked a moment in the emergence of absolutism, and more generally, it promoted an accretion of the power and legitimation of the modern state" (p. 82). He adds that public health measures, such as quarantines and sanitary cordons, "presupposed the economic, administrative, and military resources of the state" (p. 71). In other words, without effective governments, societies are unable to cope with pandemics. Also, pandemics encourage states to develop their power even more.

Throughout the last 2000 years, there have been three great plague pandemics. The first plague, the plague of Justinian, began in 541 CE and ended in 755 CE. It killed somewhere between 20 and 50 million people (Snowden, 2019, p. 35). The second plague, the Black Death, lasted an astonishing 500 years breaking out in successive waves from the 1330s to the 1830s. It is impossible to calculate the overall death toll because so many people died, but some specific outbreaks killed half of a city's population. We do know that the mortality rate of the plague (before the discovery of antibiotics) was over 50 percent (Snowden, 2019, p. 29). The final pandemic, the Modern Plague, began in the 1850s, and it has not been eradicated. The United States, for example, has an average of about six or seven cases of the plague per year. In 2018 there was only 1 reported case; in 2017, 5; in 2016, 4; and in 2015, 16, of whom 4 perished (CDC, 2021).

(continued)

The second plague is most critical for a discussion of the social contract theory, and so it should be no surprise that our three social contract theorists were thinking about the relationships between the individual and the state during the midst of terrifying outbreaks of the second plague. Hobbes (1588–1679), Locke (1632–1704), and Rousseau (1712–1788) all had personal experience with devastating European pandemics. For example, Italy was particularly hard hit during this timeframe. Milan's great plague occurred between 1629 and 1631 and killed nearly half of the population. Between 1630 and 1631, Venice lost about one-third of its population. Britain was also severely affected; London's great plague, which occurred between 1665 and 1666, killed tens of thousands. In France, Marseille's plague between 1720 and 1722 killed about 60,000 of the city's population of 100,000 (Snowden, 2019, p. 72) and did even further damage as it spread inland.[8]

So how did people behave when the Black Death came and how did governments react? Not so well. Pandemics bring out our very worst selves. Racism, hysteria, violence, scapegoating, witch-hunting, flight to the countryside, quack-science, and recommitment to religion were common responses—all behaviors we saw during the COVID-19 pandemic. In Milan, the plague was blamed on Spain (they were at war), and four Spaniards were rounded up and tortured to death in public. Other common culprits were Jews, prostitutes, witches, and any type of foreigner. Similarly racist and scapegoating behavior was widely reported during the COVID-19 pandemic. For example, Asians in the United States reported increased racist acts against them (Rabin, 2022), and both Africans and African-Americans in China were subjected to COVID-induced racism (Williamson & Wang, 2020). During the Black Death, people also fled from cities, the epicenters of infection, due to mass hysteria and false notions about how the disease spread (polluted air or sin, they thought). Of course, flight only served to spread the disease to rural communities that could have avoided infection entirely. Again, the similarities with the COVID-19 pandemic are clear to see, although people living in the seventeenth century did not have the benefit of modern medicine to guide their actions. Of course, with no scientific explanations to draw upon, quackery and religious fervor seemed to be worthy of pursuit. Magical potions and holy cures were hawked to both the rich and the poor. People thought that if they turned away from sin, God would save them, and many elaborate churches and monuments were built after the plague disappeared. During the COVID-19 pandemic, people turned to magical bullets to protect themselves from disease. Quack doctors still plied their trade to the gullible, and the religious still turned to prayer as a weapon against infection (Taylor, 2021).

(continued)

---

[8] Much like today, wealthy city-dwellers fled to the countryside in order to avoid infection; however, the strategy did not work since they simply facilitated the further spread of the disease into villages that would have otherwise been disease-free.

These behaviors certainly do not make one trust in the fundamental rationality or inherent kindness of human beings. And unfortunately it gets worse. We do have some first-hand accounts of the plague. Boccaccio's *Decameron* (1353) was written as a response to the plague of Florence in 1348. He describes the breakdown of social relations in the section "Day the First" as follows. The people of Florence:

> [...] died not all, yet neither did they all escape; nay, many of each way of thinking and in every place sickened of the plague and languished on all sides, well nigh abandoned, having themselves, what while they were whole, set the example to those who abode in health. Indeed, leaving be that townsman avoided townsman and that well nigh no neighbor took thought unto other and that kinsfolk seldom or never visited one another and held no converse together save from afar, this tribulation had stricken such terror to the hearts of all, men and women alike, that brother forsook brother, uncle nephew and sister brother and oftentimes wife husband; nay (what is yet more extraordinary and well nigh incredible) fathers and mothers refused to visit or tend their very children, as they had not been theirs. (para. 6–7)

During a pandemic, the hysteria and fear is so great that people lose their moral bearings and forget what it means to be human. Unfortunately, these troubling responses to pandemic-induced trauma persist to this very day.

Throughout history, normal people have reacted to pandemics in a variety of helpful and unhelpful ways; governments have also been forced to react to pandemics, and they have done so in a variety of helpful and unhelpful ways. As with COVID-19, some measures enacted during the Black Death were productive and others counterproductive. The important historical point that needs to be stressed is that *pandemics and government power have evolved together*.

Effective government responses to pandemics have also required the existence of strong governments, so in some ways, as Snowden argues, pandemics and the modern nation state grew together, almost symbiotically. In order to exert control over a hysterical population, one requires institutions that can enforce the rules. States need public health authorities to make rules, and they also need soldiers, sailors, militia, police, and other government agents to compel obedience. Furthermore, they need doctors, nurses, cleaners, grave diggers, and record keepers. All of these form the apparatus of modern states. Without the Black Death, one can argue, the modern state would have taken a different—perhaps a less bureaucratic and centralized—form.

As each state experienced and then recovered from the plague, new institutions and bureaucracies were created. Snowden (2019) describes a number of these developments in *Epidemics and Society*. In Italy, some of the first important measures were taken, beginning with the creation of boards of health, which were given strong emergency powers to cope with pandemics. The Italians created the concept of the quarantine, which comes from the word *quaranta* or 40. They did not know why 40 days was an appropriate

(continued)

amount of time to require ships from foreign shores to wait before docking, but sometimes public health measures can be effective even if they are based on false premises. Lazarettos, barracks to isolate sailors in normal times as well as the sick during pandemics, were also built. The practice of the sanitary cordon was also introduced. It required soldiers to guard borders in order to enforce containment and prevent the arrival of outsiders. Furthermore, the Italians practiced contact-tracing. Government agents would scour cities to identify infected people, and in some instances, all of the inhabitants of a home would be locked inside under guard until the plague passed. Gatherings were banned and even church services were forbidden. Just like during our modern COVID-19 pandemic, people were not able to mourn their dead at funerals, which piled trauma upon trauma. Of course, businesses were also forced to close and cities facing plague were confronted with the prospect of economic ruin. In short, the experience of the Black Death echoes our own experience of COVID-19.

Pandemic disease and civil society have evolved together over the course of centuries. Pandemics have shaped the societies in which we live in numerous ways, and there are many tensions that have yet to be resolved. During a public health crisis, emergency laws are passed that grant power to the authorities at the cost of civil liberties. Some of these power grabs can be justified based on the extent of the threat, and others may really be government overreach. However, it is important to weigh these measures against the aim of the social contract as articulated by Hobbes, Locke, and Rousseau: It is in one's own real self-interest to live within a social contract. It is better to live in civil society than in the state of nature, where the life of man really is "solitary, poor, nasty, brutish and short."

Discuss
- **How well prepared are you as an individual for future pandemic restrictions? What restrictions would you consent to? What restrictions would you disobey? Why?**
- **During the next pandemic, would you prefer to live self-sufficiently in an isolated house in the middle of nowhere (i.e., in the state of nature) or in a city with hospitals, police, grocery stores, etc. (i.e., in a civilized society with a social contract)? Why?**
- **Social contract theory provides a robust defense for increased public health powers during a pandemic. Still, many public health measures were criticized during the COVID-19 pandemic. Take one example of these measures–such as lockdowns, mandatory masking, or compulsory testing. Imagine you are discussing the measure with someone who is opposed to it. Use the social contract theory to justify the rightness of the measure providing specific concepts from the theory.**

5.6 Conclusion

Jean-Jacques Rousseau famously said, "Man is born free, and everywhere he is in chains." Rousseau's concepts of freedom and bondage are both paradoxical and counterintuitive: Freedom enslaves people, and chains free them; self-interest is slavery, and the greater good is freedom. Rousseau might have called his book *The Virtue of Bondage* instead of *The Social Contract*.

We will see in the next chapter that Ayn Rand uses a similar counterintuitive technique at the beginning of *The Virtue of Selfishness*. The concept of selfishness, she says, is profoundly misunderstood by the vast majority of people: Selfishness is a good thing, and altruism is a great evil; selfishness is freedom, and altruism is bondage. The Randian egoists are in some respects the modern descendants of the old social contract theorists, albeit with an egotistical slant. Rousseau and Locke were committed to good and just societies. Egoists and libertarians insist that less government is better government and that individuals should be allowed to exercise as much personal freedom as possible in their personal affairs, with as little governmental oversight and interference as possible. Egoists assume that personal freedom (the right to live how one chooses to live) is the most important end of power; furthermore, the only legitimate *telos* or goal of government is to secure and protect individual freedom and personal property.

So Rand and Rousseau are both obsessed with the concepts of freedom and self-interest, but they could not disagree more in the definitions of the words. Rand argues that ensuring personal freedom—the freedom to live as one chooses—is the most important end of political power; Rousseau argues that empowering the general will—the greater good of society as a whole—is the most important end.

Boiled down to its essence, our exploration of social contract theory returns us to the theme of the ends of power. Is ensuring personal freedom, the liberty to follow one's own self-interest, the single and most important end of power? Or are there other equally important or even more important goals, such as justice, equality, or the greater good of the community? Your answer hinges on your interpretation of Rousseau's paradox: *Do chains enslave us or do they, in fact, free us?*

Box 5.5 Criteria for Evaluating Ethical Theories: Part 3

In the previous two chapters, we discussed five key criteria for evaluating ethical theories. Use this opportunity to evaluate the strengths and weaknesses of social contract theory according to those criteria before learning more about criteria 6 and 7.

1. Does the theory have an appropriate scope for who belongs in our moral community?
2. Does the theory exhibit an appropriate degree of rational consistency?
3. Does the theory align with "common sense"?
4. Does the theory adequately explain issues about moral distance?
5. Does the moral theory have an appropriate *telos* or ultimate goal?

(continued)

6. Does the theory clearly delineate obligatory actions and supererogatory ones?

We have seen that one advantage of the social contract theory is that it identifies appropriate and inappropriate actions solely with reference to the law. One can be a good citizen simply by obeying the law, which is the legal and ethical obligation of the citizen. Additional actions that go above and beyond the law—being a kind neighbor or a volunteer at a homeless shelter—are not obligatory. The previous ethical theories that we have discussed have not set such a distinction between obligatory and *supererogatory* actions.

Take giving to the poor as an example. Utilitarians argue that there is only ever one way to live one's life and only ever a single solution to any moral dilemma. The utilitarian Peter Singer insists that we donate *all* of our excess money to alleviate poverty and hunger; if we do not do so, we are not good people. A social contract approach would certainly praise someone for being so charitable; however, such a person would be regarded as going beyond any normal standard of behavior. After all, good citizens who pay their taxes (some of which is donated by the government to alleviate poverty and hunger) are being sufficiently good and are not required to give any more.

Lying is another example. The duty not to lie is absolute in Kant's system. Any lie you tell is wrong. A social contract approach would acknowledge that truth-telling is good, especially when it comes to contracts and legal proceedings. Indeed, truth telling is legally enforceable, and lying under oath is a crime. However, outside of legal requirements, it is perfectly fine to lie—to your spouse, for example, if you are having an affair. Is this how a solid system of ethics is supposed to work?

In short, the social contract sets the base level of proper ethical conduct. The question for you is this: Is this base level an appropriate standard for ethical behavior? Or do you need to do more than follow the laws of the land in order to consider yourself to be a good person?

7. Can the theory adapt to and account for the emergence of new technologies?

For any ethical theory to be effective, it must be comprehensive. It should be able to assess new developments in world history that were not present at the time the theory was created. Some theories seem to be more adaptable to historical and technological change than others. Let's look at two examples in technology—human cloning and using nuclear weapons—in light of Kantian deontology, utilitarianism, and social contract theory. Can these theories tell us what is right or wrong?

Human cloning is the "artificial" creation of people using the exact same DNA as a donor. Kant argued that we should act according to universal laws and that we should always treat people as ends in themselves, never as a

(continued)

means to an end. So does that help us understand the ethics of human cloning? Is cloning using people as means to an end and therefore forbidden? Or is it acceptable if the clone is considered to be a full person with the full list of rights and dignity of any other rational creature? Utilitarians argue that we should always act in such a way as to increase the happiness of as many creatures as possible. So, does this rule prevent us from cloning? Could we make clones in order to harvest their organs and, thus, save ourselves? Social contract theory tells us that morality is circumscribed by the law—behaviors are right if they promote the common good and wrong if they don't. Furthermore, we decide both who is in our community and also who receives the rights, privileges, and protections of being in it; we can also decide those we wish to exclude. Maybe human clones would be given full rights and maybe not. It would be our choice. Of course, the clones—if rational—could potentially rebel and form their own society. Can any of the ethical theories that we have learned about give us a clear answer to the question: Is it right or wrong to clone humans?

Moving on to the development of nuclear weapons, which our major philosophers in history could scarcely imagine, do their theories help us to assess appropriate use? Kant would argue that the killing of innocents is always wrong because it violates the absolute dignity of all human beings. He would be very clear about this. Utilitarians, however, have no such absolute standard. The use of nuclear weapons and the killing of innocents could be justified if certain conditions are met, namely, if the consequences lead to more overall happiness. And what does social contract theory say? Since the rights and privileges bestowed by the social contract are limited to those people within the community, innocent human beings in other societies outside of the contract lack basic rights.

In conclusion, an ideal ethical theory ought to be able to assess the morality of new technologies. If it cannot do so or if it provides unclear analyses, then perhaps the theory has a fundamental weakness.

References

Bittner, J. (2020, March 17). Germany has more than enough ventilators. it should share them. *New York Times*. https://www.nytimes.com/2020/03/17/opinion/coronavirus-europe-germany. html. Accessed 8 Nov 2021.

Boccaccio, G. (1353). *Decameron* (J. Payne, Trans.). Project Gutenberg. 2021. https://www.gutenberg.org/files/23700/23700-h/23700-h.htm

CDC. (2021, May 27). National Center for Emerging and Zoonotic Infectious Diseases (NCEZID), Division of Vector-Borne Diseases (DVBD). Plague in the United States. https://www.cdc.gov/plague/maps/index.html. Accessed 30 Aug 2022.

Farrer, M. (2022, August 31). China places millions into Covid lockdown again as economy continues to struggle. *The Guardian*. https://www.theguardian.com/world/2022/aug/31/china-places-millions-into-covid-lockdown-again-as-economy-continues-to-struggle. Accessed 31 Aug 2022.

Hobbes, T. (1651). *Leviathan*. Project Gutenberg. 2021. https://www.gutenberg.org/files/3207/3207-h/3207-h.htm

Holpuch, A. (2022, July 20). Covid-related international travel restrictions continue to wane. *New York Times*. https://www.nytimes.com/2022/07/20/travel/covid-related-international-travel-restrictions-continue-to-wane.html. Accessed 31 Aug 2022.

Lefton, B. (2021, March 3). Japan's travel ban has American baseball players in limbo. *New York Times*. https://www.nytimes.com/2021/03/03/sports/baseball/japan-eric-thames-colin-rea.html. Accessed 5 Mar 2021.

Locke, J. (1689). *Two treatises of government*. Project Gutenberg. 2021. https://www.gutenberg.org/files/7370/7370-h/7370-h.htm#

Locke, J. (1690). *An essay concerning human understanding*. Project Gutenberg. 2017. https://www.gutenberg.org/files/10615/10615-h/10615-h.htm

McGuirk, R. (2021, June 1). Australian court upholds ban on most international travel. *AP News*. https://apnews.com/article/asia-pacific-australia-lifestyle-travel-coronavirus-pandemic-a1d239e80be05c8cf393ec67d1b6cce2. Accessed 5 June 2021.

Pillai, S. (2021, May 7). Australia's decision to ban its citizens from returning from India—Is it legal? Is it moral? Is it just? *ABC*. https://www.abc.net.au/religion/is-australias-india-travel-ban-legal-moral-just/13335360. Accessed 10 May 2021.

Plato. (360 BCE). *Crito* (B. Jowett, Trans.). Project Gutenberg. 1999. https://www.gutenberg.org/files/1657/1657-h/1657-h.htm

Rabin, R. C. (2022, February 25). U.S. minorities experienced high rates of Covid-related discrimination, a study finds. *New York Times*. https://www.nytimes.com/2022/02/25/health/covid-racial-ethnic-discrimination.html. Accessed 31 Aug 2022.

Rand, A. (1964). *The virtue of selfishness: A new concept of egoism*. Signet.

Robbins, R., Weiland, N., & Jewett, C. (2022, January 6). Lifesaving Covid treatments face rationing as virus surges again. *New York Times*. https://www.nytimes.com/2022/01/06/business/covid-paxlovid-antibodies-omicron.html. Accessed 31 Aug 2022.

Rousseau, J. (1762). *The social contract and discourses*. Project Gutenberg. 1920. https://www.gutenberg.org/files/46333/46333-h/46333-h.htm

Sheikh, K. (2020, April 2). Essential drug supplies for virus patients are running low. *New York Times*. https://www.nytimes.com/2020/04/02/health/coronavirus-drug-shortages.html. Accessed 5 Nov 2021.

Snowden, F. M. (2019). *Epidemics and society: From the Black Death to the present*. Yale UP.

Taylor, D. B. (2021, July 15). Homeopathic doctor is charged with selling fake Covid-19 vaccine cards. *New York Times*. https://www.nytimes.com/2021/07/15/us/julie-mazi-napa.html. Accessed 31 Aug 2022.

Wang, V. (2021, October 27). Why China is the world's last 'zero Covid' holdout. *New York Times*. https://www.nytimes.com/2021/10/27/world/asia/china-zero-covid-virus.html. Accessed 27 Oct 2021.

Williamson, E., & Wang, V. (2020, June 2). 'We need help': Coronavirus fuels racism against black Americans in China. *New York Times*. https://www.nytimes.com/2020/06/02/us/politics/african-americans-china-coronavirus.html. Accessed 31 Aug 2021.

Yuan, L. (2022, January 13). The army of millions who enforce China's zero-Covid policy, at all costs. *New York Times*. https://www.nytimes.com/2022/01/12/business/china-zero-covid-policy-xian.html. Accessed 30 Aug 2022.

Chapter 6
Egoism and Altruism: Is Selfishness a Virtue?

6.1 An Introduction to Egoism

Having explored what are often considered to be three main options in ethics—Kantian deontology, utilitarianism, and the social contract theory—we turn now to perhaps the most controversial of ethical theories, ethical egoism, which is the belief that individuals *should* always follow their own self-interest and never sacrifice themselves for the benefit of others. The theory insists that human beings ought to be selfish. Ayn Rand (1905–1982), the twentieth-century thinker, novelist, and advocate of selfishness, famously argued, "If any civilization is to survive, it is the morality of altruism that men have to reject."[1] This is a frankly counterintuitive and radical proposition: It is morally right to be selfish and morally wrong to be the opposite—*altruistic*. She goes so far as to insist that the morality of altruism would lead to the end of civilized society. Her statement might come as a shock to some given that most people believe that collaboration, teamwork, cooperation, and self-sacrifice—in short, altruism—are the keys to thriving societies and healthy social contracts.

The dispute about egoism and altruism is one of the perennial dilemmas in Western thought, and we might remember the theme being raised in Chap. 2, when a basic question about human nature was asked: Are human beings, by nature, selfish and egoistic or unselfish and altruistic? Ethical egoists answer the question by refusing to accept the either/or nature of it. Egoists would argue that it is irrelevant if we *are* selfish by nature. The important question is *should* we be selfish, and they argue quite forcefully that we should be. Both in times of peace and health and also in times of war and disease, we should always be selfish.

---

[1] This quotation from the lecture "Faith and Force: The Destroyers of the Modern World," which is now commonly cited, was given by Rand during a lecture at Yale University in 1960.

A. Sola, *Ethics and Pandemics*, Springer Series in Public Health and Health
Policy Ethics, https://doi.org/10.1007/978-3-031-33207-4_6

As with all basic disputes in this book, it is important to keep an open mind when considering the ideas presented in this chapter. After all, being selfish is frowned upon in many societies, and you might consider egoism to be a theory that ought to be rejected immediately. Also when considering the merits of selfishness, you should beware of the rigid nature of dichotomies, which tend to close off the rich possibilities of thinking past the conflict. Perhaps, as Hegel argues, there is a way to move beyond the simple contradiction between egoism and altruism, a path that is hidden because our normal ways of thinking have become stale and rigid.

Like most philosophical debates that address fundamental questions about human existence, the debate between egoism and altruism is long and complex. It has its origins in the philosophy of ancient Greece, but it appears in a variety of intellectual, religious, and political traditions. In this chapter, we will explore those traditions before turning to an assessment of the debates about egoism and altruism in contemporary politics. Then we will learn about the "objectivist" theory of Ayn Rand and the development of the modern version of ethical egoism. Next, we will assess the strengths and weaknesses of the theory, before seeing if ethical egoism can teach us any lessons about ethics during pandemics, specifically HIV/AIDS and COVID-19.

6.2   The Greek Tradition

The subject of selfishness was much debated in ancient Greece, particularly in light of the accumulation of wealth, power, and status—also known as "external goods." Some Greeks, like Plato, believed that the selfish acquisition of wealth led to problems within communities. They noted that disparity in wealth often causes hatred and division between the haves and have-nots. Aristotle, however, allowed for a good deal of selfishness because caring for oneself is a *prerequisite* for living a full, healthy, and happy life. Diogenes and Epicurus agreed that living a happy life was important but insisted that the selfish acquisition of external goods actually leads to unhappiness not happiness. Lastly, Aristippus, the great hedonist, argued that the selfish pursuit of pleasure was the only way to achieve happiness.

6.2.1   Plato

In Plato's vision of the ideal state presented in *The Republic* (375 BCE), he insisted that the leaders (also known as Guardians or Philosopher Rulers) and their younger assistants (called Auxiliaries) should be forbidden from acquiring wealth and property. Preventing the political rulers from acquiring wealth was a key aspect of his ideal state, and he is quite clear about the rules for the Guardians:

> In the first place, none of them should have any property of his own beyond what is abso-
> lutely necessary; neither should they have a private house or store closed against anyone
> who has a mind to enter; their provisions should be only such as are required by trained
> warriors, who are men of temperance and courage; they should agree to receive from the
> citizens a fixed rate of pay, enough to meet the expenses of the year and no more; and they
> will go to mess and live together like soldiers in a camp.[…]. And they alone of all the
> citizens may not touch or handle silver or gold, or be under the same roof with them, or
> wear them, or drink from them. And this will be their salvation, and they will be the saviors
> of the State. But should they ever acquire homes or lands or moneys of their own, they will
> become housekeepers and husbandmen instead of guardians, enemies and tyrants instead of
> allies of the other citizens; hating and being hated, plotting and being plotted against, they
> will pass their whole life in much greater terror of internal than of external enemies, and the
> hour of ruin, both to themselves and to the rest of the State, will be at hand. (III, para. 396)

The conjunction of wealth and power was (and still is) a fundamental source of
conflict in societies, so Plato thought it wise to remove wealth from the equation.
However, Plato noted another potential source of conflict. If the leaders have to live
a life of austerity, they might not be happy in their positions of power because they
might not realize any (selfish) personal benefit from their status. They might look at
other rulers in other lands who have great wealth and become envious and unhappy.

Plato thought not. He believed that the Guardians would be perfectly happy people:

> Our guardians may very likely be the happiest of men; but that our aim in founding the State
> was not the disproportionate happiness of any one class, but the greatest happiness of the
> whole; we thought that in a State which is ordered with a view to the good of the whole we
> should be most likely to find justice, and in the ill-ordered State injustice: and, having found
> them, we might then decide which of the two is the happier. (IV, para. 6)

Like the social contract thinkers, Plato believes that an ordered state in which justice
reigns is happier than a chaotic and disorderly one. He also reckons that the
Guardians will be happy as individuals and as a class because they will be instru-
mental in developing a happy, healthy, and just society as a whole. If their people
are happy, so will they be, despite the fact that they cannot selfishly accumulate
personal wealth. It seems, then, that Plato clearly advocates an altruistic vision of
the ideal state: The Guardians are meant to care unselfishly for the overall happiness
of the community, not their own happiness.

At this point in the argument, an advocate of selfishness might object as follows: *Plato argues that the Guardians will become happy by being unselfish themselves and creating a happy community. So Plato is arguing that their own
happiness is their ultimate purpose. Is that not really a selfish goal masquerading
as an altruistic one? In short, the Guardians do not desire a happy community for
the sake of the community; they desire a happy community to guarantee their own
happiness.*

We see here the problem of setting up a simplistic dichotomy between egoism
and altruism. Oftentimes, people may appear to promote the common good, but
upon closer inspection their motives could be described as being selfish after all.

6.2.2   Aristotle

Continuing with the Greek tradition of selfishness and altruism, Plato's student Aristotle took a more measured view on the "selfish" acquisition of wealth, power, and status (we will cover Aristotle in depth in the next chapter on virtue ethics). Aristotle, like Plato, focused a significant part of his philosophy on achieving personal happiness or *eudaimonia*, which he might have even considered a basic human right in the modern sense of the term (although he would not have recognized a concept of universal human rights back then). However, he did not believe that taking care of yourself and following your own self-interest were problematic. Indeed, in order to achieve happiness, one needs to acquire external goods. He writes in the *Nicomachean Ethics* (350 BCE), "Yet evidently, as we said, [*eudaimonia*] needs the external goods as well; for it is impossible, or not easy, to do noble acts without the proper equipment. In many actions we use friends and riches and political power as instruments" (I, VIII, para. 6). For Aristotle, being a little bit selfish allows people to achieve their full potential as human beings.

Aristotle's concept of "the golden mean" also helps us to determine a sensible middle ground in the debate about egoism and altruism. He believed that a virtue exists as a mean between two extremes. Certainly, being completely and totally selfish in the extreme would be considered a vice. However, can you be *selfless* in the extreme, to the point that it becomes a vice? Aristotle believes that you can. If you were to give away all of your wealth, you would be as poor as the poorest people and lose your ability to help others. Also, sacrificing your wealth, power, and status would prevent you from realizing your full potential as a human being, because these external goods are required to achieve happiness. Total selflessness, therefore, would also be considered to be an extreme form of a virtue because it would reduce your maximum life potential. In sum, Aristotle would argue that a balance between care for yourself and care for others would be a prudent position to take when choosing the values that shape your life.

6.2.3   Diogenes

Greek philosophers continued to develop ideas about the accumulation of wealth, power, and status as well as the effect these desires have on personal happiness. The famous cynic Diogenes (c. 412–323 BCE), for example, insisted that possessions were the root cause of unhappiness. He owned nothing except a cup and a spoon, but he eventually realized that even *they* were unnecessary possessions when he saw a child using his cupped hands to drink water and a crust of bread to eat lentils; he would even embrace marble statues in order to remind himself that the warmth of human companionship was a luxury that could be renounced.[2] Diogenes believed

---

[2] These stories are related by Diogenes Läertius in *Lives of Eminent Philosophers*, which was probably written sometime in the third century CE. Diogenes Läertius is not to be confused with Diogenes, the cynical philosopher.

that those with no wealth, power, or status would be the most content because no one could take anything from them. Of course, an egoist could still say that shunning these external goods, which conventionally selfish people desire, has the self-interested objective of guaranteeing one's own personal happiness.

6.2.4   Epicurus

The Athenian philosopher Epicurus (341–270 BCE) also focused his philosophical efforts on helping people achieve happiness through controlling their desire to maximize pleasure. He insisted that moderation of one's desires was the key to achieving real happiness mostly because we tend to be disappointed and frustrated when we are unable to enjoy the luxuries that we are accustomed to experiencing. Of the correct diet, he writes, "To accustom one's self, therefore, to simple and inexpensive habits is a great ingredient in the perfecting of health, and makes a man free from hesitation with respect to the necessary uses of life. And when we, on certain occasions, fall in with more sumptuous fare, it makes us in a better disposition towards it, and renders us fearless with respect to fortune" (as cited in Diogenes Läertius , X, XXVII, para. 6). Epicurus believed that prudence, simplicity, and moderation were the most important virtues. Controlling one's desires for luxuries would prevent the pain that results from the inability to achieve those desires. In short, Epicurus maintains that being unselfish when it comes to luxurious living and the acquisition of wealth, power, and status would lead to happiness. As with Plato's and Diogenes' philosophies, an egoist critic may point out that Epicurus' philosophy of being unselfish, prudent, and moderate has ultimately a selfish goal: achieving personal happiness. Furthermore, since Epicurus almost entirely avoids discussions about the nature of a just and happy society, it seems that his philosophy of the happy individual is, at its core, an egoistic philosophy.

6.2.5   Aristippus

In stark contrast to other schools of thought in ancient Greece were the hedonists, who insisted openly and proudly that the selfish maximization of one's own pleasure was the correct way to live one's life. The first great hedonist was Aristippus (c. 530–350 BCE) who constructed his philosophy around two fundamental facts of life: creatures seek out pleasure, which they enjoy, and avoid pain, which they do not. He thought that seeking pleasure is the single, most simple explanation for *everything* we do. Aristippus went even further by suggesting that this fact was a law of nature—all creatures selfishly maximize their own pleasure, even when they appear to be unselfish. In short, we are all selfish by nature, so we should not fight that fact by forcing ourselves to be unselfish.

Let's test the theory that we are all really selfish despite any claims to the contrary. Mother Teresa is widely regarded as being the epitome of unselfishness. She gave away all of her money and spent her entire life caring for the poor and sick. Surely, she was not being selfish! Aristippus would argue that she actually took pleasure from her actions and that she was indeed acting selfishly. After all, she wanted to be rewarded for her actions by going to Heaven, and maybe she even took pleasure from behaving in a saintly fashion. The pleasure she received from helping poor people and having faith in God was greater than the pleasure she received from other activities, so of course she chose what gave her the most pleasure.

Let's consider another example, the Giving Pledge, which has been signed by billionaires, such as Gates, Buffett, Branson, Zuckerberg, and many others, promising to give away half of their wealth to charity. Are they being altruistic or selfish? It is interesting to observe here that altruistic thinkers have different standards for generosity. The famous contemporary utilitarian philosopher Peter Singer insists that the quantity of wealth we give away is irrelevant, as was noted in Chap. 4. Singer (1999) argues in "The Singer Solution to World Poverty" that people should donate to charity all of the money that they do not spend on necessities. He calculated that the average American household spends $30,000 per year on necessities. The rest is spent on luxuries, which, by definition, people do not need. All of the additional money, he argues, should be spent on charitable giving. This would mean that Gates and Buffet would have to give away not half of their billions, but essentially all of it—only retaining $30,000 (or the equivalent adjusted for inflation) per year for their own needs—in order to be considered moral people.

Leaving Singer's radical critique aside for the moment, some billionaires are becoming increasingly self-critical and aware of the global problems caused by wealth inequality, and they openly support the idea of the ultra-rich paying higher taxes (Feuer, 2015). Of course, critics of this new seemingly altruistic trend argue that billionaires are engaged in a highly orchestrated public relations maneuver in order to head off growing opposition to wealth inequality, highlighted by the Occupy Wall Street protests, which began in New York in 2011 and were exposed even further by the COVID-19 pandemic. Indeed, the wealth of the ultra-rich increased by over $10 trillion in the first year of the pandemic (Neate, 2020). It may be impossible to determine if the ultra-rich are truly being altruistic or if they are selfishly trying to protect their own interests; however, it is important to note that the conflict between altruism and egoism is not necessarily as clear as it is assumed to be. Although some might argue that they are being unselfish when they give away billions of dollars, Aristippus would argue that they too are being selfish, just like Mother Teresa and the rest of us. No one is exempt from Aristippus' egoistic law of nature. He would argue that the ultra-rich generate a great deal of pleasure from giving away their money, molding the lives of millions of human beings, and putting their stamp on world history—in short, they exchange their wealth for other external goods, namely, power and status, which are pleasurable things to possess. Donating money is what the givers most want to do. If keeping their money made them happier, Aristippus would argue, then they would keep it.

In modern terms, Aristippus' theory is called *psychological egoism*, the belief that all people always act according to their own self-interest. The theory has many proponents for the reasons enumerated above: No matter what people *claim* their motives are for performing unselfish actions, their true motives, which are often hidden even from themselves, are always selfish and self-interested.

However, critics of psychological egoism would point to numerous examples of people not behaving selfishly. For example, soldiers jump on live grenades in order to save their comrades; people rush into burning buildings to save children, the elderly, and even their pets; parents often sacrifice themselves for the benefit of their children. During the COVID-19 pandemic, doctors and nurses continued to work long hours without appropriate PPE and risked their own health and well-being in order to care for others; teachers, at great risk to themselves, braved classrooms with unvaccinated and unmasked students in order to continue educating the next generation; first responders continued to rescue members of the public, placing themselves intentionally in harm's way; and grocery store clerks, pharmacists, bankers, waiters, bartenders, and restaurateurs all continued to work in high-risk environments in order to keep society healthy, sane, and fed. It would be difficult to describe those behaviors as being either selfish or self-interested. After all, how is contracting a novel respiratory virus and then dying in one's own self-interest? When looking at all the evidence, it seems that Aristippus' law—that we always act selfishly to secure our own pleasure—does not stand up to scrutiny.

A final point that hedonists make is that the goal of maximizing pleasure does not require any *context*. Indeed, if one only focuses on maximizing one's own pleasure, other potentially stressful sociopolitical issues can be avoided. Aristippus argues as follows: If you only seek your own pleasure, it does not matter if you live in a democratic society or a dictatorship; it does not matter if you live in a communist or a capitalist state; it does not matter if the natural world is exploited or preserved; nor does it matter if you live in a theocratic state or one that upholds freedom of religion. Indeed, you could be an enslaved person or a free person and still experience more pleasure than kings, queens, and emperors who have the stress of rule weighing on their minds. For hedonists, if pleasure is your only goal, then you adapt to the prevailing conditions and maximize your pleasure within them.

Having explored the theme of selfishness and unselfishness in the Greek tradition, some tensions in the dichotomy can already be seen. For Plato, the Guardians were required to be unselfish with respect to money, but one can reinterpret this mandatory unselfishness as really being selfish: the Guardians would achieve happiness *for themselves* as a consequence of their unselfishness. For Aristotle, the virtue of caring for one's self is as important as the virtue of caring for others, if one wishes to become a fully developed and *eudaimonic* individual. Both Diogenes and Epicurus insisted that controlling one's selfish desires for wealth, power, and status, as well as limiting one's reliance on pleasurable luxuries, would lead to happiness in the long term. Again, the overall goal of personal happiness here could be determined as being a selfish goal. Lastly, the hedonists were very open to the proposition that we should actively seek pleasure. In fact, they insisted that we all behave selfishly, no matter what other theories might argue. In short, while the Greek tradition may have established the dichotomy between altruism and egoism, the ideas overlap in a variety of ways, clouding the arguments and preventing simple resolution.

6.3 The Christian Tradition

Along with the Greek tradition, the Christian tradition has also shaped modern views about egoism and altruism. Some theologians argue that Jesus took the side of altruism against egoism, of selflessness over selfishness. However, others disagree with that assessment. Religious texts are always open to interpretation, and this is also the case with the themes of wealth accumulation, care for the self, and care for others as represented in the Bible. The passages below will illustrate the slippery nature of biblical interpretation.

In the Book of Luke 12:33, Jesus seems to command the renunciation of one's wealth: "Sell your possessions, and give to the needy. Provide yourselves with moneybags that do not grow old, with a treasure in the heavens that does not fail, where no thief approaches and no moth destroys." This passage seems to require Christians to give all of their money to the poor.

However, in Philippians 2:4, we see the following: "Let each of you look not only to his own interests, but also to the interests of others." This passage seems to suggest an Aristotelian balance between caring for the self and caring for others. Indeed, it suggests that one should look out for his own interests as a precursor to looking out for others' interests. Is that a selfish approach?

Next, 1 Corinthians 10:24 seems to contradict Philippians: "Let no one seek his own good, but the good of his neighbor." Also, Galatians 6:2 says, "Bear one another's burdens, and so fulfill the law of Christ." These passages indicate that care for others should supersede care for self.

However, 1 Timothy 6: 17–19 is more circumspect: "As for the rich in this present age, charge them not to be haughty, nor to set their hopes on the uncertainty of riches, but on God, who richly provides us with everything to enjoy. They are to do good, to be rich in good works, to be generous and ready to share, thus storing up treasure for themselves as a good foundation for the future, so that they may take hold of that which is truly life." Again, this passage seems to recall an Aristotelian balance. The rich should not necessarily make themselves as poor as the poorest, but they *should* be kind and generous because they have the external goods that give them the ability to do so. The Giving Pledge seems to be justified by this passage: Billionaires do not necessarily have to give away all of their wealth, but they should share their wealth and do good works.

Even the Golden Rule from Mark 12:31—"Love your neighbor as yourself"— and Jesus' famous command from Matthew 7:12 "Do unto others as you would have them do unto you" lend themselves to multiple interpretations. While the passages might seem to advocate altruism, loving one's neighbor as one's self implies that *one must care for the self as a necessary component of caring for others*. In short, one could argue (and many Christian thinkers have argued) that some selfishness, defined as the appropriate care for the self, is perfectly in line with Jesus' commands.

In the present age, much debate persists about the true meaning of Jesus' teachings. Some theologians insist that the right way to live a Christian life is to be completely altruistic; others insist that wealth accumulation and at least some measure of egoism is perfectly fine as well. The Bible, unfortunately, does not provide unequivocal guidance on these matters, and these disagreements about the appropriate way to live one's life have done much to shape our perceptions of the relationship between the individual and the community. This immensely complicated relationship has confounded philosophers and theologians for centuries, but perhaps a new field of ethics, relational ethics, can begin to shed some additional light on the problem.

Box 6.3.1: Interdisciplinary Perspective #13: Medical Ethics

Relational Ethics: A Modern Approach to Medical Ethics and Traditional Ethics

We have seen in this chapter and throughout this book that the history of ideas constantly evolves—dialectically, as Hegel argued. Certain ideas are ascendant at one time, and then they are challenged and revised. New ideas are created, building on what has come before. One important and fairly new field is relational ethics, a discipline that begins with the core idea that ethics must be a communal or relational concept precisely because *no one exists independently*. All moral agents exist within and as part of a network of individuals, communities, and political structures. In other words, relational ethics is directly opposed to any concept of ethics that takes the individual as its central focus. In this respect, it is antithetical to egoism. Rather than accepting the possibility of a dichotomy or conflict between the individual and the community, it begins with the insight that individuals are always already a part of a community.

There are echoes of Kant, the utilitarians, and the social contract thinkers in relational ethics. For example, Kant notes that morality can only exist because of Reason, which only humans have. Further, he notes in his second formulation of the categorical imperative that we should never treat other human beings as a means to an end, since doing so destroys the moral universe. How we treat others—our *relationships* with others—is a key feature of Kant's theory. Still Kant's strict deontology—his absolute moral rules—are so rigid that exceptions can never be made in your moral decision-making, even if you have a personal relationship with someone. For example, he would argue that you should not lie to your friend (e.g., about a bad haircut decision), even if telling this little white lie might be in the best interest of your relationship in the long-term.

Utilitarians concentrate explicitly on the good of the whole community rather than the good of the individual. However, they argue that personal relationships should have no bearing on your ethical decision-making. Indeed, personal relationships often lead us to make immoral decisions, at least

(continued)

according to strict utilitarians such as Peter Singer, who argues that we should not spend money on gifts for our own children when that money ought to be used to save the lives of poor children in faraway lands.

Lastly, the social contract thinkers also focus on ethical relationships among citizens in a community. However, the social contract is so focused on following the laws that it has a blind spot when it comes to extra-legal interactions among citizens. So, if adultery and deception are not illegal where you live, then lying to your partner about your extra-marital affair is not explicitly wrong, at least within the framework of the theory. However, relational ethics would certainly characterize your behavior as being problematic.

Relational ethics identifies these weaknesses and blind spots in the traditional ethical theories and seeks to correct them. Building on these insights from the past, relational ethics turbocharges the community and relationship orientation of ethics. Rather than focusing solely on individual actions and consequences, relational ethics considers the impact of actions on relationships, communities, and larger social structures. This approach recognizes that ethical decisions are not made in a rational vacuum, but are influenced and shaped by the relational networks we have with others. This change of focus yields important insights about medical ethics during pandemics.

In order to illustrate these relational insights, we will begin by outlining the four traditional principles of medical ethics, which govern the relationship between the medical professional and a patient.

- Autonomy: Medical professionals must respect patients' right to self-determination and allow them to make informed decisions about their own healthcare.
- Beneficence: They are obligated to act in the best interest of their patients, promoting their well-being.
- Nonmaleficence: They are obliged to avoid causing harm to the patient, including refraining from providing treatments that could cause more harm than good.
- Justice: Healthcare professionals must seek the fair distribution of resources and benefits within society, ensuring equal access to quality healthcare for all, regardless of social, economic, or demographic status.

There is nothing at all problematic about these principles in normal treatment situations. One might describe the principles as being patient-centric in the most positive sense. However, in a pandemic context, some of these principles might need to be altered by broader relational considerations. Most importantly, pandemics require a rebalancing of values away from the exclusive good of the individual patient to the inclusive good of the community as a whole.

Let us consider an example that shows how the four traditional principles can conflict with public health priorities during the COVID-19 pandemic.

(continued)

Let's say you are a healthcare professional and one of your patients comes to see you with mild flu-like symptoms. She is Tina, a single mother who is living paycheck to paycheck. You give her a test, which is positive for COVID-19. It is the height of the pandemic. She immediately freaks out when her positive test is returned. If she cannot work, she cannot earn money, and she will not be able to feed her family. You note that she does not have severe symptoms, and she agrees. She believes that she can still go to work. You caution her that she is highly contagious and that she should quarantine herself for 10 days for the good of the community. She insists that her primary duty is to her family. Therefore, she decides that she will take precautions to ensure that she does not spread the virus, but she will nevertheless go to work. Her stress about her finances and her anxiety levels are so high that she feels that the only option is to continue working. Is Tina being selfish? Should you pressure her to change her mind?

It is worth noting that the Tina example is not a theoretical game. We already know that the COVID-19 virus causes direct physiological damage to the brain and the nervous system. But research has also shown that well-intentioned pandemic prevention measures—such as extreme lockdowns and quarantine measures—had serious unintended consequences that further harmed public health. Among the long list of secondary negative effects of lockdowns and quarantines are a general increase in anxiety and depression; an increase in fear of losing one's job and stress about one's ability to sustain oneself and a family; an increase in feelings of sadness and loneliness; an increase in domestic abuse and violence against partners; an increase in drug and alcohol abuse; and an increase in microaggressions in social settings and hate crimes, particularly against Asians (Pandey et al., 2021, p. 162). Furthermore, it has been shown that pandemic lockdowns disproportionately harm working mothers (Alon et al., 2020, pp. 1–2), just like Tina.

Returning to her, our previous ethical theories certainly tell her what *she* ought to do. However, they do not address what *you*, the healthcare professional, should do. Traditional theories would focus on the rightness or wrongness of Tina's decision and completely ignore the relationship you have with Tina as well as the unique characteristics of Tina's situation. For example, Kant, citing absolute moral rules, would insist that Tina quarantine herself because the rule—all people who are infectious should quarantine during a pandemic in order to stop the spread—is a reasonable universal law. The utilitarian approach would be the same. Whatever financial stress and anxiety Tina might have is less than the greater harm she may cause by starting a new chain of infections. According to the social contract, if the law dictates that one must quarantine, then Tina has no choice in the matter—she must quarantine. Note that all of these "solutions" depersonalize Tina and ignore her anxiety and personal circumstances; they focus on the inescapable logic of their theoretical framework while dismissing her fears and concerns.

(continued)

So what should you, the healthcare professional, do in this situation? Do the four principles of medical ethics help? Well, if you must respect patient autonomy, as the principle demands, then should you simply accept Tina's decision to return to work in a highly contagious state? Doing so would not necessarily harm her, your patient, but it might harm the community. Or do you insist that she quarantine herself, reminding her of the harm she might inadvertently cause to others if she infects them? Second, the principle of beneficence is also troubling in Tina's case. Maybe it is in Tina's self-interest to return to work, but is her self-interest more important than the interest of the community? Next, the principle of nonmaleficence requires that you not harm your patient, but forcing her to quarantine *will* harm her and her family, especially if they have financial difficulties because she can't work; also, not working will increase her stress and anxiety. Lastly, the principle of justice forces the medical professional to seek fair and equitable health outcomes for all. Here, Tina is suffering from resource scarcity and financial insecurity. She cannot afford not to work. You do understand that. At the same time, it is part of your professional duty to protect the community at large. It seems that the four principles do not offer a clear solution to this problem.

The question now becomes this: Does the relational approach provide a more satisfactory response to Tina's predicament? Some thinkers believe it does. David Ian Jeffrey (2020) suggests that the COVID-19 pandemic has highlighted the weaknesses of the four traditional principles of medical ethics. Specifically, since healthcare professionals have to shift their focus from the good of the patient to the good of the community, they have a tendency to appear to be cold utilitarians, particularly when arguing for strict lockdown measures that emphasize the good of the community over the good of the individual. He argues that relational ethics—with its focus on mutual respect, trust, solidarity, and reciprocity—can "soften" the seeming harshness of strict lockdowns (Jeffrey, 2020, p. 495). Cheryl Pollard (2015) notes that healthcare professionals often adopt an oppositional power relationship with their patients, a relationship that can be counterproductive. She argues that the traditional view of caring *for* patients—which places the specialized professional above the patient—should be substituted for the more relational concept of negotiating *with* patients about their options (p.362). Most importantly, it means treating patients as unique *individuals*, not as general *patients* (p. 364). In Tina's case, it would mean perhaps fully embracing her financial concerns as being fully part of her—not something that can be dismissed through reference to the abstract principles of Immanuel Kant or John Stuart Mill.

This insight about the patient-professional relationship raises the issue of the importance of embodied knowledge in relational knowledge. Embodied knowledge does not reference abstract theoretical principles; instead, it seeks a holistic understanding of a situation, including the particular circumstances of the patient. Again, relational ethics encourages the professional to

(continued)

understand the unique predicament of the patient. Pollard (2015) suggests that the professional-patient relationship should be an embodied one, in which each person in the relationship mutually respects the other (p. 367). In short, a relational approach to Tina's pandemic predicament suggests that you should not engage with her solely with reference to the four principles, nor with reference to the traditional ethical theories discussed so far in this book. Instead, you should meet her where she is and discover a solution to her predicament that works for her, her family, and the community at large.

Discuss

- **Evaluate Tina's predicament and evaluate your role as a healthcare professional. How would you address Tina's concerns about herself and her family? How would you balance your professional responsibility to protect the good of the community with your competing responsibility to your patient?**
- **Do you find a relational ethics approach more satisfying than a deontological, utilitarian, or social contract approach? Why or why not? Provide concrete examples to support your conclusion.**

6.4 Ayn Rand and Objectivism

We will now continue exploring the important question of how the individual relates to other human beings through looking at ethical egoism, which, unlike relational ethics, argues that the individual must be the core of any ethical theory. The contemporary version of ethical egoism is a product of Ayn Rand's development of a philosophy that she called objectivism. Rand was born Alissa Zinovievna Rosenbaum in St. Petersburg, Russia, in 1905. She lived through the Communist Revolution, but supported neither the communists nor the tsarists. She studied philosophy as well as literature and screenwriting, attending Petrograd State University and the State University for Cinematography. Her family had already moved to the States when she acquired a permit to visit them in Chicago in 1925, but she did not want to return to the USSR, whose political system she despised. She stayed in the States, living in Chicago and Los Angeles. Eventually, she moved to New York in 1951 where she died in 1982.

During her life, she wrote a series of controversial novels, the most important being *The Fountainhead* (1943) and *Atlas Shrugged* (1957). In them she developed her own theory of egoist ethics which is explained through the voices of her characters. This fictional approach to expressing her theory put her outside of mainstream Anglo-American philosophy, and many traditional academic philosophers refused to and still refuse to recognize her status as a philosopher because she did not publish systemic philosophical treatises. However, she did produce something like a traditional philosophical book, *The Virtue of Selfishness: A New Concept of Egoism* (1964), in which her controversial ethical position is presented in a more traditional form. We turn to the ideas in that book now.

Rand begins *The Virtue of Selfishness* with this cryptic passage:

> The title of this book may evoke the kind of question that I hear once in a while: "Why do you use the word 'selfishness' to denote virtuous qualities of character, when that word antagonizes so many people to whom it does not mean the things you mean?"
>
> To those who ask it, my answer is: "For the reason that makes you afraid of it." (p. 5)

You might begin to recognize some key echoes of ideas already discussed in this book. First, you may hear Aristotle echoed in the phrase "virtuous qualities of character." Such an echo is intended, for Rand was fond of his virtue ethics calling him "the greatest of all philosophers" (p.11). Indeed, one of Rand's goals in the book is to redefine selfishness as a virtue instead of a vice.

Second, you may sense that Rand seeks to move beyond the "straitjacket of names;" she seeks to move beyond a simple dichotomy of selfishness and its opposite: altruism. The intellectual effort to move beyond simple contradictions, you may remember, is a key Hegelian idea that was presented in the introduction. Simple dichotomies are easy for many to understand: good vs. evil, Republican vs. Democrat, capitalist vs. communist; selfish vs. unselfish. However, moving beyond these name-pairs often antagonizes both sides and makes everyone *afraid*.

From the very beginning of her book, Rand seeks to set her ideas apart from the mainstream, in direct opposition to the thoughts of most people. She means to antagonize her readers. It is no surprise, then, that she is such a controversial figure—both loved and despised. Let us now analyze the political climate in the United States, which will help us explore the tensions between altruism and egoism, tensions that Rand helped to expose.

Box 6.4.1: Interdisciplinary Perspective #14: Political Science

COVID-19 and the Contemporary Political Climate in the United States
Currently in the modern capitalist Western world and particularly in the United States, the debate about egoism and altruism can be seen in all manner of political debates about taxation or wealth redistribution, about social services or entitlements such as healthcare, and indeed about the basic economic principles on which Western life depends. On the altruistic side are those who believe that the role of the state is to secure the common good, sometimes at the expense of individual wealth and freedom; on the egoist side are those who believe that the role of the state is to secure the freedom of the individual, who must not be forced to sacrifice his or her own life for the common good. The debate about egoism and altruism even expands into foreign policy with the national self-interest standing in for individual self-interest and the common good of the world standing in for the common good of a specific nation state.

(continued)

The general tendency in the United States is to see Democrats supporting the idea of altruism and the common good and Republicans supporting that of egoism and individual freedom (although, of course, these positions are incredibly nuanced and complex). John F. Kennedy's famous inaugural address delivered on 20 January 1961 sums up the dichotomy nicely, invoking egoism on one side and altruism on the other: "Ask not what your country can do for you—ask what you can do for your country." The egoist might retort: "I do not ask what my country can do for me—I simply ask it to stay out of my affairs." Similar left-right divides exist in Britain, Germany, France, Italy, the Netherlands, Sweden, Australia, and a number of other liberal democracies; however, all have their own unique cultural, historical, and economic contexts which shape the exact character of the debates.

Let's focus for a moment on the COVID-19 pandemic and policy debates in the United States. A perennial debate in American politics revolves around the appropriate level of taxation, which proponents of low taxes call "wealth redistribution," intending to summon the ghosts of revolutionary communists. Republicans have called for lower taxes for years, arguing that high taxes punish "job creators." As advocates of trickle-down economics, many Republicans suggest that reducing taxes and regulation of business will eventually benefit those further down the wealth ladder. However, many Democrats, particularly progressive ones, insist that it is the duty of the government to redistribute wealth to help the unfortunate. Higher taxation of the wealthy helps to stabilize society and reduces tensions between the haves and have-nots.

These familiar conflicts were seen during the COVID-19 pandemic, when politicians on both sides were forced to face a severe economic downturn and mass unemployment. The government ordered a shutdown of the economy with the promise that laid-off workers and shuttered businesses would be given financial assistance to weather the storm, and so Congress passed the CARES Act, a two trillion-dollar aid package to support workers, families, and businesses, which President Trump signed into law on 27 March 2020 (Cochrane, 2020). Although the passage of the CARES Act provides evidence of a momentary alignment of interests between Republicans and Democrats, additional aid packages were held up due to the long-standing ideological differences between the parties. On 15 May 2020, Democrats, who controlled the House of Representatives, passed the HEROES Act, a three trillion-dollar aid package, with more money for workers, families, students, emergency workers, and businesses among other initiatives. However, the Senate, which at the time was controlled by Republicans, declined to move forward with the legislation. Mitch McConnell, the Republican Senate Majority Leader at the time, said that the bill was DOA—dead on arrival, a term used to describe legislation that would not even be moved to the Senate floor for a vote (Bailey, 2020). One Republican concern was that people who receive additional money from the government would be incentivized to stay at home and not

(continued)

return to work, further harming the chances for a swift economic recovery. More importantly, they generally believe it is not the government's role to increase the *dependence* of citizens on the state; it is instead the role of government to make people more independent, more self-interested, and more self-directed. In short, the brief period of political bipartisanship was destined to be short-lived, given the historical conflicts between party ideologies.[3]

Another long-standing political debate in the United States centers on social services, particularly healthcare. The controversy about Obama Care or the Affordable Care Act, which was President Obama's effort to increase the number of Americans with health insurance through a complex series of initiatives, is based on two contradictory positions. On the one hand, supporters of Obama Care argue that it will create stronger, healthier communities by increasing the number of people with health insurance. Of course, opponents say that people should not be forced by the government to subsidize the costs of their do-nothing neighbors—the so-called social parasites, moochers, and welfare moms derided by some politicians. Regarding other entitlements from welfare to Medicare to Social Security, Democrats insist that these policies make for stable communities, while Republicans focus on individual choice, wanting people to have as much control as possible over their own healthcare, their own money, and their own retirement needs. It is important to note that both sides—if their motives are indeed pure—share the same goal of building a stronger and happier America. The differences arise from the methods employed to achieve it.

During the COVID-19 pandemic, the inequalities of the US healthcare system were further exposed. Historically speaking, pandemics have always swamped hospitals and stressed fragile public health systems (Snowden, 2019, p. 77). Indeed, in the absence of a healthcare system that includes everyone—a government-run national healthcare model like Britain's NHS or a model that requires everyone to have health insurance like Germany's *gesetzliche Krankenversicherung* system—pandemics prove even more difficult to manage, especially for underserved communities. People in the United States without any health insurance may be less likely to see a doctor because they are fearful of the costs. If they do not see a doctor at an appropriate stage in an illness, then there may be serious consequences. Furthermore, in poor areas, there may be distrust of so-called safety-net hospitals, which serve the poor but are not as well-equipped as hospitals that serve paying customers. There are many reasons why certain communities are more heavily exposed to

(continued)

---

[3] It may be interesting to note that there are different ways that nations deal with unemployment during economic crises. Germany, for example, has a *Kurzarbeit* (shortened work) model which allows businesses to retain workers during a downturn. Instead of firing workers, the employees work reduced hours—for example, half of their normal hours—and receive half of their pay from the employer. However, the government tops up their salaries, so they retain normal income levels despite their shortened hours.

pandemics than others, but a major factor in the United States is race. ProPublica, a non-for-profit foundation supporting investigative journalism, studied the first 100 COVID-19 deaths in Chicago and confirmed some harsh realities about being poor and black in the city (Eldeib et al., 2020). Seventy of the first 100 dead were black people, even though the city's population is only 30% black. The report shows that, unfortunately, being black and poor are two factors that increase your chances of dying from COVID-19 in Chicago. When asked by the journalists to comment on the problem, Dr. David Ansell of the Rush University Medical Center on the city's near-east side, said, "I'm not surprised because every natural disaster will peel back the day-to-day covers over society and reveal the social fault lines that decide in some ways who gets to live and who gets to die. And in the United States, those vulnerabilities are often at the intersection of race and health" (as cited in Eldeib et al., 2020). While some diseases are equal opportunity—in that they strike the rich and poor, young and old, healthy and sick, black and white at similar rates—COVID-19 hits urban blacks particularly hard, not due to the biological predisposition of the virus itself, but due to the public health inequalities that prevent timely and appropriate treatment as well as deficiencies in public health education and other factors. These factors also explain the high rates of HIV in black communities. Maybe COVID-19 will serve as the catalyst that pushes the United States to change its healthcare system to make it more equitable for everyone, but many on the right will object to any change in federal law that requires universal coverage. However, the logic of egoists is that the government should stay out of a citizen's private and independent decision to have health insurance or to decline it.

These domestic policy debates bleed into foreign policy, with some arguing that the United States should try to build a more peaceful and more secure world order, even at the expense of American blood and treasure—an altruistic goal. Opponents, the isolationists, take the egoist's position that the United States should secure its own borders and focus its money on building a stronger America at home. In *The Virtue of Selfishness*, Ayn Rand (1964) weighs in on national selfishness as follows: "It is not a free nation's duty to liberate other nations at the price of self-sacrifice, but a free nation has the right to do it, when and if it so chooses" (p. 99). The critical point, which we will explore below, is whether or not free nations as well as free individuals have a moral duty to help others. Rand clearly says that no such duty exists. The political debate about international humanitarian assistance is clouded. It is difficult to say on which side the two parties stand because some Republicans and many Democrats broadly agree that it is America's *duty* to intervene for humanitarian reasons, but others on both the left and right reject such a notion for a wide variety of different reasons. Libertarians like the late Ron Paul and to some extent his son Rand (named after Ayn Rand) insist that America should not be engaged in conflicts around the world because doing so is financially wasteful

(continued)

and often counterproductive. Many on the left share Paul's skepticism, insisting that the military is too big and too intertwined with big business already; the military-industrial complex does not serve the nation nor does it uphold humanitarian principles. Curiously enough, the man who coined the term military-industrial complex was both a Republican and a general—Dwight D. Eisenhower. Suffice it to say that the altruism-egoism dichotomy is sufficiently complex and clouded that neither political party can necessarily claim ideological purity on the matter.

Nevertheless, the COVID-19 pandemic further highlighted ideological differences. President Trump had already established an "America First" approach to international relations when he was elected in 2016, and the COVID-19 pandemic provided him with an opportunity to double down on that policy. One of his complaints was directed at international institutions, such as the World Health Organization, which he blamed for colluding with China to prevent transparent and swift notification regarding the spread of the virus so the rest of the world could be better prepared (Gebrekidan et al., 2020). On the other hand, many Democrats and some Republicans wished to support international institutions further, seeing the pandemic as a global problem that required a coordinated global response. Furthermore, President Trump viewed the development of a vaccine as well as the production of tests, treatments, ventilators, and PPE as a national effort, isolated from the rest of the world (Goodman et al., 2020). In these policy disagreements, one sees the egoistic approach in private ethics mirrored in international policy. If, as Hobbes said, there is competition for resources among individuals in the state of nature, then for Trump, the planet was a battlefield in which nations constantly compete for scarce resources. Hobbes indicated that there is no justice, no morality, no right or wrong in the state of nature. If a nation's leader views the community of nations as being in such a state, then logically there would be no right or wrong, no justice, in how one nation treats another.

Discuss

- **American policy debates are much more nuanced and complex than that described above, but they all center on a fundamental moral question: Should a society be centered on community-oriented, altruistic principles or individual-oriented, egotistical principles? Drawing the analogy from domestic policy to international relations, should a nation's foreign policy be guided by altruistic or egoistic principles?**
- **As we prepare for the next global pandemic, how should we understand our own nation's potential moral obligations to other countries? Should countries with excess resources always share them? Or are there compelling reasons to stockpile resources exclusively for one's own citizens?**

6.5   Ethical Egoism and the Virtue of Selfishness

Let us return to the philosophy of Ayn Rand, who insisted that the only just society is one devoted to protecting individual rights, particularly the right of individuals to be selfish and self-interested. Randian ethical egoism marks a departure from previous versions of egoism in that it reframes the debate about selfishness. Instead of saying, like the hedonists, that all people *are* egoistic and self-interested by nature, ethical egoists insist that all people *should be* egoistic and self-interested. In other words, they accept the fact that people have the freedom to choose to behave altruistically, but they should not do so. This shift in language from the *is* to the *ought* is important and highlights a critical difference between two major categories of ethics: descriptive and normative ethical theories. Descriptive theories explain how people think about ethics—what ethics are from an objective perspective. Normative theories, on the other hand, tell us what ethics should be—how we should behave. Psychological egoism is a descriptive theory, and ethical egoism is normative. Kant's theory, utilitarianism, and virtue theory are also normative theories, while psychological egoism is descriptive. Rand's argument is normative: People *should* follow their own self-interest even if they have an evolutionary predisposition to being altruistic.

In *The Virtue of Selfishness* (1964), she argues that people have come to regard selfishness as evil without actually considering the meaning of the word; furthermore, they have not considered the *normative* question of whether or not people should be selfish. Indeed, she cites the dictionary definition of selfishness as "concern with one's own interests." The definition, however, "does not include a moral evaluation; it does not tell us whether concern with one's own interests is good or evil; nor does it tell us what constitutes man's actual interests. It is the task of ethics to answer such questions" (p. 5). Rand here argues that the common mode of thinking is tautological, i.e., it engages in circular thinking and is therefore illogical. If selfishness = evil, then a tautology is created: evil = evil. This is not an argument in the sense that logicians use the word. However, if we define selfishness appropriately, then it might be easier to determine if concern with one's own interests is indeed evil. She asks the prescriptive or normative ethical question: *Should we be concerned with our own self-interest?* Her task is to show that indeed we should.

In order to make her case, she criticizes the opposite of selfishness, altruism, which, she insists, is the default moral position in contemporary society: "Altruism declares that any action taken for the benefit of others is good, and any action taken for one's own benefit is evil" (p. 6). The ethics of altruism forbids doing anything for oneself, and this dogma confuses many common sense moral issues. Rand provides examples to support her view, noting that both a law-abiding entrepreneur and also a thief are equally "selfish" for wanting to become rich, at least in the view of altruists.

Rand's position is that the ethics of altruism has a blind spot: it fails to see value in the sacrifice of individuals *for themselves and for their own goals* as being worthy of praise. In a certain respect, egoists wish to reinstate Aristotle's value system— that the care for self is an important goal in life, perhaps the most important goal in life. Altruism does not permit people to achieve their dreams and therefore under-mines the dignity of individuals rather than respecting it. In their haste to be com-munity-minded and respectful of others, altruists actually weaken the dignity and value of individuals. The solution, Rand argues, is to engage the idea of altruism in open intellectual warfare: "To rebel against so devastating an evil, one has to rebel against its basic premise" (p. 7).

Rand then defines her *telos* of morality: "The purpose of morality is to define man's proper values and interests, that *concern with his own interests* is the essence of a moral existence, and that *man must be the beneficiary of his own moral actions*" (p. 7). Critically, Rand does not condone recklessness and stupidity. She explains that the egoist does not have "a right to do as he pleases," but he "must always be the beneficiary of his action" and "must act for his own *rational* self-interest" (p. 8). In this respect, egoists must follow strict rules of behavior—selfish and self-interested, but rational behavior.

At this point, Rand has established that selfishness, now redefined as rational self-interest, is the correct moral stance we must take with regard to our own lives. Next, she takes the leap to social organization:

> The basic *social* principle of the Objectivist ethics is that just as life is an end in itself, so every living human being is an end in himself, not the means to the ends or the welfare of others—and, therefore, that man must live for his own sake, neither sacrificing himself to others nor sacrificing others to himself. To live for his own sake means that the achievement of his own happiness is man's highest moral purpose. (p. 23)

Echoes of Aristotle's theory of happiness, conceived as fulfillment of oneself, can be observed here. There are also echoes of Immanuel Kant—all human beings are ends in themselves. Social rules, she concludes, must be constructed in order to allow every individual to achieve his or her own happiness and in order to protect the priceless dignity of the human subject.

In these passages, Rand has set out the goals of her ideal Objectivist Republic, goals that are much different from Plato's. Whereas Plato prizes community happi-ness, Rand prizes individual happiness. Whereas Plato sees community well-being as the guarantor of social happiness, Rand sees individual well-being as the guaran-tor of social happiness. In this dichotomy between Plato and Rand, we see the great historical differences between altruism and egoism sharply drawn. Before evaluat-ing the strengths and weaknesses of the ethics of egoism, it is important to consider an entirely different perspective, namely, the biological basis for selfish and altruis-tic actions.

Box 6.5.1: Interdisciplinary Perspective #15: Evolutionary Biology

Have We Evolved to Be Selfish or Altruistic?
Our previous discussion of egoism and altruism has focused on the philo-sophical nature of the dispute, covering over two millennia of thought on the subject from Aristotle to Ayn Rand. Throughout this book, you have also been

(continued)

encouraged to think about your own empirical observations of human beings during the COVID-19 pandemic in order to assemble evidence to support a hypothesis that people are fundamentally good or evil. However, perhaps a completely different perspective—a scientific perspective—can shed further light on this conundrum.

The discipline of evolutionary biology provides us with a completely different set of assumptions and definitions about the words *selfish* and *altruistic*. There is nothing immoral about selfishness from the standpoint of natural selection. Indeed, the goal of any creature is to reproduce its DNA as much as possible. Viruses do this, as do insects, fish, and mammals. A selfish action in nature could be described as one that benefits the creature by ensuring its survival and opportunity to reproduce. Doing whatever one can to ensure one's own survival in order to reproduce is, hence, *amoral*—outside the realm of ethics. Even the social contract theorists recognized that self-preservation is the basic right of all human beings, a natural right.

An altruistic action is, from a biological perspective, one that benefits another creature at its own expense, understood as reducing the likelihood that the creature could survive and reproduce. The only criterion to evaluate this behavior scientifically is with the concept of *reproductive fitness*: Does the action increase or decrease the chance of an organism to reproduce (Okasha, 2020)? For example, a well-fed dog, Spot, could be said to be biologically altruistic if he does not eat his food but allows another starving dog, Rover, to eat it. Not eating would decrease the chances of Spot having more puppies and increase the chances for Rover. However, most dogs would eat as much food as possible and, therefore, would be engaging in behavior that increases their own reproductive fitness. From an ethical perspective, we humans might consider Spot to be selfish for overeating and denying poor Rover some food; from a biological perspective, it would be difficult to judge Spot. Similarly, from a moral perspective, the COVID-19 virus may be selfish for debilitating and killing millions of humans (and other animals), but from a biological perspective, all it is doing is replicating its DNA, which is naturally what all organisms do.

But can we reduce all actions by all organisms to the narrow concept of reproductive fitness? Throughout the natural world, many creatures do not actually exhibit behaviors that increase their reproductive fitness. Biologists have noted that a number of species exhibit altruistic behavior. For example, vampire bats regurgitate food they have eaten to feed other bats who have failed to find food in their nightly hunting expeditions; worker bees and worker ants are sterile and only serve the queen and the colony as a whole (Okasha, 2020). How can these behaviors be explained? Biologists developed a concept of kin selection to explain the selective altruism that we see in these behaviors. The vampire bats, for example, exhibit their altruistic feeding behavior only with bats with whom they nest. The implication is that by

(continued)

feeding members of their own social group, they are more likely to receive assistance if they are starving in the future, increasing the whole group's reproductive fitness in the long term. In this view, being an altruistic bat is actually in the bat's own long-term self-interest.

Here, we see the same argument that is used by psychological egoists who try to redefine Mother Teresa's charitable behavior as being self-interested. We can also redefine the vampire bat's behavior as being not altruistic but self-interested. If the theory of kin selection is indeed true, it explains seemingly altruistic behaviors in humans in self-interested terms. We do tend to care for our own families, friends, and communities more than strangers on the other side of the world. However, we do these things to benefit ourselves in the long run. Like vampire bats, we are charitable to others in our own community because it will increase the chances of receiving future benefits, whereas helping a starving baby in a war zone far away might yield nothing.

Is caring for our kinship group—a behavior that favors limited altruism directed toward members of our own social group—an evolutionary trait that we have inherited? Let's say we do have such a gene. Does that then invalidate the claims by utilitarian thinkers, such as Peter Singer, who demand that we take a purely rational approach to our care for others by recognizing that there is no *moral* difference between a starving neighbor next door and a starving baby far away—despite our evolutionary tendency to treat them differently? Is Kant also wrong to insist on a purely rational approach to ethics?

In short, can we use evolutionary biology as an *excuse* for abandoning the role of reason in ethics? Or do we look at evolutionary biology and realize that *reason* should be the central focus of ethics?

Discuss

- **Evolutionary biology provides a different perspective on selfish and altruistic behaviors in nature. Is the capacity to think rationally, however, a special human trait that should force us to form ethical theories on the firm foundation of reason while abandoning biological explanations of appropriate behavior?**

6.6 Criticisms and Defenses of Ethical Egoism

Our discussion of Ayn Rand has included important social, political, and economic concerns, as well as ethical concerns that affect the decisions individuals must make about the conduct of their own lives. We turn now to the individual ethical theory that has been developed from Rand's wider philosophical outlook. Contemporary philosophers call this ethical egoism—the simple normative viewpoint that individuals should follow their own self-interest. We might call this theory a *personal ethical theory*, a way to conduct one's life without necessarily assessing the wider social implications. Other theories—namely, utilitarianism with its single moral goal of creating as much happiness as possible for as many creatures as possible—are deliberately conceived more widely to include society as a whole.

When assessing ethical egoism, it is helpful to turn to some of the criticisms as well as the defenses of the theory. The criticisms can be summarized as follows: (1) Egoism condones doing evil; (2) egoism does not meet the minimum standards of a moral theory because it does not consider the perspective of others; (3) egoism has an inappropriately narrow moral scope; (4) egoism misunderstands the role of cooperation in achieving happiness; (5) egoism does not recognize the priceless dignity of individuals.

(1) Egoism Condones Doing Evil

The most significant criticism of ethical egoism is that it tells people that they should be evil, if and only if being evil is truly in their self-interest. If you could benefit from taking advantage of others, egoists would tell you to do so. For example, used-car salesmen should lie about the condition of cars they sell in order to maximize their profits. Medical doctors should prescribe expensive but unnecessary treatments for their patients in order to maximize pay-outs from insurance companies and pad their own wallets. Men should sexually harass women at the workplace for their own selfish pleasure. Self-proclaimed healers should sell quack medicines to the public. During the COVID-19 pandemic, the CDC flagged hundreds of businesses for selling phony products that claimed to prevent infection or treat the disease, including Silver Sol's tincture with real silver, Corona-Cure Coronavirus Infection Prevention Nasal Spray, and Halosense's Salt Therapy products (CDC, 2022). Egoists argue that these dubious sales strategies are not necessarily wrong if they are in the self-interest of the seller, which gives critics of egoism a clear reason to reject the theory.

How would egoists defend themselves? First of all, they would deny that any of the behaviors described above are really in the self-interest of the people doing them. Dishonest car salespeople might lose customers and their businesses if they develop a bad reputation; doctors might be sued and lose their medical licenses for prescribing unnecessary procedures; and men who harass women might be subject to complaints and grievances and eventually lose their jobs as well.

So, one important defense of egoism is that it is a perfectly normal and *common sense ethical theory*. It says that being virtuous and following society's normal ethical codes are usually in one's self-interest. Liars, cheats, thieves, and sexists are usually discovered, and their lives end up in tatters. Therefore, it is usually in one's rational self-interest to obey the law and follow the normal rules of society. Furthermore, an egoist might summon Kant's critique of utilitarianism here and argue that we never know the consequences of our actions with absolute certainty, so the prudent course of action—the course that is really in one's own rational self-interest when faced with an uncertain future—is to obey the law and follow the rules.

Still, a critic of egoism would retort as follows: While most of the time, egoists would suggest that we follow the rules and obey the law, this is not *always*
the case. Indeed, nothing in ethical egoism suggests that someone should not
break the law if he or she can benefit from such behavior without adverse consequences. Indeed, many argue the point of a strong ethical theory is to raise the
bar on goodness, to force us to be good even when it is not in our self-interest to
do so. However, when egoism is confronted with really tough decisions, it tells
us to be selfish. This might be the most damning critique of egoism.

(2) Egoism Does Not Consider Other Perspectives

Continuing with this line of thinking, ethical egoism seems to contradict
some of the most basic and sensible concepts in ethical thinking: the idea that
one should consider the perspective of others. Indeed, some would argue that
the minimum standard of an ethical theory is that it should account for conflicts
between people. Egoism is one-sided, but common sense morality is multifac-
eted. Egoists consider themselves to be the center of the universe, but most ethical thinking rests on the idea of acknowledging the rights of others—and their
well-being must be considered as well. Critics of ethical egoism insist that it is
not an ethical theory at all because there is no room for the consideration
of others.

Nearly every common sense moral rule—established either by religious tradition or by legal statute—has to do with treatment of others. Thou shall not
steal from others (because it hurts them). Thou shall not bear false witness
against others (because it hurts them). Thou shall not murder others (because it
hurts them). Ethical egoists turn these simple insights on their heads. Thou shall
not steal from others (because doing so might hurt you if you're caught). Thou
shall not bear false witness (because doing so might hurt you if your lies are
discovered). Thou shall not kill (because doing so might hurt you if you're
thrown in jail). At no point does the ethical egoist acknowledge the rights and
interests of others as being valuable in and of themselves. This is another damning criticism of the theory.

(3) Egoism Has an Inappropriately Narrow Moral Scope

Connected to criticism (2) is the idea of moral scope. We have already seen
that different ethical theories conceive of the moral community in different
ways. For example, Kant reduced the moral community to those who possess
the faculty of reason, thereby eliminating animals from the moral community.
Utilitarians, on the other hand, create a much wider moral community based on
any organism's ability to feel pleasure and pain. Therefore, non-human animals
are part of the utilitarian moral community and worthy of moral consideration.
Furthermore, utilitarians insist that everyone counts the same in the moral community, reducing the concept of moral distance. So a starving person on the
other side of the world should count the same in one's moral thinking as a starving neighbor, and future generations may deserve the same moral consideration
as those living the present.

Another powerful criticism of egoism is that it reduces the moral community
to one. The only thing worthy of moral consideration is the individual, namely,

you. There are no other members of the community—not your spouse, your child, your neighbor, and certainly not other species or generations yet to come.

(4) Egoism Misunderstands the Role of Cooperation in Achieving Happiness

Another criticism of egoism is this: Since it rejects altruism completely, it does not recognize important insights from the social contract thinkers, who state that cooperation is often in one's long-term self-interest, as can be seen in the decision to move from solitary, barbaric life to life in law-abiding communities. Advocates of egoism, such as Ayn Rand, state quite explicitly that altruism is the bane of human civilization. This belief flies directly in the face of the Platonic belief that good societies must be interested in the good of every member of the community, not simply the good of a specific class. Egoists seem to say the opposite. The role of a good government is to be exclusively concerned with individual happiness; in other words, a good government must allow individuals to live freely and develop their full potential.

However, egoists would argue that one should behave altruistically and seek cooperation, when doing so is in one's own self-interest. Indeed, they would argue that living in a civilized society is in one's own self-interest, so one should behave in a civilized way—only insofar as doing so is in one's own self-interest. There is still another argument that egoists use to support it. They suggest that egoists may adopt altruistic ethics in their own lives. However, by being altruistic, egoists might still be making long-term calculations about their own self-interest. After all, if behaving altruistically leads to great personal benefits, then altruistic behaviors are still, at the end of the day, selfish behaviors.

(5) Egoism Does Not Recognize the Priceless Dignity of Individuals

Along with the criticism (2) above, critics suggest that egoism does not respect the dignity of individuals in the way that, say, Kant does. Kant, we remember, insists that all rational human beings have rights that can never be violated for any reason and without exception. Egoists seem to say that you should only be concerned about your own rights and your own dignity, even at the expense of others.

However, egoists respond rather strenuously that their theory is the only one that actually prizes human dignity. Community-minded ethics of altruism— such as utilitarianism, socialism, and communism—insist that the individual may be sacrificed for the good of the community. And so we see Plato forbidding the Guardians from accumulating wealth, while socialists nationalize it, and communists abolish it. An egoist like Ayn Rand argues that these political philosophies actually undermine the priceless dignity of individuals, because they insist that the achievements, the labor, and the creativity of the individual must be sacrificed on the altar of the community.

In short, ethical egoism is not a theory that can be dismissed without thorough analysis. While many find the implications of the theory disturbing, supporters insist that it is a common sense theory that guarantees individual freedom. Furthermore, they argue, the freedom of individuals to make their own decisions about their own lives must be the bedrock of the entire moral universe, the *telos* of ethics. After all, without this freedom, what is the point of living? Framed in this way, egoism seems to be the only ethical theory that respects the importance of individual freedom by refusing to require the sacrifice of one human being for the sake of another. But how would this theory work in practice during a pandemic? We can explore this question through a historical comparison of HIV/AIDS and COVID-19.

Box 6.6.1: Interdisciplinary Perspective #16: History

A Comparison of the HIV/AIDS Pandemic and COVID-19

HIV and COVID-19 have many important differences, but they also have a lot in common. Both are zoonotic diseases that crossed the species barrier and became deadly in human beings. HIV is thought to have come from the practice of eating bush meat—perhaps monkeys or chimpanzees—in some cultures in Africa (Sharp & Hahn, 2011). COVID-19 may have come from the practice of eating exotic animals in some parts of China. However, it is important to note that both scientists and intelligence agencies have still not conclusively determined the specific origin of COVID-19 (DNI, 2021, p. 1.). The fact that a precise origin is unknown—and the fact that new diseases often cause hysterical responses in the public—has led to a wide variety of conspiracy theories about the origins of HIV, and we have seen the spread of similar conspiracies about the origins of COVID-19.[4]

In addition to their zoonotic origins, the two diseases both progress in stages. HIV first has an incubation period, which is then followed by a period of infection. HIV is particularly dangerous because after the first period of infection, during which time patients exhibit mild symptoms, the disease seems to go away. However, if infected people are unaware that they have HIV, they can continue to spread the disease for years before more serious symptoms return and an accurate diagnosis is made. COVID-19 also progresses in stages, and one may be asymptomatic but still contagious. The fact that people can unknowingly infect others presents one major ethical and legal dilemma, which we have already seen in the case of Typhoid Mary in Chap. 3.

Unlike COVID-19, which is transmitted through respiratory droplets, HIV is primarily transmitted through blood, semen, and vaginal secretions. Sweat and saliva contain only minimal traces of the virus. Hence, HIV is considered to be a sexually transmitted disease (STD) even though the disease can be

(continued)

---

[4] At time of writing, the debate about the origins is still ongoing, with some reports indicating that the virus was accidentally leaked from a lab in Wuhan and others identifying the transmitting species as the raccoon dog. It may be that the true origins will remain forever shrouded in mystery. However, knowing or not knowing the origins does not affect this ethical analysis.

transmitted through drug users sharing needles, blood transfusions, and accidents with sharp objects at medical clinics. Obviously, improper testing of donated blood can also lead to infection. Most devastating for families, mothers can pass the disease on to their fetuses. It is important to note that HIV is not a "gay" disease, and the medical historian Frank M. Snowden (2019) reminds us that "globally, heterosexual intercourse has been the dominant mode of transmission, with women more susceptible to infection than men" (p. 412). HIV (the human immunodeficiency virus) progresses in four stages and becomes AIDS (acquired immunodeficiency syndrome) in either stage three or four, when the white blood cell count reaches a critically low number.

Like COVID-19, HIV/AIDS is a global disease, but the country most affected is South Africa. Recent HIV/AIDS statistics from the UN AIDS Program make for tragic reading (UN, 2021). Nearly 8 million South Africans live with HIV out of a population of nearly 58 million. About 18% of adults (aged 15–49) have HIV, and roughly 48,000 died from AIDS-related illnesses in 2021. However, due to improved public health initiatives developed over the past two decades—specifically mass testing and sex education—90% of South Africans are aware that they either have or do not have HIV, which means that the numbers should begin to decrease through proper treatment and the adoption of appropriate measures to prevent further transmission. The obvious lesson to learn from HIV-prevention efforts in South Africa is that pandemics can be managed and contained through proven measures, such as effective public health education and mass testing.

The history of HIV in the United States is intriguing because it illustrates the complex relationship between public health and politics, on the one hand, and ethics and religious morality, on the other. HIV first arrived in the United States well before the epidemic came to prominent public attention in the 1980s. It may have been brought to the United States by Haitian immigrants who had previously worked in the Democratic Republic of Congo (Snowden, 2019, p. 430). By 1981 doctors began noticing clusters of rare diseases, which were only common in patients who were already suffering from immunosuppression. They suspected that the rare diseases might be the result of an unknown virus affecting their immune systems. In 1984, that virus was discovered and named HIV. However, public opinion about the virus had already become twisted. During the 3 years between the discovery of the syndrome and the discovery of the virus itself, the disease had already acquired two names that shaped public perception in discriminatory and destructive ways. The first term was gay-related immunodeficiency (GRID) or the gay plague because it was most commonly found in homosexuals, and the second was the 4H disease because it was mostly found in Haitians, hemophiliacs, heroin addicts, and homosexuals.

The identification of the virus with homosexuality shaped the response to the disease in the United States due to the religious views of a large portion of

(continued)

the American public as well as the conservatism of the political leadership. In the view of many conservative Christians, homosexuality was a sin, and HIV was a punishment for that sin. The solution to halting the spread of HIV, therefore, was not grounded in proven public health measures such as sexual education, prophylaxis, and testing; instead, many argued that homosexuals should stop "sinning." These religious explanations for disease have been common throughout the history of pandemic disease (see the interdisciplinary perspective on the Black Death in Chap. 5).

Attitudes toward HIV and homosexuality are slowly changing, but HIV is still an epidemic in the United States. Now, however, the epidemic demographics look a lot different than they did in the 1980s and 1990s. According to the US Department of Health and Human Services HIV information site, approximately 1.2 million Americans are currently infected with HIV, and about 6 in 7 people are aware that they have it—a rate of 87% awareness, which is slightly lower than the rate in South Africa (HHS, 2021). By the turn of the millennium, the black community—gay and straight—in the United States was suffering particularly elevated levels of HIV, but public opinion still focused on the white homosexual, who was still the poster child of HIV. Between 2010 and 2016, new cases among white homosexuals dropped significantly as did new cases among intravenous drug users. However, cases among black homosexuals are holding steady, and those among Latino homosexuals are rising significantly. Nevertheless, no matter who you are and where you come from, HHS still strongly recommends that sexually active people in high-risk groups get tested yearly, at a minimum, and more often, when appropriate.

A comparison between HIV and COVID-19 shows the profound difference in reactions from politicians, religious leaders, and the general public. During the onset of a new pandemic, people are fearful and hysterical. A common way of dealing with fear is through blaming others. Scaremongers proclaim, "We were free of this disease, until foreigners arrived and infected us." During the Black Death, Jews, witches, prostitutes, and foreigners were blamed. During the HIV epidemic, homosexuals, Haitians, heroin users, homeless people, and prostitutes were blamed. During the COVID-19 pandemic, depending on where you lived, blame could potentially be assigned to any number of groups: Christians, Muslims, Jews, Asians, blacks, Latinos, drug users, prostitutes, witches, Republicans, Democrats, the Chinese Communist Party, or, indeed, Bill Gates. The scientific fact about disease transmission is that we can all be held responsible for being potential disease vectors simply because we are carbon-based organisms that interact with other creatures in a shared environment.

Despite this fact, public perception and politics play an important role in the public health response to a pandemic. In the case of HIV, a general climate of homophobia prevented politicians throughout every level of the US

(continued)

government from taking the epidemic seriously. Many lives were lost because politicians refused to accept the advice of public health experts who wanted to take important public health measures to prevent the spread of HIV. In short, rather than providing money for HIV testing, condoms, and sex education, politicians chose to promote celibacy, abstinence, or monogamous and heterosexual sex, preferably after marriage. The results of these policy positions still reverberate today. Pandemics typically require someone to blame, mostly in order to help leaders avoid scrutiny for their own ineffective responses. As mentioned in this book several times already, COVID-19 has been frequently blamed on Asians, who were unfortunately scapegoated in much the same way as homosexuals were during the height of HIV.

With this general background, we can now explore some legal and ethical perspectives on both HIV and COVID-19 in light of this chapter's discussion of altruism and egoism.

Testing, Safe Behavior, and Personal Choice
Testing is one of the major dilemmas raised by HIV. Although there are no laws requiring everyone to be tested (i.e., no legal obligation), is there still an ethical obligation to get tested? Since you may have HIV without knowing it, is it negligent to avoid a simple test that would reveal your status and prevent unintentional infection?

From an altruistic perspective, you should indeed be proactive about protecting your own sexual health as well the health of your partners. So, if you are sexually active with multiple partners, you should get tested for HIV and the whole range of other STDs regularly. Furthermore, you would be required to practice safe sex practices to account for the periods of time during which you may be infected but unaware. Similarly, if you lived during the height of the COVID-19 pandemic, testing would have been advisable so you knew your status and could behave appropriately around others. If testing were unavailable and you were therefore unaware of your status, you should have also practiced safe behavior—which would mean wearing a mask and maintaining your social distance especially when feeling poorly—in order to avoid unintentionally infecting others.

From an egoist perspective, the position is slightly more complicated. An egoist would tell you to follow your own rational self-interest in theory, but what does that mean in practice? Well, it would be in your own self-interest to know if your sexual partners have HIV, and it would be in your own self-interest to know your own health status. Therefore, you should still get tested, and you should follow safe-sex practices. The same applies for COVID-19. It was probably in your self-interest not to get sick, so you should have at the very least protected yourself by following prevention practices. So it seems that even egoists should be wearing masks and social distancing in order to protect themselves while also practicing safe sex for the same reason. We see

(continued)

here an echo of the second objection to ethical egoism mentioned above. Most ethical theories argue that we should not mistreat others because doing so harms them, but egoism turns this principle on its head, arguing that we should not mistreat others because doing so might harm ourselves.

Egoism becomes more complicated in a different scenario. If you know you have HIV, are you morally obligated to inform your sexual partners that you have it? Furthermore, are you morally obligated to prevent the spread to your partners? Is it in your rational self-interest to do so? In the absence of laws criminalizing such behavior—going to jail would not be in your self-interest—spreading a disease simply due to selfishness is not expressly forbidden by the ethics of egoism. And this is precisely why many philosophers have issues with egoism: It does not adequately explain our obligations to others if our own self-interest is not affected by our action or inaction. Similarly with COVID-19, being careful may have not been in your own self-interest, so there may have been no other obligation to alter your behavior to prevent the spread of the disease.

This analysis about private ethics pushes our discussion to the much more complex role of the government in compelling citizens to practice safe pandemic behaviors.

HIV, COVID-19, and Criminalizing Behavior when Vaccines Are Unavailable

In theory, well-run and competent autocracies with capable security forces should have no problem controlling pandemics. After all, tyrants can simply impose and enforce draconian rules that prevent the spread of disease, and they do not have to worry about pesky lawsuits, public protests, or negative media coverage. A concrete example is China's zero-COVID strategy with its complete lockdowns of massive cities policed by millions of police, soldiers, and volunteers (Yuan, 2022). Liberal democracies, on the other hand, have many more challenges with pandemic control because free societies are not inclined to overregulate personal freedoms or control citizens by force. For example, now that homosexuality is no longer criminalized in much of the West, governments are not allowed to execute, castrate, jail, or isolate homosexuals in order to prevent the spread of HIV, but an autocracy would have no such trouble.

Furthermore, liberal societies do not ban other risky behaviors, such as eating fatty foods, drinking alcohol, or cycling without a helmet. Some behaviors are, however, regulated if they cause harm to others. For example, although smoking isn't banned, secondhand smoke harms others, so smoking in public places has been restricted in many countries.

There is a very real tension between public health and private freedom, and liberal democracies have to navigate a tricky path between the two positions during a pandemic. If we could rely on our fellow citizens to behave in the

(continued)

right ways, we would not need laws. Unfortunately, as John Locke argued (see Chap. 5), laws are required to protect society from the degenerate people who would cause us harm.

Banning people from having sex has never worked. During the height of the HIV epidemic, it was not productive for officials to suggest celibacy as a remedy. Testing and sex education were more successful options. However, since HIV is so dangerous, it raises the question of a citizen's legal obligation to inform partners of their status. According to the CDC (2021), currently 35 states in the United States "have laws that criminalize HIV exposure." Four states require intravenous drug users to disclose their HIV status (if known) to those with whom they share needles, and 12 states require disclosure of one's HIV-positive status (if known) to sexual partners. Sentencing guidelines vary, but one may face up to life in prison for violating the disclosure law. Disclosure is one matter, but intentional infection is another. General criminal laws, such as reckless endangerment and attempted murder, can be used to prosecute people for intentionally infecting people with HIV. Furthermore, 11 states have statutes that criminalize biting and spitting with the intent of infecting someone with HIV.

Turning to COVID-19, we can begin to assess the laws a liberal democracy might pass in order to protect public health while preserving individual freedom as much as possible. Comparing past and current HIV regulations with COVID-19 provides some useful historical context. The five scenarios below explore public health laws during times when vaccines are not available—which is unfortunately still the case with HIV. Afterward, we will explore the legal environment when vaccines are available.

- **Intentional or reckless spread of HIV/COVID-19**
  Regarding criminal liability, if you know you have HIV (or any other disease), intentionally infecting a victim is a criminal offense throughout the world (NAM, 2020). Intentional infection can be considered attempted murder or reckless endangerment under general criminal statutes. Laws that criminalize intentional infection are not controversial, since intentionally harming people either through physical violence or through the sinister and depraved action of spreading disease violates basic standards of civilized society. However, there are at least 75 countries (as of 2020) with laws that further criminalize the intentional or reckless spread of HIV specifically, laws that many human rights advocates argue are discriminatory and stigmatizing since intentional disease spreading is already penalized under existing statutes (NAM, 2020).
  Using the same line of legal reasoning, if you knew you had COVID-19 and you spat or coughed on someone with the intent to infect, you may have committed the crimes of attempted murder or reckless endangerment. Some cases of intentional and reckless exposure were reported during

(continued)

COVID-19 (BBC, 2020). However, intentionality is difficult to prove in court, since there is a subtle distinction between knowing that there is a risk of causing harm and intending to cause harm. And even if intent can be proven conclusively, it would be almost impossible to prove that the victim was infected specifically by the intentional spitter and not by another innocent person, since a respiratory disease like COVID-19 pervades the environment and it is hard to pinpoint the exact place, time, and circumstance of an infection. Lastly, criminalizing coughing and spitting could lead to a number of confusing legal situations. Imagine you had a dispute with a COVID-positive neighbor who then coughed or spat in your general direction: Should you report him for intentionally trying to infect you? How could his true intent be proven in court?

- **Mandatory testing for HIV/COVID-19**
  In most Western democracies, mandatory testing for HIV is not required for the average citizen in normal circumstances. However, in certain circumstances, it is required. For example, soldiers are required to undergo testing because they have a high risk of contact with bleeding comrades in unsanitary environments. Also, blood and organ donors must be tested for obvious medical reasons, but these rules are based on risk levels and pathways of transmission, which are considerably different for COVID-19. For non-citizens, HIV testing rules are more diverse. Countries around the world have changed their approach to HIV/AIDS over the years. For example, the United States used to have an HIV testing requirement for visa applications but no longer does. On 4 January 2010, the rule removing the requirement for HIV testing officially changed. The US Department of State (2009) notified the public of the rule change as follows: "The CDC has determined that allowing non-US citizens with HIV infection to enter the United States will not pose a health risk to the American public because HIV is preventable and not spread through casual contact or day-to-day activities." In other words, non-citizens are no longer required to prove with a test that they do not have HIV in order to enter.
  Testing was required by nearly every country for international travel throughout the COVID-19 pandemic. Such requirements disappeared when the public health danger decreased, which is exactly what happened with HIV. During COVID-19, positive tests upon arrival in a new country often led to involuntary quarantines, and we have already seen that this has been an accepted practice for preventing disease spread since the Black Death. But what about citizens living their lives in their own countries? As with HIV, it may have been reasonable from a public health perspective to require people in certain professions to undergo COVID testing in order to prevent further infection, especially among vulnerable people. For example, workers in high-risk environments where the transmission of and exposure to respiratory droplets is elevated could be required to submit to

(continued)

regular testing. At various stages in the COVID-19 pandemic, many countries in Europe implemented testing requirements not only for workers but also for all citizens who wished to engage in social life, and so tests were required to access bars, restaurants, cinemas, public transportation, etc. However, the argument that everyone should be tested in order to live their lives presents both practical and logistical problems. These rules also raise concerns about civil liberties. Nevertheless, mandatory testing has a distinct public health advantage in that it ensures that people know their disease status. And since public health authorities seem to believe that human beings are often altruistic, the assumption is that most people who know they are sick will act in such a way as to avoid infecting others.

- **Unintentionally spreading HIV/COVID-19**
  If regular HIV testing is not mandatory for all citizens, then the government has in effect decided to accept a certain level of disease transmission from those who do not realize they are infected. In this permissive legal environment, unintentional spreading cannot be criminalized. Instead, public health institutions hope that safe sex practices will prevent unintentional spread of HIV, and the historical data shows that governments have been fairly successful at reducing levels of infection.

  As with HIV, in the absence of rules requiring universal COVID-19 testing, a state has in effect accepted the fact that the disease will be spread by otherwise careful and law-abiding citizens who are completely unaware of their status. It would be difficult to prosecute people for living their normal lives and unintentionally infecting people without clear laws requiring regular tests. Again, this position *presumes*, rightly or wrongly, that human beings are for the most part altruistic and will behave appropriately.

- **Compulsory prophylactic measures to prevent transmission of HIV/ COVID-19**
  Although governments could require universal HIV testing for their own citizens, they have not done so. There is another option: compulsory prophylaxis, the legal obligation to act in such a way as to prevent spread. In the case of HIV, such a law might require mandatory condom use. Indeed, a law requiring condoms in adult films was proposed in California in 2016, but the measure was not passed (La Ganga, 2016). It seems that some liberal societies do not wish to wade too deeply into the debate about regulating people's sexual behavior (homosexuality aside).

  Since liberal governments do not require sex with condoms to prevent HIV transmission, it is curious that many liberal democracies required the wearing of masks to prevent the transmission of COVID-19. There is a reason for the discrepancy, namely, the difference in how the diseases are spread. HIV is difficult to transmit when going about one's day-to-day activities because it is spread through blood and sexual secretions. COVID-19, on the other hand, is transmitted via droplets that permeate public spaces.

(continued)

Since every disease is different, it seems reasonable to enact disease-specific regulations. With the expected onslaught of new respiratory diseases, we might be facing a new normal of disease-specific, government-mandated mask wearing. Mask mandating in various forms may become increasingly common throughout much of the world, although they have also been heavily criticized for the following reasons: Masks in schools harm children's development; they cause even further discrimination against minority groups; they cause other health problems in people with respiratory illnesses; they violate individual freedom; they are expensive; etc. It remains to be seen what the future will hold when the next deadly respiratory virus spreads around the world.

- **Compulsory disclosure of HIV/COVID-19 status**
  Another legal issue raised by HIV is the compulsory disclosure rule. Advocates of privacy and equality insist that compulsory disclosure of one's HIV status leads to discrimination in public life, in private relationships, and at work. This further stigmatizes the disease and actually proves harmful to preventing the spread of HIV, since people who are fearful of the consequences of a positive test result might never get tested in the first place. Germany handles the legal problem in an interesting way (Deutsche AIDS Hilfe, n.d.). While you can be held criminally accountable for intentional or negligent transmission for causing bodily injury, you are not *legally obligated* to inform a sexual partner about your HIV status. Instead, you have to demonstrate that you are not negligent by protecting your partner through the use of condoms. Furthermore, if you choose not to use condoms, the legal recommendation is that you and your partner document that decision with a witness. Germany's policy requires each partner to consent to any risky behavior, but does not require someone who is HIV positive to inform a partner proactively. As HIV has become less stigmatized, countries have relaxed their disclosure laws, and liberal democracies now tend to avoid such laws because they violate the medical privacy rights of individuals and are also ineffective in preventing the further spread of the disease. In short, what we can learn from HIV is that medical privacy laws promote better public health in the long run since privacy prevents the negative consequences of public shaming (see Chap. 2).
  Interestingly enough, COVID-19 never had the same type of stigma attached to it as HIV. When someone caught COVID, as nearly everyone did, no one assumed that the person was negligent or engaged in transgressive behavior. Also, since COVID is not a lifelong ailment (long-COVID notwithstanding), having COVID was often interpreted as being "good" for one's health due to the generation of antibodies. Indeed, many people who had COVID were not ashamed to reveal it to everyone, whereas with HIV, there is often some measure of fear and shame attached to one's status. With COVID, the key controversy was not about the disclosure of

(continued)

one's current infection status; it was about the disclosure of one's vaccine status.

Of course, another important factual difference between HIV and COVID-19 is that HIV is often transmitted through private activities that still have some social stigma attached to them, namely, intravenous drug use and homosexual sex (although there is significantly less stigma now attached to the latter activity). Casual transmission—defined as the transmission of a disease through normal interactions in the public sphere—is practically impossible with HIV. COVID-19, on the other hand, is spread through the most normal social behaviors—breathing, talking, and touching things in the public sphere. The inescapable fact of casual transmission led many policy makers to insist on measures that forced people to prove their COVID status. These were highly controversial decisions. During future pandemics, mandatory disclosure rules will certainly be similarly controversial.

HIV, COVID-19, and Criminalizing Behavior when Vaccines Are Available

All of the points above bring us once again to the controversy over compulsory vaccination. There is currently no FDA-approved vaccine for HIV although two candidates, Imbokodo and Mosaico, are in the later stages of testing (HHS, n.d.). If a vaccine were to obtain approval, we would be forced to reconsider some of the examples described in the section above:

- **Unintentional Transmission**
  Should people be considered criminally negligent for unintentionally transmitting HIV because they chose not to be vaccinated? If so, why should people not be considered to be criminally negligent for unintentionally transmitting COVID-19 if they chose not to be vaccinated? Is there a rationally consistent principle that distinguishes these two situations?
- **Prophylaxis**
  What if this hypothetical HIV vaccine leads to so-called breakthrough infections in a small percentage of cases, as has happened with the various COVID-19 vaccines? Would being vaccinated mean that you have no further legal obligations to engage in safe sex?
- **Work-Specific Regulations**
  Should those who work in high-HIV-risk settings—such as doctors, dentists, nurses, soldiers, and adult-film actors—be compelled to be vaccinated? Again, is there a principle that would distinguish an HIV vaccine mandate from a COVID mandate?
- **International Travel Rules**
  Many countries already have vaccine requirements for immigrants and visa applicants for many diseases. The United States, for example, requires vaccines for mumps, measles, rubella, polio, tetanus and diphtheria,

(continued)

pertussis, haemophilus influenzae type B (Hib), hepatitis A and B, rotavirus, meningococcal disease, varicella, pneumococcal disease, and seasonal influenza (CDC, 2012). Should an HIV vaccine be added to the list? It is hard to argue against such a rule given the fact that non-citizens have fewer rights than citizens in most social contracts. Therefore, nations have sufficient legal authority to create any number of requirements before opening their doors to those outside of their social contract, and COVID passports, such as the EU's CovPass, have already been used to regulate travel during COVID-19.

- **Medical Privacy and Disclosure**
  The stigma attached to HIV led policy makers to realize that maintaining privacy was an effective way to reduce infections. Presumably, an HIV vaccine would destigmatize the disease even further. However, a broader question remains: Should vaccination status—for a hypothetical HIV vaccine—be a private medical matter? Should you be forced to reveal your vaccine status to anyone who asks? These same questions were asked about COVID-19 vaccines. For example, in many European countries, people were required to use the CovPass to reveal their vaccine status often multiple times a day—not to the police or medical professionals, but to the cinema clerk, the hairstylist, the shop owner, the postal clerk, the waiter, the bartender, or the bus driver. There are at least two significant objections to these policies. First, they undermine medical privacy by forcing people to reveal private medical information to strangers. Second, these rules force "normal" working people to become, in effect, public health police although they have no training in law enforcement or pandemic prevention. If it is appropriate for a bartender to demand evidence of your COVID vaccine status, would it also be appropriate for him or her to ask you for evidence of your HIV vaccine status?

The legal environment, as we have seen, is incredibly complicated. You could spend a lifetime developing a system that perfectly balances civil liberties and public health orders. However, you can also determine how to live your life during a pandemic in a much easier way, by asking yourself if you want to be a pandemic altruist or a pandemic egoist. Even though the government might not require you to get tested, wear a condom, practice social distancing, or wear a face mask, egoists would argue that it may still be in your own rational self-interest to adopt these behaviors in order to protect yourself from unnecessary exposure to any disease. Altruists would advocate the same risk-avoidance practices, not for their own safety but for the health and well-being of others. In short, you can be selfish or altruistic during a pandemic and arrive at the same conclusions.

(continued)

Discuss

- An altruist and an egoist might adopt the *same* pandemic behaviors but for different reasons. Take condoms and HIV: Altruists would wear them in order to protect others, and egoists would wear them in order to protect themselves. And what about masks and COVID-19? Again, altruists would wear them in order to protect others, and egoists would wear them in order to protect themselves. Think about a future pandemic. Would you be extra safe in order to protect yourself or in order to protect others?
- From an ethical perspective, does moral motivation—the reason why we choose a certain course of action over another—even matter if people choose to perform the same action anyway?

6.7 Conclusion

This chapter has shown that the debate about egoism and altruism has a long and rich history in Western thought, a debate that is far from being resolved in a neat and tidy way. Indeed, tensions between altruism and egoism color nearly all of the decisions we make in life—decisions that affect our private and professional lives.

- To what extent do I sacrifice my own goals for those of my family, my friends, my community, and my planet?
- To what extent do I bend the rules to further my own self-interest?
- To what extent do I support policies that prize wider social happiness above my own?
- Is it our moral *duty* to help others or is helping others merely a strategy to use in order to maximize our own self-interest?
- Am I really an evil person if I reject the altruistic idea that one *must* help others in order to be considered a good person?

We began this chapter with a quotation from Ayn Rand which stated unequivocally that the ethics of altruism would spell the end of human civilization. This is certainly a controversial position because many people argue precisely the opposite— the ethics of egoism will spell the end of human civilization. Perhaps there is no way to resolve these diametrically opposed attitudes, but in order to move forward as a civilized species, the dichotomy cannot be left unchallenged. Hopefully, we can formulate ideas that will help us move beyond this most disturbing and destructive dispute. In the next chapter, we will look at one final ethical theory that might help us move beyond binaries of altruism and egoism, good and evil. In fact, we will ask if describing actions as being *right* or *wrong* is even necessary.

Box 6.8: Criteria for Evaluating Ethical Theories: Part 4
In the previous three chapters, we discussed seven key criteria for evaluating
ethical theories. Use this opportunity to evaluate the strengths and weaknesses
of ethical egoism according to those criteria before learning about the next
criteria.

(1) Does the theory have an appropriate scope for who belongs in our moral
community?
(2) Does the theory exhibit an appropriate degree of rational consistency?
(3) Does the theory align with "common sense"?
(4) Does the theory adequately explain issues about moral distance?
(5) Does the theory have an appropriate telos or ultimate goal?
(6) Does the theory clearly delineate obligatory actions and supererogatory ones?
(7) Can the theory adapt to and account for the emergence of new
technologies?
(8) Can the theory be easily applied to different situations by providing clear-
cut solutions?

We recall with utilitarianism that the calculation of consequences can be an
exceedingly difficult and complicated undertaking. For example, when deciding to shut down businesses to halt the spread of a pandemic, one must balance all of the pain and suffering caused by shutting down with all the pain
and suffering caused by keeping them open. As one calculates all of the financial costs and emotional toll as well as the loss of life, a clear-cut decision
might be impossible to calculate. So utilitarianism might fail the ease-of-
application test because it does not provide clear-cut solutions.

What about egoism? The theory is certainly clear in its most basic form.
You should always follow your own rational self-interest in all circumstances.
This maxim is clear and straightforward, but it rapidly becomes vague and
mysterious when put into practice. Self-interest is open to interpretation, and
people often make mistakes when they believe they are following it. You can
be deceived into thinking something is good for you when, in fact, it is bad for
you. As with utilitarianism, sometimes the consequences of our decisions are
unknowable. If your self-interest is indeed rational, clear, and well defined,
then ethical egoism provides clear-cut solutions to any problems; however, if
it is not, then the theory might also fail this test.

Kant, on the other hand, provides a way out of the maze by arguing that
one should always follow absolute rules and never be bothered with nuance or
exceptions. Is this absolutist approach actually better for its simplicity and
decisiveness?

(9) Does the theory account for conflicts of interest?
Conflicts of interest are a fact of life. Indeed, one can view the whole of
human history as one huge bubbling cauldron of conflicts of interest. Many

(continued)

argue that the whole point of ethics should be to help us resolve those conflicts. Social contract theory, for example, takes conflicts of interest as a fundamental fact of life. The point of the theory is to figure out the appropriate way to resolve conflicts. Utilitarianism also acknowledges that conflicts of interest exist between the individual and the wider moral community. It then argues that these conflicts should be resolved by choosing actions that lead to the greatest benefits for all, even if this means an individual's rights or self-interest might be violated.

What does Rand think about conflicts of interest? Well, she flatly denies the existence of these conflicts with only one qualification. She writes, "There is no conflict of interests among men who do not desire the unearned, who do not make sacrifices nor accept them, who deal with one another as *traders*, giving value for value" (1964, p. 28). So, among rational people, Rand argues that there are no conflicts of interest. How can that be?

Let's imagine that two children require a lifesaving drug, but Jane, a pharmacist, only has one dose. The children's mothers appear at Jane's pharmacy at the same time, both needing the drug. Jane needs to decide who gets it. One mother is rich and the other is poor. The rich mother says she will pay twice the amount for the drug, but the poor mother can only pay the list price. Jane does not know what to do. She has something of great value that someone else also values, so she decides to sell the drug at double the price to the rich mother. However, the poor mother ambushes the rich mother in the parking lot and steals the drug.

This hypothetical scenario seems to reveal a very real three-way conflict of interest. However, Rand would argue either (1) that there is, in fact, no conflict of interest here because everyone is rationally following their own self-interest or (2) that these women are being irrational, which is why the conflict exists. Surely, something has gone wrong with an ethical theory if it (1) refuses to acknowledge the existence of conflicts of interest or (2) that it explains conflicts by simply arguing that people are behaving irrationally.

So, where do you stand on conflicts of interest? Do other theories deal with conflicts in a better way? Should a strong ethical theory make resolving conflicts of interest its primary feature?

References

Alon, T., et al. (2020). *The impact of COVID-19 on gender equality* (NBER working paper series). National Bureau for Economic Research. https://www.nber.org/system/files/working_papers/w26947/w26947.pdf. Accessed 5 Feb 2023.

Aristotle. (350 BCE). *Nicomachean ethics*. Trans. W. D. Ross. The Internet Classics Archive. 2009. http://classics.mit.edu/Aristotle/nicomachaen.1.i.html

Bailey, P. M. (2020, May 14). Do we need HEROES? Yarmuth, McConnell at odds over $3T coronavirus relief bill. *The Courier Journal*. https://eu.courier-journal.com/story/news/politics/2020/05/14/heroes-act-mcconnell-yarmuth-odds-over-need-covid-19-bill/5191256002/. Accessed 4 Sept 2022.

BBC. (2020, May 12). Coronavirus: Victoria ticket worker dies after being spat at. *BBC.com*. 12 May 2020. https://www.bbc.com/news/uk-england-london-52616071. Accessed 12 May 2020.

CDC. (2012, March 29). New *vaccination criteria for U.S. Immigration*. https://www.cdc.gov/immigrantrefugeehealth/laws-regs/vaccination-immigration/revised-vaccination-immigration-faq.html. Accessed 6 Sept 2022.

CDC. (2021, December 22). HIV and STD Criminal *Law*. https://www.cdc.gov/hiv/policies/ law/states/exposure.html. Accessed 6 Sept 2022.

CDC. (2022, August 8). *Fraudulent COVID-19 products*. https://www.fda.gov/consumers/health-fraud-scams/fraudulent-coronavirus-disease-2019-covid-19-products. Accessed 6 Sept 2022.

Cochrane, E. (2020, March 30). Nancy pelosi is already talking about the next stimulus bill for coronavirus relief. *New York Times*. https://www.nytimes.com/2020/03/30/us/politics/coronavirus-stimulus-relief-congress.html. Accessed 31 Aug 2022.

Deutsche Aids Hilfe. (n.d.). *Criminal law*. Aidshilfe.de. https://en.aidshilfe.de/criminal-law. Accessed 6 Sept 2022.

Diogenes Läertius. (c. 3rd C. CE). *Lives and opinions of the eminent philosophers*. Trans. C. D. Yonge. 1915. Project Gutenberg. https://www.gutenberg.org/files/57342/57342-h/57342-h.htm

DNI. (2021). *Updated assessment on COVID-19 origins*. Office of the Director of National Intelligence. https://www.odni.gov/files/ODNI/documents/assessments/Declassified-Assessment-on-COVID-19-Origins.pdf. Accessed 6 Sept 2022.

Eldeib, D., et al. (2020, May 5). The first 100: COVID-19 took Black lives first. It didn't have to. *ProPublica Illinois*. https://features.propublica.org/chicago-first-deaths/covid-coronavirus-took-black-lives-first/. Accessed Sept 2022.

Feuer, A. (2015, July 3). Billionaires to the barricades. *New York Times*. https://www.nytimes.com/2015/07/05/opinion/sunday/billionaires-to-the-barricades.html. Accessed 31 Aug 2022.

Gebrekidan, S. et al. (2020, November 2). In hunt for virus source, W.H.O. Let China take charge. *New York Times*. https://www.nytimes.com/2020/11/02/world/who-china-coronavirus.html. Accessed 19 Sept 2022.

Goodman, S. et al. (2020, April 10). A new front for nationalism: The global battle against a virus. *New York Times*. https://www.nytimes.com/2020/04/10/business/coronavirus-vaccine-nationalism.html. Accessed 19 Sept 2022.

HHS. (2021, June 2). Data and trends. US Statistics. *HIV.gov*. https://www.hiv.gov/hiv-basics/overview/data-and-trends/statistics. 16 Jan 2020. Accessed 6 Sept 2022.

HHS. (n.d.). HIV vaccines. *HIV.gov*. https://www.hiv.gov/hiv-basics/hiv-prevention/potential-future-options/hiv-vaccines. Accessed 6 Sept 2022.

Jeffrey, D. I. (2020). Relational ethical approaches to the COVDI-19 pandemic. *Journal of Medical Ethics, 46*, 495–498. https://doi.org/10.1136/medethics-2020-106264

La Ganga, M. L. (2016, October 18). Why a porn star is fighting California's condom law: 'It's a women's rights issue'. *The Guardian*. https://www.theguardian.com/us-news/2016/oct/18/porn-tasha-reign-california-condom-law-proposition-60. Accessed 6 Sept 2022.

NAM. (2020, June). *HIV criminalization laws around the world*. https://www.aidsmap.com/about-hiv/hiv-criminalisation-laws-around-world. Accessed 6 Sept 2022.

Neate, R. (2020, October 7). Billionaires' wealth rises to $10.2 trillion amid Covid crisis. *The Guardian*. https://www.theguardian.com/business/2020/oct/07/covid-19-crisis-boosts-the-fortunes-of-worlds-billionaires. Accessed 20 Oct 2020.

Okasha, S. (2020). Biological altruism. In E. N. Zalta (Ed.), *The Stanford encyclopedia of philosophy* (Summer 2020 Ed.). https://plato.stanford.edu/archives/sum2020/entries/altruism-biological/. Accessed 5 Sept. 2022.

Pandey, K., et al. (2021, November). Mental health issues during and after COVID-19 vaccine era. *Brain Research Bulletin, 176*, 161–173. https://doi.org/10.1016/j.brainresbull.2021.08.012

Plato. (375 BCE). *The Republic*. Trans. B. Jowett. Project Gutenberg. 2021. https://www.gutenberg.org/files/1497/1497-h/1497-h.htm

Pollard, C. L. (2015). What is the right thing to do: Use of a relational ethic framework to guide clinical decision-making. *International Journal of Caring Sciences, 8*, 362–368.

Rand, A. (1943). *The fountainhead*. Bobbs Merrill.

Rand, A. (1957). *Atlas shrugged*. Random House.

Rand, A. (1964). *The virtue of selfishness: A new concept of egoism*. Signet.

Sharp, P. M., & Hahn, B. H. (2011). Origins of HIV and the AIDS pandemic. *Cold Spring Harbor Perspectives in Medicine*. https://doi.org/10.1101/cshperspect.a006841

Singer, P. (1999, September 5). The singer solution to world poverty. *New York Times Magazine*. https://www.nytimes.com/1999/09/05/magazine/the-singer-solution-to-world-poverty.html. Accessed 28 Aug 2022.

Snowden, F. M. (2019). *Epidemics and society: From the black death to the present*. Yale University Press.

UN. (2021). *Aids program*. South Africa data. https://www.unaids.org/en/regionscountries/countries/southafrica. Accessed 27 Aug 2022.

US Department of State. (2009, December 15). Removal of HIV infection from the CDC list of communicable diseases of public health significance – Questions and Answers (Q&As). https://travel.state.gov/content/dam/visas/HIV_QandAs.pdf. Accessed 6 Sept 2022.

Yuan, L. (2022, January 13). The army of millions who enforce China's zero-covid policy, at all costs. *New York Times*. https://www.nytimes.com/2022/01/12/business/china-zero-covid-policy-xian.html. Accessed 6 Sept 2022.

Chapter 7
Virtue Ethics: An Alternative to Theories of Right Action

7.1 Virtue Ethics and the Problem of Motives

John Stuart Mill paints the following moral picture in his seminal book *Utilitarianism* (1863): "He who saves a fellow creature from drowning does what is morally right, whether his motive be duty, or the hope of being paid for his trouble" (II, para. 19). Mill's simple assertion raises some important ideas about morality, ideas that have been neglected in this book until now. In his brief albeit profound scenario, Mill suggests that the person who saves his fellow creature from drowning has performed the right action regardless of his motives—be they humane and selfless or mercenary and selfish.

However, some of you might reject Mill's blunt claim. He raises the specter of motivation as an important part of moral thinking, but he swiftly banishes the implications of the idea in one simple phrase. In effect, Mill says, "Right actions are right and wrong actions are wrong, regardless of the motives of the actor." Is Mill correct to ignore motives so quickly? After all, do pure motives make a moral action even more worthy of praise? And do impure motives make a moral action less worthy of praise? Conversely, do pure motives make an immoral action less worthy of condemnation? In short, Mill suggests that we should praise a saint and a serial killer equally for saving a fellow creature from drowning. But what if the serial killer only saved the man in order to murder him later? Mill would claim that the first action is right (saving the man) but that the second action is wrong (murdering him)—and that the two actions are absolutely unconnected from an ethical perspective. Clearly,

---

[1] According to the various laws and treaties about war, uniformed soldiers on all sides of a conflict are indeed morally equal, provided they do not commit war crimes. In other words, killing an enemy is not murder during war. Furthermore, prisoners of war are accorded a significant number of rights. For additional information about the moral equivalence of soldiers, see Sola (2009).

[2] A simple Google search reveals a number of COVID-risk calculators from reputable institutions, such as Harvard, the British Heart Foundation, and UNICEF.

A. Sola, *Ethics and Pandemics*, Springer Series in Public Health and Health Policy Ethics, https://doi.org/10.1007/978-3-031-33207-4_7

there is something deeply troubling with Mill's view that motivation should play no part in our analysis of this situation.

Let's look at a real-world legal case from Great Britain in order to think through the implications of moral motivation. Frances Inglis was convicted of murder for "killing" her son Thomas in 2010 (Pidd, 2010). Thomas had been left in a vegetative state after a tragic accident. Spending time by his side every day, Frances became convinced that he was not simply asleep in a coma but that he was in great pain. Legally, he could only be *allowed to die* by removing his feeding tube, which would lead to a slow death by starvation and dehydration, but she wanted him to die peacefully and painlessly, so she acquired heroin and injected him with a fatal dose. Thomas died. Frances was arrested, tried, and convicted of murder. She received the mandatory minimum sentence of 9 years, which was reduced to 5 years after an appeal. In her trial, no one accused her of being malicious or having evil motives. Indeed, quite the opposite was true. She was described by the judge as being a good mother, and her family, friends, and supporters agreed with that assessment. Furthermore, she felt no remorse for her actions and was unwavering in her belief that she did the right thing. However, the judge stated, "We must underline that the law of murder does not distinguish between murder committed for malevolent reasons and murder motivated by familial love [...]. Subject to well-established partial defences, like provocation or diminished responsibility, mercy killing is murder" (as cited in Davies, 2010).

The Inglis case illustrates a number of important legal complexities, but it is equally important for what it reveals about moral motivation and questions of character. Should Frances' pure motives absolve her of blame for ending her son's life? Should one even consider her motives when weighing the justice of her decision? Furthermore, should her good character, her possession of important virtues such as being a devoted and caring mother, count for nothing in the ethical calculus?

7.2   Motivation—> Action—> Consequence

The overwhelmingly dominant tendency of ethical thinking is to conceive of ethics as a system of rule-following when considering the correct course of action. The Ten Commandments is a good example of act-based morality: Thou shall not kill; thou shall not steal; thou shall not commit adultery; etc. Modern legal systems also

Table 7.1 The ethical timeline

Timeline	Motivation—>	Action—>	Consequence
Theory	Virtue ethics	Deontology	Utilitarianism
Thinker	Aristotle	Kant	Mill
Type	Theory of virtue	Theory of right action	Theory of right action
Concern	Virtuous being	Correct doing	Correct doing
Focus	Agent-centered	Action-centered	Action-centered

stress the centrality of the action itself when assigning criminal blame. Laws require or prohibit certain actions: Pay your taxes; refrain from shoplifting; do not exceed the speed limit; etc. The judge in the Inglis case stressed the point that pure motives do not excuse or justify the action of murder. Kant also focuses on the universal rules of action that all must follow in his categorical imperative. Utilitarian thinkers focus on actions as well, although they stress the importance of considering the consequences of an action when determining the rightness of the action itself. Philosophers call these *theories of right action*. All of them refuse to fully address the motivation of people who follow rules or who break them. But shouldn't motivation be an important factor in evaluating an ethical decision?

When assessing decisions, it is often helpful to remember that there are three distinct phases in the process: motivation, action, and consequence. Table 7.1 shows the different terms used to describe the different moral theories and their areas of focus on the ethical timeline.

Different theories focus on different phases of the process. In the previous chapters on Kantian deontology and utilitarian consequentialism, two important positions in the timeline have been discussed. Let us turn to the concept of motivation and the virtues now.

7.3   The Return of Aristotelian Virtues

Throughout much of Western history, the virtues were seen as being of critical importance. The ancient Greek philosophers, particularly Aristotle and Plato as well as the Stoics, focused on methods to develop characteristics in children that led to the creation of good, virtuous citizens. A city-state made up of virtuous people would, of course, be a rather nice place to live. As Aristotle writes in the *Nicomachean Ethics* (350 BCE), his work in political science is focused on "making the citizens to be of a certain character, viz. good and capable of noble acts" (I, IX, para. 3). Aristotle was less concerned about creating people who performed specific "right" actions than he was with creating a mass of people who tended to behave virtuously. However, as philosophy transformed into a reason-oriented, system-focused discipline during the Enlightenment, thinkers began to create tightly constructed theories of ethics, such as Kant's and Mill's, that would provide unequivocal guidance about right and wrong action. To some extent, cultivating virtues in young people lost its prominence. However, recently virtue ethics has returned to the fore, and it is now regarded as one of the major options in ethical theory (Hursthouse & Pettigrove, 2018).

In the subsequent discussion we will explore (1) Aristotle's definition of the virtues as habitual behavior; (2) his proposition that the virtues exist as a mean between two extremes; (3) his concept of happiness or *eudaimonia*, which is the ultimate purpose or *telos* of human life; and (4) the connection between the virtues and happiness.

7.3.1   The Virtues and Habit

How do we define the virtues? Aristotle claims that there are two broad types of virtues: intellectual and moral. He writes, "Intellectual virtue in the main owes both its birth and its growth to teaching (for which reason it requires experience and time), while moral virtue comes about as a result of habit" (II, I, para. 1). People become intellectually wise through acquiring education and life experience. However, people become morally good through *doing* virtuous acts over and over again. We are already familiar with many of the moral virtues: fairness, courage, justice, industriousness, generosity, honesty, patience, tolerance, etc. And how do we become virtuous individuals? Aristotle says, "We become just by doing just acts, temperate by doing temperate acts, brave by doing brave acts" (II, I, para. 1). Crucially, virtues are not simply qualities that an individual only shows once in a while. Instead, virtues are habits of character that are routinely expressed in a person's life. So it would be impossible to consider yourself courageous if you never face situations that demand courage, nor can you consider yourself honest if you never face difficult choices about telling the truth. Aristotle insists a virtuous person is one who habitually lives a virtuous life:

> By doing the acts that we do in our transactions with other men we become just or unjust, and by doing the acts that we do in the presence of danger, and being habituated to feel fear or confidence, we become brave or cowardly [...]. It makes no small difference, then, whether we form habits of one kind or of another from our very youth; it makes a very great difference, or rather all the difference. (II, I, para. 1)

Here, Aristotle maintains that we are taught habits of virtue at a young age, since those habits make us who we really are as adults.

Unfortunately, the vast majority of people fail to engage in the activities that lead to the formation of virtuous habits. While many people know what it means to be good, they fail to act according to their principles. Aristotle writes:

> It is well said, then, that it is by doing just acts that the just man is produced, and by doing temperate acts the temperate man; without doing these no one would have even a prospect of becoming good.
>
> But most people do not do these, but take refuge in theory and think they are being philosophers and will become good in this way, behaving somewhat like patients who listen attentively to their doctors, but do none of the things they are ordered to do. (II, IV, para. 4–5)

Just as many people with health problems know they need to change their habits in order to manage their disease but fail to do so, many people know they need to practice virtuous habits in order to become good but fail to act according to their principles. A central concern of Aristotle's theory of the virtues, therefore, is to shape individuals who form virtuous habits and who actually act virtuously, not merely to teach individuals the theory of virtue so it can be discussed in a classroom.

7.3.2   The Concept of the Golden Mean

Aristotle further clarifies what the virtues are by raising the concept of the golden mean. He insists that the virtues exist between two extremes, which are vices. For example, courage is a mean between cowardliness and foolhardiness. Courageous people do not seek out danger unnecessarily in order to show off their courage, nor do they bury their head in the sand in order to avoid danger. Honest people do not go around telling everyone what they really think—"You are lazy; you have bad taste; you are uninformed"—because doing so would be tactless and impolite, turning the virtue of honesty into a vice. However, when facing difficult decisions about truth-telling, honest people would not lie or deceive in order to spare themselves pain or discomfort. Industriousness or having a solid work ethic also exists as a mean between two extremes. Laziness and sloth are frowned upon for good reason, but so is being a workaholic. Aristotle again:

> For the man who flies from and fears everything and does not stand his ground against anything becomes a coward, and the man who fears nothing at all but goes to meet every danger becomes rash; and similarly the man who indulges in every pleasure and abstains from none becomes self-indulgent, while the man who shuns every pleasure, as boors do, becomes in a way insensible; temperance and courage, then, are destroyed by excess and defect, and preserved by the mean. (II, II, para. 2)

We can see here that Aristotle was an advocate of moderation in all aspects of life, from physical activity to diet, and his view is no different with the virtues, which exist as a mean between two extremes.

In contemporary society, tolerance is another oft-debated virtue. Tolerance is often employed by cultural relativists to urge the acceptance and understanding of other cultures, for example, the unequal treatment of women in some Islamic cultures; of course, others argue that tolerance of this behavior, which they call sexism, is wrong. Virtue ethics provides a neat solution to this problem. Aristotle would argue that tolerance exists as a mean between two extremes. A person errs in one extreme when tolerating all of the harmful and destructive behavior seen in other cultures, simply because cultures are different and differences must be tolerated. However, criticizing the behavior of others simply because they are different exhibits rigidity and narrow-mindedness, which exhibits a deficiency of tolerance. Aristotle's concept of the golden mean allows us to understand the wisdom of inhabiting the middle ground between extremes and deficiencies of any virtue.

7.3.3   Eudaimonia *and* Telos*: Happiness and the Ultimate Purpose of Human Life*

We have seen that (1) virtues are habits of conduct, and (2) they exist as a mean between two extremes. The next important point to address is the value of the virtues in human life. What's the point of the theory? In order to answer that question, Aristotle first defines what the ultimate purpose or *telos* of life is.

Aristotle's method of answering this question is to ask continuously why we do such and such an activity. If the answer points to another purpose, then we have not found the ultimate purpose. Once we find something that exists for the sake of itself, then we have found the ultimate purpose. For example:

"Why do we go to school?" To learn.
"Why do we want to learn?" To get a good job.
"Why do we want a good job?" To make money.
"Why do we want to make money?" To provide for our material needs.
"Why do we want to provide for our material needs?" To be happy.
"Why do we want to be happy?"

Well, we don't want to be happy for something else. Therefore, happiness exists for itself. For Aristotle, happiness must be the *telos* or the ultimate purpose of all activities.

Aristotle calls happiness *eudaimonia*, which is a difficult word to translate, but it means happy, contented, satisfied, vital, and alert, but it also means fully developed in the sense that people who have achieved *eudaimonia* have achieved success in their public and private lives. Aristotle argues that happiness is the only end that exists for itself, not for something else:

For [happiness] we choose always for itself and never for the sake of something else, but honor, pleasure, reason, and every virtue we choose indeed for themselves (for if nothing resulted from them we should still choose each of them), but we choose them also for the sake of happiness, judging that by means of them we shall be happy. Happiness, on the other hand, no one chooses for the sake of these, nor, in general, for anything other than itself. (I, VII, para. 3)

Here, Aristotle claims that there are other valid purposes in life, for example, honor (by which he means social status or the respect of one's peers). However, he insists that we want the respect of our peers for another reason—because achieving honorable status makes us happy. The same can be said of wealth: We desire wealth because it will help us become happy. Even virtues like generosity are valuable in themselves, but we are not generous for the sake of generosity itself; we are generous because generosity leads to happiness.

Again, Aristotle insists that we don't strive to be happy in order to be wealthy, wise, powerful, or respected. Indeed, we desire them in order to be happy. Still, he is not wholly convinced that happiness is something fully internal to one's own character. In order to achieve *eudaimonia*, external goods are required, by which he means some measure of wealth, power, wisdom, health, social status, and even good looks:

Yet evidently, as we said, [*eudaimonia*] needs the external goods as well; for it is impossible, or not easy, to do noble acts without the proper equipment. In many actions we use friends and riches and political power as instruments [...]. As we said, then, [*eudaimonia*] seems to need this sort of prosperity in addition. (I, VIII, para. 6)

Aristotle identifies *eudaimonia* with both the virtues and the acquisition of external goods. He says it is wrong to think that *eudaimonia* can result merely from good fortune (e.g., being born wealthy or winning the lottery). Virtue is the key to happiness, but a virtuous person will necessarily acquire the external goods that are required to be fully happy.

It is important to mention here that virtue ethics is not opposed to being self-centered, at least a little. In order to achieve *eudaimonia* one must develop one's own virtuous character. Being concerned about one's own well-being is actually a requirement of Aristotle's model. As a result, there are a number of *self-regarding virtues*, which are distinguished from *other-regarding virtues*. Self-regarding virtues are those that benefit the possessor. Temperance, for example, benefits the individual in that the temperate person lives a healthy life. Self-reliance is considered a virtue that benefits the possessor. Frugality allows the possessor to accumulate wealth. Other-regarding virtues, by contrast, focus on those characteristics that mainly benefit others. Charity, for example, benefits others, not oneself. Justice focuses on the correct treatment of others, not the correct treatment of oneself. For Aristotle, a virtuous person must achieve a proper balance between being self-regarding and other-regarding.

Aristotle's theory of the virtues always takes the middle ground between extremes. Many thinkers insist on extreme ways of living in order to live moral lives, particularly when it comes to wealth accumulation. Some interpretations of Jesus' teachings, for example, insist that we must give all of our money and possessions to the poor in order to be good Christians. Some utilitarian thinkers, such as the contemporary philosopher Peter Singer, insist that we give all of our money in excess of what we need to meet our necessities to the poor. However, Aristotle does not see a contradiction between the possession of external goods and being a good person. Indeed, external goods give us the proper equipment we need to perform good and noble acts.

7.3.4 The Virtues and Happiness

So, we can sum up Aristotle's happiness formula as something like this:

> External goods
> +Cultivation of self-regarding virtues
> +Cultivation of other-regarding virtues
> = *Eudaimonia*

The next step in Aristotle's argument is to link more concretely the concept of virtuous activity specifically with pleasure—not hedonistic pleasure like drinking, drug use, sex, or fine dining, but true pleasure. He indicates that behaving virtuously really should make one happy—a virtuous action should be pleasurable for the actor. A good person should rejoice in being generous, fair, tolerant, courageous, and kind. Because virtuous behavior is pleasurable, the virtuous person must be happy. Virtuous people will achieve *eudaimonia*, because their virtue reinforces their happiness and vice versa. While many people may think of virtuous actions (being charitable, patient, honest) as potentially being difficult and painful, the truly virtuous person thinks the opposite:

> The man who does not rejoice in noble actions is not even good; since no one would call a man just who did not enjoy acting justly, nor any man liberal who did not enjoy liberal actions; and similarly in all other cases. If this is so, virtuous actions must be in themselves pleasant. (I, VIII, para. 3)

Here, Aristotle insists that doing the right thing should be enjoyable, which is in stark contrast to previous thinkers that we have discussed. Kant, for example, insisted that doing the right thing—following his absolute moral rules at all times—may often be painful. Also, Peter Singer, the modern utilitarian, insists that many actions required by utilitarian ethics, such as donating all of your money above $30,000 to charity, may also be painful; nevertheless, these actions must be done if you wish to consider yourself to be a good person. Aristotle strongly disagrees. Such actions, if they are indeed signs of virtuous behavior, ought to be pleasurable.

So why should we cultivate the virtues in ourselves and in others? Aristotle provides two justifications. A society of virtuous people would be a nice place to live. However, why should any of us—living in less-than-perfect societies—try to cultivate virtues? Why should we be honest, when honesty might put us at a disadvantage in a society of liars and cheats? Why should we be generous when our generosity might not be reciprocated? Why should we be courageous when putting our own careers on the line by speaking out about immoral behavior will cost us our jobs? Aristotle argues that virtuous people lead happier, fuller, more fulfilling lives. In sum, he says, "The happy man lives well and does well; for we have practically defined happiness as a sort of good life and good action" (I, VIII, para. 1).

7.4 Virtue Ethics and Its Advantages

Now that we are familiar with Aristotle's ancient theory of the virtues, we can begin to understand the modern version of the theory known as virtue ethics. Like all ethical theories, virtue ethics solves some problems that other theories do not. We will explore three of the advantages now: (1) emphasis on character and motivation, (2) accommodation of personal relationships, and (3) focus on the happiness of the individual.

Emphasis on Character and Motivation
The first important point to make is that virtue ethics resolutely avoids the entrenched method of understanding isolated actions as being either right or wrong, preferring to focus instead on which specific virtues come into play when a person makes a difficult decision. It is extremely important to keep this in mind as you assess your own personal ethics. *Virtue ethics is not a theory that focuses on praising or condemning specific actions.* Virtue ethicists suggest that the modern theories which

establish systems, rules, and laws for right action wrongly ignore a number of valuable insights that ancient theories provide.

For example, in Mill's drowning scenario, he insists that anyone who saves a fellow creature from drowning performs the right action regardless of motive. One might argue, however, that while saving others is certainly a good action, focusing on the action alone neglects important parts of the full picture, namely, motivation. If the rescuer had impure motives, then the action would be less worthy of praise, at least according to virtue ethics.

Virtue ethics also provides an important solution to the conundrum of Frances and Thomas Inglis in ways that the other act-based approaches cannot. When assessing her decision to euthanize Thomas, one may argue that Frances showed a great deal of *courage* in that she knew that she was breaking the law, but was willing to do so in order to bring her son's suffering to an end. Also, she was *honest* about her actions, never lying about what she did or denying that she performed the action. She was also *selfless* in that she believed she was acting in a way to benefit Thomas at great cost to herself. Furthermore, everyone agrees that she was a devoted and loving mother. If you believe that a 9-year prison sentence for Frances was not just, it is probably for these reasons, and virtue ethics provides the theoretical basis for that assessment.

Accommodation of Personal Relationships
Another advantage of virtue ethics is that it provides a useful corrective to the inflexibility of action-based theories when it comes to the importance of personal relationships. Some theories, like utilitarianism, insist that all people count the same—whether they are your neighbors or strangers, your child or someone else's. Utilitarianism prevents you from treating one human being as more important simply because you have a personal relationship with that person. This doctrine is called *impartiality*.

Let's look at some examples that illustrate the problems with maintaining the ideal of impartiality. The utilitarians have a single rule for evaluating the rightness or wrongness of an action: An action is right if it increases happiness and wrong if it does the opposite. Let's say you have $100 to help starving people. The $100 can help 10 poor people in your own wealthy country or 100 people in an impoverished country. Which starving people would you help? A utilitarian would insist that you help the greater number because more people would be saved and every human being counts the same. In fact, some utilitarians would say that saving the lesser number, those whom you know personally, would violate the ideal of impartiality and would therefore be immoral.

Certainly, some may protest, something is wrong with an ethical theory when it cannot, at the very least, offer a convincing argument that *any* charitable action is good, despite the fact that other charitable actions might be even more beneficial.

Here is another example involving impartiality and one's own family. Let's say two children are drowning, and you can only save one. One of the children is your own, a misbehaved brat who tortures animals, and the other is a young genius with a talent for playing the piano and finding cures for rare diseases. Who do you save?

A utilitarian would insist you save the little genius and allow your own child to drown. Saving your own child would violate the rule of impartiality. But if you chose to save your own child, would that really make you a moral monster? Furthermore, many parents buy their own children expensive birthday gifts, but that money would be better spent saving poor children from starvation. A utilitarian would insist that the money go to helping the poor, not to giving one's own child yet another unnecessary toy.

In addition to the utilitarians, Kant maintained that all people have the same priceless dignity and must be treated impartially in that respect. The murder of innocent people, Kant insisted, is the worst possible crime, and he would certainly have abhorred Truman's decision to drop the atom bombs on Hiroshima and Nagasaki because doing so killed countless innocents. How would virtue ethicists approach the A-bomb debate? First, they would acknowledge that special considerations apply to all difficult decisions. Second, they would insist that Truman's motives be taken into consideration—and his motives, many scholars suggest, were pure although there is still considerable disagreement (Walker, 2005). Third, they would acknowledge that the killing of enemy civilians should be viewed differently than the killing of one's own, simply because it is difficult and even impossible to be impartial to all people, and one's own countrymen have a different moral status than others, especially during war. Certainly, they would say, killing innocent civilians in war is a tragedy, but it may be excused and justified. In short, a virtue ethicist would not judge Truman's decision to be absolutely wrong simply because he violated the doctrine of impartiality.

So virtue ethics does not require any one of these actions described above to be either right or wrong. Indeed, virtue ethicists would find ways to justify donating money to your local community, saving your own child from drowning, giving your own child birthday presents, and sacrificing innocent civilians in war. Indeed, a virtue theorist would argue that the doctrine of impartiality is an excessive form of the virtue that we might call *fair treatment*. It is certainly important to treat people fairly, without bias, and in ways they deserve to be treated. Someone deficient in this virtue would find reasons to treat people unfairly, simply because they are different. However, impartiality can become an excessive form of the virtue because your friends and family may deserve preferential treatment for any number of reasons. Therefore, it is fully consistent with virtuous behavior to focus on being charitable to your own community, sometimes at the expense of the rest of the world.

In fact, a virtue ethicist might suggest that a moral monster is the person who donates food to people on the other side of the world, but not to a starving neighbor; the mother who saves another child from drowning, but not her own; the father who gives toys to poor children, but ignores his own; and the president who respects the lives of enemy civilians, but allows his or her own soldiers to perish.

Focus on the Happiness of the Individual

We might have noted that both Kant and Mill seemed to neglect the role of individual happiness as a fundamental theme of their theories. In Kant's theory, acting according to universal moral rules is all that matters—whether or not doing so makes one happy or not. In Mill's theory, happiness or pleasure is the overt goal, but not one's own pleasure—the goal is to make as many creatures as happy as possible, which might mean that an individual might have to sacrifice his own happiness and external goods in order to lift others up. Again, the personal happiness and fulfillment of the individual is lost. Aristotle would strongly disagree with this approach to life. Indeed, he would suggest that everyone has a path to full development, a *process* that is unique to them. Some might choose one path and others might choose different ones, but they should all be allowed to achieve their own unique *telos*.

Virtue ethics reinstates happiness of the individual as the central theme. Being virtuous, Aristotle believes, will enable each individual to become happy. A society of happy and virtuous people would also achieve the utilitarian goal of creating pleasant lives for as many people as possible. Furthermore, Aristotle is not interested in prohibiting individuals from developing their full potential as human beings. Each individual has a *telos*, a unique and ultimate purpose, that he or she should be allowed to achieve, and the life paths taken to achieve that *telos* can be wildly different.

Critically, virtue ethics allows for multiple paths to personal fulfillment within the framework of the virtues. In short, any number of different types of people can be good, happy, and fulfilled following any number of paths. For example, a banker can focus on becoming a good banker professionally while also being an upstanding citizen in public life, as well as a loving parent and steadfast friend in private life. Focusing on developing habits of virtue allows any person to become a good, fully developed, and well-rounded person. And even if bankers fail at banking, they can still be good citizens, loving parents, charitable neighbors, and caring friends, that is to say, virtuous and happy individuals.

Box 7.4.1: Interdisciplinary Perspective #17: Feminism

Ethics of Care: A Transformative Perspective on COVID-19
The rediscovery of virtue ethics in the latter half of the twentieth century corresponded with another important innovation in academia, namely, the development of feminist critiques of social hierarchies, political institutions, the economy, and the reassessment of gender bias in perhaps every academic discipline, from anthropology and art to literature and linguistics. The field of ethics was also subjected to feminist critique, and female philosophers started building a distinctly feminist school of ethics, dubbed the ethics of care (Norlock, 2019). The feminist critique is profound: Traditional Western philosophy is a discipline created mostly by men for a mostly male audience, and the exclusion of female voices has made the ethical dimension of human life much poorer for it. Rarely does one find in the history philosophy a female voice, nor does one find a male voice that actively argues against the subordination of women or other historically marginalized groups. To be sure, there are exceptions to this narrative. For example, Mary Wollstonecraft wrote her

(continued)

Vindication of the Rights of Women in 1792, and John Stuart Mill, whom we've already met, penned *The Subjection of Women* with his partner Harriet Taylor in 1869. Still, the overall tendency in ethics was to privilege a dispassionate, rational, male perspective over others. One might wonder why virtues such as compassion and empathy seem to be missing from the theories we have discussed in this book so far. Indeed, only virtue ethics explicitly considers the importance of personal relationships. Being a good person requires a number of virtues that are other-regarding, such as compassion, generosity, and care-for-others. But these so-called feminine virtues have been undervalued or simply ignored in the history of ethics, so feminist philosophers set about setting the record straight by including the excluded female voice.

One of the key innovators of feminist ethics is the philosopher and social theorist, Carol Gilligan (b. 1936). In her book *In a Different Voice* (1982), Gilligan argues that traditional ethical theories, which are often rooted in masculine perspectives and cold, rational principles, fail to fully consider the role of relationships in ethical development. She argues that women tend to approach ethical decisions differently than men, placing greater emphasis on care. She asks why these very positive virtues are not seen as being equal to so-called masculine virtues of impartiality, rule-following, and logical deduction. It is a good question. She illustrated this bias against women's perspectives in her now famous critique of Lawrence Kohberg's theory of the stages of moral development. Kohlberg argued that children pass through six levels of morality, starting with a punishment-obedience orientation and eventually arriving at the highest level, which is universal ethical principle orientation, by which he means something like an ability to think abstractly according to the Kantian categorical imperative or the Utilitarian principle of impartiality. Kohlberg further noted that focusing on relationships, which comes in his third and fourth stages, is a less developed (and hence inferior) form of moral reasoning than his later stages. Gilligan critiqued precisely this point, arguing that a focus on relationships and caring for others—so-called feminine qualities—should not be placed in a moral hierarchy beneath masculine values such as reasoning from universal principles.

The consequences of this critique are profound. If the female perspective were to be legitimized and given its due weight in the discipline of philosophy, it would lead to a new ethical system that recognizes the importance of relationships and interdependence—an ethics of care. Note here that there are many similarities between relational ethics, discussed in Chap. 6, and the ethics of care; they arise from the same feminist critique and share a focus on relationships or networks of care. However, the feminist ethics of care goes perhaps further than relational ethics because it stresses that ethics must be understood as an active process of achieving fairness and justice for all people, particularly historically marginalized groups, including women,

(continued)

minorities, and LGBTQIA+ persons. The ethics of care is not simply a theory devoid of praxis; it is active and socially transformative.

In short, the feminist critique demonstrates a three-step process to social change and ethical wholeness. The first step is to recognize and embrace the vulnerabilities of human beings. The second step is to identify clearly that many of these vulnerabilities are structural in nature, which means that social, economic, and political forces are primary causes of the vulnerabilities. The third step is to change structures in order to rectify structural inequalities.

The feminist critique yields important insights when considering both successful and unsuccessful approaches to the COVID-19 pandemic. Indeed, one conclusion drawn by many feminist theorists is that the pandemic decisively proved and legitimized their critiques of the existing social, economic, and political power structures. For example, the pandemic negatively affected women, the poor, and historically marginalized people—as well as those at the intersection of multiple vulnerabilities—more than others (Cullen & Murphy, 2020). Furthermore, many public health measures to slow the pandemic, such as social distancing and enforced lockdowns, may have been well-intentioned but were woefully incomplete precisely because they affected the *vulnerable* more than the powerful. The vulnerable population includes women, minorities, and the poor, but it also includes groups that society frequently ignores, such as prisoners, people with disabilities and mental illnesses, and the homeless (Gilson 2021, p. 89).

Vulnerability, which is often perceived to be weakness from a masculine or patriarchal perspective, is embraced as a multi-faceted virtue by feminist thinkers. They argue that vulnerability is the most basic ontological (or fundamental) condition of human beings. We start our lives as vulnerable newborns, and we will most likely end them as vulnerable geriatrics. Furthermore, we will be vulnerable at various stages throughout the middle of our lives, for example, if we get sick during a pandemic. Why then should vulnerability be understood as a weakness or a vice? Furthermore, since care-for-others is an important solution to our ontological condition of vulnerability, why should it not be considered as the most important of virtues, the virtue that precedes all others? One must hesitate to put care in a Kohlberg-esque hierarchy of virtues, but from the feminist perspective *care* is a core virtue.

Once we accept our ontological vulnerability and the fact that we will care for others and be cared for, it is hard to accept the egoist claim that we are independent egos and autonomous selves. Instead, we are part of a network of interdependent relationships. Note that this feminist insight about our vulnerability echoes the insight from relational ethics (see Chap. 6) that humans are not fundamentally egotistical individuals, but are *a priori* members of a community. Perhaps nothing has illustrated our ontological interdependence more than the COVID-19 pandemic. And this is precisely where public health and the ethics of care align most closely. Public health presupposes communal

(continued)

vulnerability and interdependence. We share the environment, we share public spaces, and we share medical resources, such as ventilators, medications, and vaccines. We share doctors, nurses, and emergency medical technicians who care for you and me.

Despite the close alignment of values, there have been significant feminist critiques of the one-size-fits-all approach to some COVID-19 pandemic measures because they failed to recognize the vulnerability of certain segments of the public. For example, the decision to forbid family members from visiting dying relatives struck many as being misguided. Even though it was perhaps the safest public health decision, it failed the care test (Feder et al., 2021). Also, general lockdowns, which were again perhaps the safest public health measures to stop contagion, imperiled the most vulnerable even more (Alon et al., 2020). Workers with the luxury to be able to work from home and still earn money were much less affected than those who had to be physically present in their work environments—delivery workers, grocery clerks, healthcare workers, food workers, firefighters, police officers, etc. An ethics-of-care approach to pandemic management would require that the special needs of these groups be taken into consideration.

One final feminist critique has to do with the language used to describe COVID-era pandemic measures. Some of the messaging about pandemic management veered into the language of masculine mastery that spoke of *vanquishing*, *conquering*, or *defeating* the virus. For feminist thinkers, this language privileges false notions of autonomy and independence above a care ethics that takes vulnerability and interdependence as its starting point. This language is harmful because it blames the vulnerable for being more susceptible to the virus: She was old, so she couldn't beat the virus; he was overweight, so he couldn't fight off the infection; she never exercised, so she was too weak to win her battle with COVID; he couldn't work from home because he did not have a white-collar job, so he got infected at work and succumbed to the virus. For feminists, this blaming-the-victim tendency in language must also be corrected.

So how does an ethics of care prove decisive in pandemic management? Gilson (2021) notes, "The alternative policies that would remedy these injustices are well known (paid sick time and paid family and medical leave, higher wages, a more equitable healthcare system rather than a multitiered one that benefits those who can pay, etc.)" (p. 97). These are the structural inequalities that can be addressed to help the vulnerable survive the next pandemic.

Effective pandemic management also requires a care-oriented communication strategy. Scholars have pointed to New Zealand Prime Minister Jacinda Ardern as a positive example of compassionate and care-centered communication; indeed, she has become a model of successful, feminist pandemic management (Voina & Stoica, 2023). They specifically cite, among other qualities, her general empathy as well as her many official statements that

(continued)

explicitly recognized the economic, social, and cultural vulnerability among her constituents. New Zealand's pandemic response, led by Ardern's care-based style of pandemic leadership (while not entirely free from criticism), shows us that there are alternatives to traditional approaches to both pandemic ethics and public health.

Discuss:
- **The ethics of care approach requires us both to critique the existing state of affairs and also to imagine an improvement. From a public health perspective, what COVID-19 prevention measures—lockdowns, economic shutdowns, forced quarantine, mandatory vaccination, travel restrictions, and so on—seem to fail the care test? Do they fail to recognize our ontological vulnerability? How and why?**
- **COVID-19 will not be the last global pandemic, so describe specific social, economic, or political changes that could be implemented in order to generate more pandemic-resilient communities.**

7.5   The Central Objection to Virtue Ethics

The goal or *telos* of feminist ethics is fairly clear: one must recognize vulnerability, accept structural inequality, and then eliminate those inequalities in order to achieve a good and just society. On the other hand, virtue ethics does not provide clear moral direction beyond vague expressions about the cultivation of the virtues. We have seen it does have three clear advantages to other theories—it focuses on character and motivation, it is concerned with personal relationships, and it has an interest in individual happiness—but critics still harbor lingering doubts about it. The most strenuous criticism of virtue ethics is that it does not offer guidance in the way most people expect to be guided when it comes to ethical decision-making. Virtue ethics refuses to provide a clear path to right action. Ethical theories are meant to offer people clear guidance about right and wrong action, but virtue ethics fails to do so. Virtue ethics, some argue, is no system of ethics at all; it is merely a system of vague and imprecise guidance, much like a compass compared to a GPS.

Not only does virtue ethics fail to provide clear guidance about right action; it also fails to provide clear guidance about the application of virtues. Earlier, I mentioned the virtue of tolerance. Some are tolerant of other cultural practices, such as the differing treatments of women, while others are intolerant of those practices. Where, then, does one draw a clear line between an excess and deficiency of tolerance in the treatment of women? Should one tolerate forbidding women from driving cars? Driving cars without a male relative as an escort? Going to school? Walking alone? Working? Having an abortion? Virtue ethics does not offer a clear answer to these questions, but traditional theories like Kant's and Mill's would.

In some ways, this "failure" of virtue ethics can also be seen as its strength. In a time when people are obsessive about single instances of wrong behavior by public figures, virtue ethics provides an admirable corrective. For example, rather than focusing on, say, a single case of marital infidelity in a politician, a virtue ethicist might simultaneously focus on the wide range of virtues that the politician possesses. The politician might habitually prove to be diligent, dependable, and decisive. In assessing that person's suitability for the job, looking at the wide range of habitual actions would be appropriate. Of course, a virtue ethicist might also see infidelity as a sign of the politician's lack of transparency and trustworthiness.

Similarly, so-called cancel culture has become rather frustrating for many public figures. When a celebrity says something controversial, social media lights up with demands for apologies for these statements (which are sometimes taken out of context and deliberately misunderstood). It would be far better for critics to take to heart the central idea of virtue ethics—namely, one ought to look for characteristics of habitual action in the offender before criticizing. Is the person a habitual racist, sexist, or jerk? If so, criticism may be justified. If not, one ought to recognize that a comment might have been misinterpreted or misunderstood.

In short, virtue ethics provides an alternative to the moral judgmentalism that is pervasive in contemporary society. This book has taken the approach that there are alternative ways of thinking, ideas that you may not have been introduced to, worldviews that most people do not accept. Virtue ethics provides an important alternative to black and white ethical thinking. Virtue ethics accepts gray areas and even embraces them.

Still, many have reasonable criticisms of virtue ethics because it does not provide clear principles to guide us when making difficult decisions. Let's explore this problem further by exploring the most difficult decision medical professionals face: deciding who deserves treatment when resources are scarce.

Box 7.5.1: Interdisciplinary Perspective #18: Medical Ethics

The Challenge of Constructing Ethical Triage Policies During the COVID-19 Pandemic

Healthcare professionals are faced with numerous personal, psychological, and ethical pressures on normal work days. However, during times of severe medical emergencies, all of these pressures increase in intensity. In the most serious of medical emergencies—the aftermath of massive attacks or during pandemics—they are faced with the problem of resource scarcity: too many patients and not enough staff or resources to treat all of them equally. If you have the resources to save the lives of only a certain number of people, whom do you save?

The most universal concept used to deal with crises is the system of triage, which is a method of allocating limited resources—specialist staff, beds, medicines, lab tests, oxygen, ventilators, etc.—to patients in an orderly and ordered way. The challenge, of course, is defining policies to identify the most

(continued)

deserving patients in all of the different situations that the real world might confront us with.

Some of these triage policies are unproblematic. For example, on the battlefield, if two soldiers are injured—one lightly and one severely—medics should treat the severely injured soldier first because the other one can wait for treatment without any long-term harm. However, in real life, these policies often become much more problematic. Let's say five soldiers are injured—a friendly soldier (i.e., a comrade) and four captured enemy soldiers, all with severe injuries. The four enemy soldiers, if treated immediately, have a better chance of survival than the single friendly. Is it then morally justified to allow four enemy soldiers (who are also human beings) to perish in order to save one friendly? This scenario raises a number of problems related to the *principle of equal treatment*, which was discussed earlier. Are enemy and friendly soldiers morally equivalent and should they be treated equally? Is it wrong to care about your own comrades more than the soldiers who were trying to kill you just moments earlier?[1] A utilitarian would suggest that personal relationships should not cloud your judgment nor should the past behavior of the enemy; therefore, you should save the greater number of enemy soldiers (human beings) at the expense of your own comrade. However, the utilitarian explanation may seem like an unsatisfactory answer. Surely, past behavior and personal relationships should inform this decision.

Hypothetical scenarios like the one above fill texts on medical ethics, but they are not merely fancy flights of the imagination with no connection to the real world. Indeed, the COVID-19 pandemic illustrated to the whole world that life and death decisions are made by medical professionals on a daily basis. The scarcity of ventilators and ICU stations, for example, forced many to make the difficult choices about who would be treated—and who would not. Some of the policies enacted by hospitals and health authorities led to bitter controversy over what equal treatment means. For example, both Alabama and Washington State were criticized for suggesting that triage decisions should consider factors such as a patient's disability status, prompting the HHS Civil Rights Office to release a statement condemning the *ruthless utilitarianism* of these policies and defending the fundamental equality of all patients (Fink, 2020). Here, again, the tension between Kant's notion of the absolute dignity of human life and the utilitarian concept of the greater good are exposed in the real world. Still, the question remains: Who deserves medical care when resources are limited?

Fortunately, there are some international principles that help guide medical professionals facing crises. Susanne Jöbges (2020) and her co-authors have provided an extremely helpful overview of the broad agreement that exists globally with regard to ethical triage. After analyzing the policies of a number of countries (from Australia to Pakistan and from South Africa to the United

(continued)

States), they identify key ethical principles in triage policies that readers of this book will already be familiar with.

First, the utilitarian concept of maximizing benefits is pervasive throughout the guidelines although the precise definition of these benefits varies. For example, we have already seen in Chap. 4 that benefits can be defined as a single life saved or as the QALY (quality-adjusted life year). When defining the maximum benefit, some nations such as Switzerland define it exclusively as preserving as many lives as possible, whereas other countries such as South Africa also include language about saving the most QALYs. Furthermore, policies in the United States expressly indicate that "maintaining the function of the healthcare system" (as cited in Jöbges et al., 2020, p. 950) should be a stated goal of triage policies, implying that medical personnel ought to receive preferential care because they can save more lives in the future after recovery—this is an explicitly utilitarian justification.

A second key principle identified by Jöbges is that of equality of treatment, the concept that everyone should receive the same treatment. Here, again, there is broad agreement among different countries that all patients deserve the best treatment available. However, there are some important variations. For example, Canada notes that COVID-19 patients should not be treated differently than patients with other illnesses, i.e., they should neither be prioritized nor demoted. In Great Britain, the guidelines note that patients with COVID-19 or other illnesses should have an equal chance of receiving the care they need provided they have an equal chance of benefiting from the care. This principle of equality is important, and many countries' guidelines specifically include anti-discriminatory language; in other words, treatment decisions should not be made based on race, class, gender, etc.

The third set of criteria seen in the surveyed countries become more problematic. Given the fact that during a pandemic sick people will overwhelm the healthcare system, decisions must be made about who should receive treatment, but they can't be made based on the type of illness (COVID or non-COVID) nor based on discriminatory factors. So, the medical criteria seen in many countries are as follows: chance of short-term survival, chance of long-term survival, and projected life span. Here, doctors are given much more flexibility to judge each patient on an individual basis. Perhaps a young patient who has a long projected life span is admitted, but she is so sick when she arrives that her chances of short-term survival are limited. Then, perhaps an older patient in the earlier stages of disease could be given priority. Comorbidities are also taken into account in this step of the process. A healthy person might be given priority over someone with asthma, diabetes, and an immunodeficiency. Regarding biological age, in Belgium, it is specifically noted that "age in itself is not a good criterion to decide on disproportionate [or unequal] care" (as cited in Jöbges et al., 2020, p. 950). However, in Italy, an age limit on treatment can be set. Switzerland specifically excludes patients

(continued)

over 85 years old if there are no ICU beds available. However, Great Britain specifically bans age limit rules as being discriminatory and, hence, unlawful.

The final set of criteria relates to so-called tie-breakers. What if two patients are identical—they have the same age, the same comorbidities, the same chance of survival in the short- and long-term, and the same projected life span—but there is only one ICU station available? Here, countries diverge quite a bit in their guidelines. Australia, for example, prioritizes disadvantaged groups in this situation. Therefore, in the above scenario, an indigenous person would get the ICU, and a white Australian would not. Belgium recommends a lottery system, so the two patients would have to flip a coin to decide who gets the ICU. Switzerland rejects the lottery and maintains the principle of first-come, first-served. So, if one patient arrived a minute before the other, he or she would get the ICU. The United States prioritizes healthcare workers, children, pregnant women, and also research volunteers. (This is one selfish reason to volunteer for vaccine trials!)

Based on the comparative analyses, Jöbges and her co-authors conclude by offering ten criteria for establishing ethical triage policies that balance the maximization of benefits with other important considerations like fairness, justice, and equality. But this chapter is focused on virtue ethics, so let us turn to its ability to add depth to the question of triage.

We have seen that virtue theory has three distinct advantages to right-action theories. Here, we focus on the first two: virtue theory supports evaluating a person's character, and it allows us to take personal relationships into account.

In the triage guidelines above, issues about a person's character are wholly excluded from treatment decisions. The fear is that medical professionals will make decisions based on arbitrary or discriminatory factors. However, one might wonder why a virtuous doctor should not be allowed to make decisions based on a patient's character. For example, let's say Sally and Sam both need the last remaining ICU. Sally is a 70-year-old grandmother, a pillar of the community, a retired scientist, and a volunteer at the local homeless shelter; however, she has serious comorbidities. Sam, on the other hand, is a perfectly healthy 25-year old ex-con, who has served time for spousal abuse, drug dealing, and cruelty to animals. The guidelines above would forbid the medical staff from considering the patients' moral characters, and Sam would get the last remaining ICU. Is that just? Shouldn't a person's character determine how he or she is treated by others?

Second, virtue ethics accommodates personal relationships; it argues—against utilitarianism—that all people are in fact not equal in the moral universe. It is okay that our friends, families, and neighbors count for more than strangers on the other side of the world. Thinking about triage again, let's say that Frank and Franny both need the final ICU bed. Franny is a young, undocumented immigrant without health insurance, and Frank is an elderly citizen

(continued)

with health insurance. Is it ethically justified to reject Franny's claim to the ICU because she is an outsider? In short, is it acceptable for a society to care for its own citizens more than others? Furthermore, it is justified to keep one's own medical resources (vaccines, ventilators, PPE, etc.) for one's own people rather than to share them equally with the rest of the world. Immigration status is not in the triage guidelines, but virtue ethics would not necessarily exclude such considerations.

We remember that the central objection to virtue ethics was that it fails to provide specific guidance to resolve specific conflicts. It refuses to tell us which specific action is right and which is wrong in any situation. Instead, it hopes that children will be raised to become virtuous adults who will make virtuous decisions. And if virtuous doctors, for example, make a bad decision, we do not conclude that they are bad doctors, but that they are good doctors who made a single "bad" decision. The triage guidelines in this section offer for the most part reasonable guidance and rational principles to guarantee the fair, just, and equitable treatment of patients in crisis situations. They provide clear guidance in the way that theories of right action demand. However, they do not consider the character of a patient, and virtue ethics suggests that character is a valuable criterion for making such decisions.

Discuss
- **Is it fair and just to exclude a person's moral character from triage decisions? If resources are scarce during a pandemic, why should we reward a convicted criminal instead of a law-abiding citizen with the last ICU bed?**
- **How could a virtue-based triage policy be designed so it could work in the real world?**

7.6 Solving Ethical Problems with Virtue Ethics

Let us carry on with an assessment of additional ways that virtue ethics can provide solutions to ethical problems we have already considered in this book. In this chapter, we have already completed the ethical timeline by accounting for motivation, having already assessed action and consequence in previous chapters. We have seen that virtue ethics addresses some important concerns that other moral theories tend to neglect. Namely, it provides a robust account of motives and character, offers a defense of treating personal relationships in a special way, and makes the happiness of individuals its central goal.

7.6.1 Stealing the Specifications of a COVID-19 Vaccine

In Chap. 3 on Kantian deontology, you were introduced to the hypothetical scenario in which a scientist sends you a USB stick with specifications to manufacture a vaccine for a new pandemic. We can return to the example now in order to determine how virtue ethics would approach the problem in an entirely different way:

> Let's say a new, terrible global pandemic has begun. However, a new vaccine has been developed and approved for emergency use, but it is protected by TRIPS. You operate a vaccine manufacturing facility in a developing country. You've tried to get licenses to produce the vaccine legally, but you've been denied. One day, you receive an anonymous letter and a USB-stick in the mail. The letter is from a disgruntled scientist at a major pharmaceutical company. She helped to develop the vaccine and believes that the vaccine specifications should be open-source and free to use during the pandemic. She says it is a violation of human dignity to put profits ahead of people. The enclosed USB-stick has all of the technical information you need to manufacture the vaccine at your facility. What would Kant do? What would you do? Why?

A virtue theorist would note that the question, with its focus on the action of stealing the specifications, is incorrectly framed. The action itself should not be the sole focus of the scenario. Instead, we should also focus on the motives and character traits of the actors. What are the motives of the scientist? Do we believe that she is honest in her claims? You also need to look closely at your own motives. Do you really want to develop the vaccine in order to do charitable and philanthropic work, or are you motivated by wealth, status, or power? If the scientist is indeed a virtuous person, then she has shown great courage by sending you the vaccine, risking her own career, and exposing herself to criminal liability in order to save the lives of others. Vicious motives, on the other hand, would certainly undermine her argument for leaking the specifications. As for your choice, it may be that producing the vaccine, though illegal, might actually showcase virtues of courage, empathy, and care for others.

A virtue-ethics approach avoids being judgmental and avoids the right-wrong dichotomy. It also provides important context to all ethical decisions by asking what the motives of the actors are. By assessing moral motivation as well as the character of the actor, we can presumably come to a variety of different conclusions in this scenario. At this point one might once again reject virtue ethics because it does not clearly tell us what the right action in this situation is. A virtue theorist might respond, "Life is complicated. There are no easy solutions, no easy answers." However, if the actors are behaving virtuously—courageously, honestly, respectfully—then we should simply describe their overall characters and not condemn their individual actions.

7.6.2   Edward Jenner and the Smallpox Vaccine

In Chap. 4 about utilitarian ethics, we discussed Edward Jenner and the development of the smallpox vaccine. You will remember that Jenner first tested the process on an 8-year-old boy. Fortunately, the boy did not die. However, a Kantian thinker would argue that testing a potentially deadly medical procedure on an innocent and perfectly healthy child was wrong—absolutely wrong. Using human beings as a means to an end undermines the dignity of life and represents the obliteration of the moral universe. Even though Jenner's discovery eventually led to the eradication of the disease, his action was despicable. A utilitarian, on the other hand, would argue that Jenner did the right thing based on the consequences of the action. Testing the vaccine on a child was a small price to pay for preventing the suffering and death of millions and millions of people. Even if the child died, it would have been worth the sacrifice. Moreover, even if Jenner had to test the procedure on one hundred, one thousand, or even one million innocent children, the eradication of smallpox is such a beneficial result that these sacrifices would be justified. These two ethical approaches provide two contradictory assessments of Jenner's action. The arguments for each assessment are clear, sound, and rationally consistent. And yet we still have two utterly different conclusions at the end of each analysis. Jenner is either a monster or a hero. It seems likes for some ethical theories 2+2=3 and for others 2+2=5, but shouldn't ethics tell us that 2+2=4? After all of the thought that the great philosophers have done over the course of thousands of years, there is very real disagreement about right and wrong behavior in the Jenner case as in many others. But shouldn't the right ethical system tell us, at the end of the day, what is truly right and wrong?

At this point in any assessment of a difficult ethical problem, virtue ethics provides some routes out of the conundrum. First, we should pause before making a judgment because many difficult ethical problems are, well, difficult to solve. If they were simple, then they wouldn't be problems at all. Second, we should assess Jenner's motivation. Did he choose to do his first test on an innocent child because he wanted fame and glory, or was he motivated by an established interest in preventing people from suffering from a horrible disease? Third, we could test the pureness of his motives by looking at his character as a human being. Was he a thoughtful, generous, caring, courageous, and prudent doctor throughout his life? Or was he a reckless quack? If his character was sound, then maybe we ought to include that fact in our assessment of his decision.

In reality, Jenner did wait a full 2 years after vaccinating the boy before testing the vaccine on additional subjects precisely because he wanted to make sure that the process was successful. A virtue theorist would certainly take this important fact into consideration and use it to show that Jenner was not a reckless doctor who sought fame and simply enjoyed playing with people's lives. After he was satisfied that the process was safe and did work, Jenner spent his whole life campaigning for universal vaccination, which provides further evidence of his altruistic commitment to saving people's lives. However, some critics might note that Jenner was not a purely virtuous person. Indeed, one of his major vices was his stubbornness. He refused to accept that his vaccination did not provide lifetime immunity, even though there was clear evidence that many people did end up getting smallpox many years after they were vaccinated (Snowden, 2019, p. 108). We now know that the smallpox vaccine requires a booster, but Jenner, being stubborn, refused to accept the fact in his own lifetime. Still, on balance, a virtue ethicist would probably look sympathetically upon Jenner's decision to conduct his first test on an innocent child because, on balance, his motives were pure.

In sum, virtue ethics—with its avoidance of action-based judgment, its openness to considering motivation, and its desire to see single ethical decisions as part of a wider portrait of a human being's general character—provides helpful ways of analyzing ethical problems that theories of right action fail to address.

Box 7.6.3: Interdisciplinary Perspective #19: History

Polio and the Cutter Vaccine Tragedy
While virtue ethics can be used to excuse or justify actions that appear to be bad on first inspection but not so bad after thorough analysis, it can also be used to show why bad actions are particularly bad. Indeed, evil motives can be used to further condemn bad actions, and many judicial systems add heftier penalties for crimes that are motivated by particularly nefarious reasons (e.g., hate-crime laws). One particularly horrifying case of bad motives leading to bad actions with even worse consequences is the Cutter Labs polio vaccine fiasco of 1955.

Polio is caused by a virus that can be transmitted through microbes traveling from hand to mouth as well as through droplets released from coughing and sneezing (yet another reason to cover your mouth and wash your hands). As with COVID-19, many infected people are asymptomatic or have very mild symptoms, but still shed the disease and infect others. Most cases of polio are not serious, but in around 1% of people the disease becomes paralytic polio, and the consequences are grave—death or lifelong disability (Estivariz et al., 2021). Since polio attacks the nerve system, it leads to paralysis in most major muscles, including the diaphragm. As a result, many polio patients spent the rest of their lives encased in iron lungs, unable to move. One man in the United States, Paul Alexander, still lives in an iron lung after contracting the polio virus as a 6-year-old boy in 1952 (McRobbie, 2020). His story is one of Stoic resilience and fortitude (see the section below) that everyone should read. Other polio victims, such as Franklin Delano Roosevelt, were either crippled or deformed, and one-third of patients who survived polio with fairly minor problems still suffered from a degenerative disorder called post-polio syndrome, which led to further physical problems as well as mental issues, including depression and memory loss. It is no wonder then that polio was regarded with ever-increasing horror and fear, since there were no effective treatments for the disease.

(continued)

Curiously, polio is a disease that also illustrates the unintended negative consequences of modern technology and scientific advancement. Before the development of sewers and water treatment systems in the nineteenth and twentieth centuries, most people were exposed to the virus as infants and were protected from severe harm because of neonatal antibodies. Furthermore, after exposure as infants, many were protected for the rest of their lives. Paradoxically, improved hygiene standards, which usually prevent the spread of infectious disease, actually created the modern polio pandemic, which became increasingly severe in the first half of the twentieth century. In 1952, the United States had over 21,000 cases of paralytic polio (Estivariz et al., 2021). In fact, in the 1950s the public hysteria was so great that Americans feared polio second only to nuclear war with the USSR (Snowden, 2019, p. 390).

During the 1940s and 1950s, scientists were making breakthroughs in their studies of polio, and on 12 April 1955, Jonas Salk's polio vaccine, an inactive polio virus administered by injection, was declared safe and effective. In the subsequent 5 years, 93 million Americans received the vaccine. (Another vaccine was also in the testing pipeline, Albert Sabin's, which used active but weakened polio virus and was administered in a sugar cube.) Polio eradication efforts have proven to be highly successful in the United States and in the industrialized West. Cases of polio dropped from the peak of 58,000 cases per year in 1952 to a mere 100 per year in the 1960s (Estivariz et al., 2021). It has been nearly non-existent since the 1980s, and there were no cases reported for 10 years between 2012 and 2022. However, a recent case diagnosed in New York has public health officials on edge (Reardon, 2022). Globally, the situation is slightly more challenging, but polio eradication efforts have been largely successful, and the polio eradication initiative of the WHO (2022) reports that the only known cases of wild polio transmission from August 2021 through August 2022 occurred in Pakistan (15 cases), Mozambique (5 cases), Afghanistan (4 cases), and Malawi (1 case).

While smallpox has been eradicated, polio still persists. Indeed, the State of New York announced a state of emergency in September 2022 due to the reappearance of polio in water (Fadulu, 2022). The reasons for polio's persistence are complicated, and the most important reason is not biological but social. Vaccines have always met with some measure of alarm. Jenner's vaccine, since it is derived from the cow, led to conspiracy theories about the effects of mixing human and animal parts. One of the more bizarre of these was that vaccinated women would be inclined to have sex with bulls (Snowden, 2019, p. 109). Others had religious objections to the vaccine, since it violates "natural laws." Vaccine conspiracy theories abound, and most of them have no basis in science. However, one sordid tale in the history of the polio vaccine has served to stoke anti-vaccination fears, despite the proven safety and success of the vaccine.

(continued)

In 1955, six companies in the United States were awarded contracts to produce Salk's vaccine for the government's mass-vaccination program. One of them was Cutter Laboratories in California. Unfortunately, about 120,000 doses of the vaccine they produced were faulty—the live polio virus was not killed in the manufacturing process. As a result, 40,000 people were infected with live polio, leading to the death and paralysis of some infected via the injection and others infected by the mini-epidemic that the infection caused (Fitzpatrick, 2006). At the end of the tragedy, 164 people were paralyzed and 10 died (Snowden, 2019, p. 396). Subsequent analysis points to a number of causes. First, the government did not oversee the process, allowing the company to self-regulate (which should serve as a warning to those who wanted to loosen regulations for the development, production, and distribution of COVID-19 and other vaccines). Second, the company culture was far from spotless. The investigation uncovered previous cases of misconduct at the company, including accusations of price fixing, safety violations, and fraud (Snowden, 2019, p. 397). However, the company was found to be not guilty of criminal negligence in the faulty production of the tainted vaccine (Fitzpatrick, 2006). The government investigation and subsequent civil cases painted a troubling picture of shady motives leading to improper actions, which, in turn, led to disastrous consequences. Virtue ethics, with its focus on motivation, highlights the vices that led to the tragedy, namely, greed and carelessness.

There is no doubt that the Cutter tragedy caused great harm to many people both directly and indirectly. The actions were bad, but the harmful consequences of the case extend not only to those infected with the faulty vaccine but also to those who still cite Cutter as a reason to distrust vaccines and government-sponsored vaccination programs. Given the overall success of polio eradication efforts and vaccinations in general (e.g., smallpox, measles, mumps, rubella, etc.), is it reasonable to distrust vaccines? Well, a virtue theorist would stress that virtues represent a mean between two extremes. There should be a healthy middle ground between complete trust and complete distrust. After all, *gullibility* and *naiveté* describe an excessive amount of trust; *skepticism* and *cynicism* describe its deficiency. We will return to the subject of healthy amounts of social trust in the next interdisciplinary perspective below.

Discuss

- **How important is the Cutter tragedy in your own assessment of the safety and reliability of government-approved vaccines?**
- **If a person who is vaccine hesitant were to cite the Cutter tragedy as reason not to get vaccinated against a new pandemic disease, how would you respond?**

(continued)

7.7   Being a Virtuous Person During a Pandemic

Turning away from the vices of greed and carelessness, let us look instead at the virtues that might help us endure the tumult and trouble of life during a pandemic. Virtue ethics, since it is not a theory of right action, provides additional guidance about living our daily lives in ways that other theories mostly ignore. Kant's theory, for example, concentrates on following absolute rules; utilitarians, on analyzing the beneficial consequences of one's action; the social contact, on following the law; and egoism, on following one's own self-interest. These are surely helpful pieces of advice, but the one-liners obscure the richness and diversity of lived experience. Virtue ethics offers a more useful way of guiding our behavior and shaping our habits of character both in normal times and also in times of crisis.

In order to identify specific pandemic-appropriate virtues, we turn to another ancient school of thought, the Stoics, who were a group of ancient Greek and Roman philosophers who made as their philosophical goal the calm acceptance of life's challenges. Founded by Zeno of Citium in the fourth century BCE, Stoicism has three central concepts, which, when practiced faithfully, can help one live a life of inner peace in a world of turmoil. First, we should stop trying to control things we cannot control. Second, we cause ourselves unhappiness by not accepting our lack of control over external events. Third, there is only one thing we can control, namely, our own mental attitude. The Stoics argued that if we train our minds to overcome our immediate emotional reactions to negative external forces, we can eventually find inner peace.

In addition to Zeno, there were two other great Stoic philosophers in antiquity, one an emperor and the other an enslaved person. The Roman Emperor Marcus Aurelius (121–180 CE) was arguably the most powerful man on the planet in the second century; his vast empire ranged from the British Isles to the Arabian Peninsula. The other great Stoic, Epictetus (51–135 CE), had no title for he was an enslaved person. (One advantage of the philosophy of Stoicism is that it is equally helpful for the powerful and the powerless.) Both Stoics made their mark on history—Aurelius for being the most virtuous of emperors and Epictetus for writing a short handbook of Stoic philosophy, the *Enchiridion*, which was the training manual for the Roman legions; however, it is also a useful guide for people living during pandemics. Aristotle mentioned the importance of developing self-regarding and other-regarding virtues, and the Stoics built upon this insight. The key self-regarding Stoic virtues are resilience, Stoic resignation, fortitude, and discipline; the key other-regarding virtue is generosity of spirit.

7.7.1 Resilience

One key pandemic virtue is resilience, the ability to adapt to misfortune and overcome obstacles in life without sinking into despair and self-pity. During a pandemic, many of the institutions that guide and structure our lives break down. For instance, during COVID-19, schools and universities were forced to cancel face-to-face classes and move to online classrooms. Many students at all levels (as well as teachers and parents) found this change to be a challenge. Countless workers lost their jobs, causing terrible emotional and economic hardship for families. Many people lost their loved ones to the virus, piling grief upon hardship, and many millions became terribly sick themselves. Furthermore, we saw an increase in mental health problems, drug use, and alcoholism, all linked to the pandemic (HHS, 2022).

Epictetus urges us to use a comparative technique to help us put our own troubles into perspective and build up our resilience. Typically, when bad things happen to other people, we react much differently than when bad things happen to ourselves. In the *Enchiridion*, Epictetus (c. 135) asks us to ponder the significance of that difference:

> The will of nature may be learned from things upon which we are all agreed. As when our neighbor's boy has broken a cup, or the like, we are ready at once to say, "These are casualties that will happen"; be assured, then, that when your own cup is likewise broken, you ought to be affected just as when another's cup was broken. (para. 16)

Epictetus was stern and possibly even a little extreme; nevertheless, the exercise of comparing how we react to the misfortunes of others with how we react to our own misfortune helps us develop our resilience. We all too often think, "Oh, what terrible tragedy that X happened to Jane, but she should really get over it and get on with her life." Indeed, all of us have experienced illness. If you have ever been very sick, you probably felt sorry for yourself—much more than when you heard that others were sick. Epictetus encourages us to be equally stern with ourselves; doing so builds our resilience to misfortune. Resilience, therefore, is a self-regarding virtue; however, we establish it through scrutinizing our attitude toward others.

7.7.2 Stoic Resignation

Another way Stoic tranquility can be achieved is through relinquishing our desire to control what we cannot control—this is another self-regarding virtue that nevertheless requires us to look at how we view others and how others view us. In a society that prizes the doers, go-getters, entrepreneurs, high achievers, and activists, in a society that says we should be the masters of our fates and the shapers of our futures, Epictetus tells us something different. His simplest commandment is this: "Demand not that events should happen as you wish; but wish them to happen as they do happen, and you will go on well" (para. 8). Some of the shame that we feel for not being "successful" comes from the expectation that we ought to overcome every obstacle, that we ought to work harder, and that we ought to be more *resilient*. However, this is not what the Stoics mean by resilience. While they do advocate not feeling sorry for ourselves, they also want us to accept the fact that bad stuff happens. Indeed, success in Stoicism is not defined as the acquisition of wealth, power, or status, which is the definition of success in many societies; success is the ability to be calm, tranquil, and self-contained despite misfortune.

Many societies shame "failure." When we are constantly told that money, power, and status are the only signifiers of success, it is easy to lose sight of the fact that pursuing these goals will not necessarily bring happiness. This type of socially mandated model of success is really not in our control. A society that denigrates otherwise hardworking and resilient people who had a bad break and need some help to get on their feet again, a society that fails to recognize that the healthy can become sick, the worker can become unemployed, and the happy can become sad, all due to circumstances outside of their control, a society that sets up an ideology of *success, at all cost,* despite the odds, despite the obstacles, despite the challenges—such a society actually reinforces people's unhappiness. Epictetus actively worked against such a view, writing, "There are things which are within our power, and there are things which are beyond our power. Within our power are opinion, aim, desire, aversion, and, in one word, whatever affairs are our own. Beyond our power are body, property, reputation, office, and, in one word, whatever are not properly our own affairs" (para. 1). Although it would be good if social expectations were different, one cannot control social expectation that we are failures if we do not acquire a house in the country, a new SUV, and a position of power. The Stoics would remind us that we should eliminate our desire to achieve the things that society says we should desire. Instead, we should desire to overcome desire. We do this by remembering that we cannot control many things that happen to us—pandemic disease being one of them—and all of the hardships that might come. We should therefore reject the aspirations of a superficial society as well as our own complicity in the system. Doing so will help us achieve Stoic happiness.

7.7.3 Discipline

The third self-regarding virtue that one can cultivate during a pandemic is discipline, particularly when it comes to personal hygiene and the protection of others as well as oneself. Sometimes it is easy to lapse into unsafe behaviors given the constant concentration required to maintain social distancing and hygiene. However, discipline is also required to regulate one's own actions and behaviors when dealing with others. In other words, discipline creates the habits that turn us into good people. In the *Nicomachean Ethics*, Aristotle (350 BCE) stressed that this is not an intellectual endeavor; it is a practical activity:

> By doing the acts that we do in our transactions with other men we become just or unjust, and by doing the acts that we do in the presence of danger, and being habituated to feel fear

or confidence, we become brave or cowardly...Thus, in one word, states of character arise out of like activities. (II, I, para. 4)

Being disciplined, acting consistently in ways that turn daily actions into character traits, is particularly important during times of crisis. The Stoics also insisted on the importance of discipline in order to create virtuous habits of character. Epictetus writes in the *Enchiridion*, "Upon every accident, remember to turn toward yourself and inquire what faculty you have for its use. If you encounter [...] pain, then fortitude; if reviling, then patience. And when thus habituated, the phenomena of existence will not overwhelm you" (para. 10). Since we can inoculate ourselves from diseases of the body, the Stoics argue, we can inoculate ourselves from diseases of the mind through habituating ourselves to calm.

7.7.4 Fortitude

Fortitude, the final self-regarding virtue, is the ability to resist suffering and pain, something that Epictetus knew all too well. One of his masters tortured him for an error made by another enslaved person. His leg was bound to a rack and twisted until it snapped. Epictetus, however, refused to think of pain or disease as an impediment to his choice to live in a state of emotional tranquility. "Sickness," he wrote, "is an impediment to the body, but not to the will unless itself pleases. Lameness is an impediment to the leg, but not to the will; and say this to yourself with regard to everything that happens. For you will find it to be an impediment to something else, but not truly to yourself" (para. 9). When you are sick, Epictetus reminds you that you still have the ability to make choices about your own mental attitude, even though you are unable to control the biological fact of disease.

7.7.5 Generosity of Spirit

The previous virtues are self-regarding virtues, but the Stoics also advocated the development of an important other-regarding virtue, which can be called generosity of spirit. Pandemics stress us out, and many people we may encounter in public life can be infuriating: the joggers who spit and cough as they pass you in the park, the shoppers at the supermarket who touch every fruit and vegetable before choosing the first one they touched, the bus riders who refuse to wear masks when they know they are gravely ill, the billionaires who complain about having to isolate on their superyachts, the police officer who wields his authority like a monster, the people who glare at you with suspicion behind every mask, the doctors and nurses who don't take your concerns seriously, the colleagues at work who snap at you, the boss who doesn't appreciate your efforts, and the busy-body neighbor who reports you to the police for meeting up with friends. Faced with this constant barrage of frustration, it is easy to lose our self-control. When we lose our self-control, we neglect the virtue of generosity of spirit, with all that it entails—practicing the virtues of kindness, patience, and forgiveness.

Marcus Aurelius also had to deal with these common frustrations that are all too familiar to all of us. As the Roman Emperor, he could have dealt with annoying people by simply executing them, but he did not do so. Instead, he maintained his calm through practicing an extreme morning routine. The first thing he did every morning was to remind himself that he would meet lots of annoying people. He writes in his *Meditations* (c. 170 CE), a journal that was meant to guide his own attitude through his difficult days running the empire and waging war, "In the morning say to thyself, This day I shalt have to do with an idle curious man, with an unthankful man, a railer, a crafty, false, or an envious man; an unsociable, uncharitable man" (I, para. 15). By preparing himself every morning for the likely stresses of life, he was able to cultivate his Stoic resilience. He would suggest to all of us living today that if we begin the morning expecting everything to be great, we will probably end up being disappointed and lose our self-control.

So how did Marcus Aurelius deal with his daily parade of nasty people? This is the remainder of his morning memo:

> All these ill qualities have happened unto them, through ignorance of that which is truly good and truly bad. But I that understand the nature of that which is good, that it only is to be desired, and of that which is bad, that it only is truly odious and shameful: who know moreover, that this transgressor, whosoever he be, is my kinsman, not by the same blood and seed, but by participation of the same reason, and of the same divine particle; How can I either be hurt by any of those, since it is not in their power to make me incur anything that is truly reproachful? or angry, and ill affected towards him, who by nature is so near unto me? For we are all born to be fellow-workers, as the feet, the hands, and the eyelids; as the rows of the upper and under teeth: for such therefore to be in opposition, is against nature; and what is it to chafe at, and to be averse from, but to be in opposition? (I, para. 15)

Marcus Aurelius reminded himself every morning that he had to maintain his generosity of spirit even in the worst of times, because to be vexed by others is to be vexed by oneself, to be angry with others is to be angry with oneself, to be frustrated by others is to be frustrated by oneself. The Stoics argue that we all have it in our power to control our attitudes and our emotions. By being generous with the flaws of others, we might be able to be more generous to ourselves.

Like Marcus Aurelius, Epictetus reminds us in the *Enchiridion* that we should always prepare ourselves in advance for likely aggravations when interacting with the public, and he adds the same advice. We should focus on mastering our emotions, which he calls staying in a mental state that is in harmony with the nature of the activity:

> When you set about any action, remind yourself of what nature the action is. If you are going to bathe, represent to yourself the incidents usual in the bath—some persons pouring out, others pushing in, others scolding, others pilfering. And thus you will more safely go about this action if you say to yourself, "I will now go to bathe and keep my own will in harmony with nature." And so with regard to every other action. For thus, if any impediment arises in bathing, you will be able to say, "It was not only to bathe that I desired, but to keep

my will in harmony with nature; and I shall not keep it thus if I am out of humor at things that happen." (para. 4)

Everyone experiences aggravation caused by others. Epictetus reminds us that we can and should prepare for likely problems—at the grocery store, on the streets, in the parks, or at the swimming pool—so we can maintain our tranquility and self-control. Regarding judging others, he writes:

Everything has two handles: one by which it may be borne, another by which it cannot. If your brother acts unjustly, do not lay hold on the affair by the handle of his injustice, for by that it cannot be borne, but rather by the opposite—that he is your brother, that he was brought up with you; and thus you will lay hold on it as it is to be borne. (para. 43)

Carrying your brothers and sisters by their handles of justice is the same as maintaining your generosity of spirit, which is arguably one of the most valuable virtues to cultivate during a global pandemic. In fact, recent studies show that having a more charitable view of our fellow human beings—trusting each other—might help us all overcome the aggravations of pandemics a little bit better.

Box 7.7.6: Interdisciplinary Perspective #20: Public Health Communications

Developing the Virtue of Trust During Pandemics and Infodemics

Virtue ethics teaches us that every virtue exists as a mean between two extremes. With the virtue of trust, the excessive form is total gullibility (believing everything people in authority say) and the deficient form is complete skepticism (rejecting everything they say). Public reactions to the COVID-19 pandemic fell everywhere on this spectrum. For example, people who are vaccine hesitant accused the vaccinated of being *gullible* and *naïve* fools, pointing out that vaccinated people still got infected. The vaccinated, on the other hand, accused the opposition of being *skeptical* and *cynical* fools who preferred to believe Internet conspiracy theories rather than medical experts. People who refused to mask argued that masks (aka face diapers) did not prevent infection and represented an unreasonable violation of personal freedom that even caused psychological harm to people like students and young children. People who masked argued that the opposition were ignorant, selfish wackos who were willfully spreading the disease. Clearly, what we experienced during the COVID-19 pandemic was a collapse of the virtue of trust—trust in each other and trust in authorities. Rather than arguing that one side is right and the other side is wrong, virtue ethics suggests that a golden mean between these two extremes should be established: a healthy trust balanced by a healthy skepticism.

Scientists have been studying the role that both interpersonal trust and governmental trust play in the pandemic, and their findings are important to reflect upon. In February 2022, *The Lancet* published a large comparative analysis of 177 countries in order to establish a basic understanding of factors

(continued)

that led some countries to have better pandemic health outcomes than others. The study came to a number of interesting conclusions. First, the authors—known as the COVID-19 National Preparedness Collaborators (2022)—show that public health policies do influence the lowering of infection rates. In short, mask mandates and social distancing rules did work; however, other factors that policy makers could not immediately influence also had an important role. For example, smoking rates, air pollution, climate variations, altitude, and body mass all had effects on COVID-19 infection rates (p. 1505).

Another interesting finding—the one that made headlines—was that higher levels of trust in the government and in one's fellow citizens led to fewer COVID-19 infections. The authors, citing Denmark as an example of a high-trust society, note that if all people in all nations had the same level of trust in their government as the Danes, there would have been 12.9 % fewer infections around the world; furthermore, if all people in all nations had the same level of trust in each other as the Danes do, there would have been 40.3% fewer infections around the world (p. 1508). The conclusion a virtue theorist would draw is that trusting others (provided they deserve your trust) can improve your health and reduce pandemic dangers for both yourself and society as whole.

The final critical point made by the authors of the article is a hopeful one. Trust can in fact be increased. Reducing social inequality (both real and perceived) can help to build interpersonal trust. Furthermore, governmental trust can be increased in a number of ways. Most importantly, the authors suggest that public health professionals should take the lead in communicating advice to the population as opposed to politicians, who may cause people to ignore sound public health advice. They note that "trust is a shared resource that enables networks of people to do collectively what individual actors cannot" (p. 1508). A global pandemic is by definition a shared crisis that affects everyone on the planet. Trust is the shared weapon we have to treat the sick, protect the vulnerable, advance the science, manufacture the tests, create the cures, and deliver the treatments to everyone in need.

Unfortunately, trust was in short supply throughout the COVID-19 pandemic. Why was this? In addition to the conventional reasons (corrupt governments, inequality, political divisions, discrimination, etc.), the COVID-19 pandemic was also the first *infodemic*—the first social media plague. An infodemic is characterized by information overload in our modern media environment. Traditional sources of news and public health advice, such as government health experts, major newspapers, and television broadcasters, competed for viewership with practically anyone with a smartphone and a social media profile. For a significant number of people, an official press release from the Centers for Disease Control and Prevention carried no more weight than an Instagram post from a teenage influencer.

(continued)

As a result of the infodemic, scholars have been focusing on the role of public health communications during pandemics. How should the authorities communicate rapidly changing information? What media should they use to disseminate information? How should disinformation be countered? How should they describe the level of risk and the level of uncertainty? Have there been any lessons learned about public health communication strategies due to COVID-19? This important academic discipline is still maturing, but scholars have offered some significant initial insights.

The first important insight is to clearly define the *telos* or ultimate goal of public health communications: *behavioral change*. The goal is not simply to provide information; it is to convince people that they need to change their behaviors voluntarily for the specific purpose of reducing or eliminating the spread of a disease. Furthermore, the behavioral changes need to occur rapidly in the population. Viruses do not wait for bureaucracies to coordinate their messaging before infecting their next victim. Time is of the essence.

Once the overall goal is articulated precisely—rapid, widespread behavioral change—scholars can draw upon a wide array of existing scientific literature in the disciplines of psychology, marketing, information literacy, anthropology, and communication theory in order to achieve more effective outcomes. Fortunately, this work is being done now in order to prepare for future pandemics. For example, scholars released an article in *Frontiers in Public Health* that identifies useful guidelines for sustainable behavior change (Porat et al., 2020). The authors use the case study of mask advice to illustrate the prevalence of confusing messaging about the COVID-19 pandemic. They note that contradictory guidance was given by different public health institutions. Furthermore, the advice changed quite a bit—wear a mask; don't wear a mask; wear it inside but not outside; masks might contribute to a false sense of security making people forget other good hygiene practices; people touch their masks too much causing accidental contagion; some people can't wear masks for medical reasons leading to mask shaming; supplies of good masks are limited, so only medical professionals should wear them; there are unintended mental health consequences of mask wearing; some cheap masks don't work; etc. (Porat et al., 2020, p. 3). Given the abundance of contradictory guidance—and the list above incorporates only expert guidance not the opinions of celebrities, politicians, and social media influencers—it is no wonder that people felt confused about the effectiveness of mask wearing, and if you traveled around the world during the pandemic, you would have seen vast differences in mask-wearing behaviors. To put it another way, if the messaging was meant to lead to sustainable behavior change, it did not occur. If public health guidance as simple as mask-wearing leads to confusion, it is no wonder that masks became a political hot potato. Was the science on masks bad? Was the public simply mistrustful? Or was the messaging poor? Well, it was probably a combination of all of the above.

(continued)

Let's focus now on positive lessons learned about public health communications as a result of COVID-19. First, psychological studies have shown that autonomous motivation is more effective at leading to behavioral change than external regulation (Porat et al., p. 6). With external regulation, people change their behavior in order to avoid punishment. We saw in Chap. 3 that some countries like China resorted to public shaming and other punishments in order to motivate people to change their behaviors. However, psychologists note that external regulation has a number of unintended consequences; it causes mental health issues, and the desired changes in behavior do not last. More effective is autonomous motivation, in which "one supports or identifies with the virtue or importance of a behavior" (Porat et al., p. 6). For example, if people learn to associate mask wearing with the virtues of social responsibility, solidarity, trust, and concern for others, they are much more likely to adopt mask wearing in the long-term, despite the fact that the behavior change comes with some discomfort. Critically, the change cannot be forced upon people by the authorities (external regulation), as this would be counterproductive in the long term. Therefore, messaging by public health authorities should stress autonomy and avoid the language of punishment, shame, and guilt.

Another important insight about creating long-lasting behavioral change echoes Rousseau's social theory concept from Chap. 5: "Man must be forced to be free." This paradox highlights the fact that we can actually be more free within the constraints of a social contract than we are if we live in the wild and uncivilized state of nature where we are constantly fearful for our lives even though we have all of the natural liberties of wild animals. This concept helps with behavior change as well. Indeed, studies show that people are more likely to follow pandemic restrictions if they are given options within those restrictions (Porat et al., p. 6). Tools like COVID-Risk Calculators are helpful for people to identify their options for seeing friends and socializing during a pandemic.[2] Public health messaging should, therefore, focus on the free choices one has within the restrictions rather than the restrictions themselves.

Lastly, public health messaging that focuses on the creation of a feeling of solidarity—in other words, interpersonal and governmental trust—is extremely helpful in leading to pandemic behavioral change (Porat et al., p. 9). The idea that "everyone is in this together" can be a powerful tool in motivating people to change their behavior. Language that encourages division, on the other hand, leads to behavior that undermines pandemic mitigation efforts. The feelings of solidarity, once developed, are so powerful that violations of pandemic restrictions by political leaders have profound repercussions. For example, Boris Johnson, the Prime Minister of Great Britain, was forced to resign at least partly due the Partygate scandal, which was caused by revelations of alcohol-fueled parties at his residence, while the rest of the country was suffering alone in lockdown (Allegretti, 2022). So, a final

(continued)

recommendation for public health messaging during a pandemic is to focus on developing feelings of social trust and solidarity.

Aristotle claimed that a happy society should cultivate virtues in its citizens who, in turn, reinforce the happiness of society as a whole. By definition, virtuous citizens are trustworthy and deserving of our trust. Perhaps the best way to mitigate the threat of future pandemics, then, is to invest more resources in creating a virtuous citizenry. Such a society would be filled with virtuous political leaders, policy makers, and public health professionals, people who see the good of society as fundamentally connected with their own virtuous habits of character. It would also be filled with a virtuous public, willing to trust the guidance of experts.

However, since all virtues exist as a mean, a virtuous citizenry should also engage in healthy skepticism by demanding the highest levels of transparency, honesty, and professionalism from the health authorities who are granted power over citizens' personal freedoms. Perhaps, this seems like a utopian vision that will be impossible to achieve. However, as was noted in Chap. 2 of this book, the universe is rich enough to provide us with data to support whatever we want to see. If we choose to see alienation, division, and despair, there is plenty of evidence to support that conclusion. However, if we choose to see virtue, reconciliation, and hope, we might be able to imagine a better future and then create it.

Discuss
- **Evaluate your own levels of interpersonal and governmental trust. How do you react to official public health advice about any number of diseases, from the flu to STDs? Are you skeptical? Have you been gullible? Are you trustful?**
- **Has your attitude towards your fellow citizens changed because of the pandemic? How will you react to public health advice during future pandemics?**
- **From a public health perspective, what communication strategies would you use in order to increase social trust during the next global pandemic? What communications groundwork should be laid in the public health space right now to enhance the social trust that will be needed to combat the next global pandemic?**

7.8 Conclusion

In this chapter, we have seen both that virtue ethics with its focus on moral motivation provides an important corrective to theories of right action and also that virtue ethics prizes the happiness of individuals. We have just seen in the preceding section about Stoicism that one important method of achieving happiness is to relinquish the desire to control things that are not in our control. The desire to control everything might explain why theories of right action come to contradictory conclusions when assessing the same dilemma (e.g., Jenner's choice). Virtue ethics demands a more nuanced consideration of any ethical dilemma. It refuses to provide clear answers—and this lack of certainty, this avoidance of closure, this refusal to solve dilemmas through the application of rigid principles is simultaneously both the greatest strength and the greatest weakness of virtue ethics.

In some respects, the theories of right action are control-based systems of reason and logical rigidity. These theories attempt to create single principles of reason that can crush the complexity out of our lived experiences, which are emotional experiences as well as intellectual experiences. For example, Kant wanted to control the complexity of life with his grand categorical imperative; the utilitarians wanted to control the fate of the world through creating a mathematical formula that would calculate the greatest happiness for all; and the social contract theorists wanted to control the development of governments through the creation of laws that control human behavior while securing the benefits of civilization. Egoists allow for a bit more nuance in determining one's own life goals, although Ayn Rand still insisted that the hammer of "rational self-interest" should be used to pound out the correct path in one's life.

The approach of rational domination in ethics has its corollaries in our anthropocentric attitude toward the environment as well as our techno-medical approach to the eradication of microbes. We wish to manage toxic run-off not by eliminating it, but by enclosing it, treating it, or purifying it with a new form of technology with its own problematic side effects. We wish to manage global warming by spreading tin foil in the clouds or launching an atmospheric solar shield. And we wish to eliminate disease through eradicating mosquitoes, developing new treatments, or creating new vaccines. Failing biological domination of a microbe, we resort to technical and (anti)social measures, by locking people in their homes, shutting down public life, and monitoring people's movements. And still the microbes win.

The Stoics would argue that all of these measures—all of these well-meaning approaches intended to secure public health, protect the environment, and enhance the common good—betray our obsession with domination, our compulsion to use reason, science, and data sets to manage a world that stubbornly refuses to be measured, weighed, counted, shaped, and defined, a natural world that refuses to accept that it ought to be *improved* by the one and only species that is fixated on controlling it. The Stoics, of course, tell us that we should stop trying to control the world because the world doesn't make us unhappy, *our desire to control it does.*

As with the technological and scientific reason, right-action ethical reason takes control as its guiding principle. The Stoics might look on the theories in this book as an attempt to control things that are out of our control, a hopeless effort to define human experience in rigid formulations, an impossible desire to regulate and manage human behavior. Maybe we should follow the Stoics advice and forget about control—whether it be through the application of reason, the dictation of moral rules, or the promulgation of laws and regulations—and focus instead on accepting our lack of control. Would this make us happier and more virtuous individuals? Would this help us to reconcile the differences that separate individuals, communities, and nations? Would this also help us reconcile our alienation from the natural world? Relinquishing control is a valid approach to living our lives. And if the Stoics are right, it may be the only free choice we ever really have.

Box 7.9: Criteria for Evaluating Ethical Theories: Part 5
In the previous four chapters, we discussed nine key criteria for evaluating ethical theories. Use this opportunity to evaluate the strengths and weaknesses of virtue ethics according to those criteria before learning about the remaining criteria.

1. Does the theory have an appropriate scope for who belongs in our moral community?
2. Does the theory exhibit an appropriate degree of rational consistency?
3. Does the theory align with "common sense"?
4. Does the theory adequately explain issues about moral distance?
5. Does the theory have an appropriate telos or ultimate goal?
6. Does the theory clearly delineate obligatory actions and supererogatory ones?
7. Can the theory adapt to and account for the emergence of new technologies?
8. Can the theory be easily applied to different situations by providing clear-cut solutions?
9. Does the theory account for conflicts of interest?
10. Does the theory explain the importance of motivation in assessing ethical decisions?

We have seen in other ethical theories that moral motivation is omitted or obscured. Instead, other theories focus on right action. Virtue ethics, however, takes motivation as a central tool in evaluating the ethical decision-making process. Do you think that motivation should be an important element in a strong ethical theory? Or should we really reduce the complicating factors and focus on the action itself? Lastly, is it best to focus on the consequences of an action, because consequences are all that really matter in the real world?

11. Does the theory include personal happiness or personal fulfillment as a central concern?

Some ethical theories diminish the importance of individual happiness and others make it a priority. In Kant's theory, emotional fulfillment is not as important as the requirement to be rational. Feelings of tenderness, care, and love fall by the wayside. The utilitarians make happiness their primary goal, but find it hard to accept that the care of one's own child should be of greater value than the care for the world's starving children. The social contract, with

(continued)

its focus on just communities and equitable power structures, also avoids the concept of personal fulfillment. At best, social contract theorists argue that the ability to attain emotional fulfillment may be one positive result of living in a stable society. Egoists, however, do insist that personal fulfillment is the central goal of the theory. Being self-interested, taking care of the self, is the only foundation on which a healthy society can rest. Virtue ethics also prioritizes personal fulfillment as a central theme.

The central question for you is this: Should an ethical theory elevate your own happiness above other important goals, such as the common good, the happiness of all human and non-human animals, the reduction of suffering, the creation of stable societies, or a clean environment?

12. Does the theory envision the creation of the kind of world you want to live in?

The final evaluation criterion is arguably the most important, based on your assumptions about human nature. For example, if you believe that we are fallen creatures, maybe you have no sense of hope in ethical progress, in which case you might not think that we have the power to shape a better community. However, if you think that we can overcome our differences and achieve something better, then an ethical theory should provide a clear vision of that world or, at the very least, a clear path to a better one.

Kant envisions perhaps an impossible world of pure reason, full of logical creatures who do no wrong. This might be a cold, yet peaceful place. Utilitarianism envisions a happier world for all creatures, but sometimes that happiness can be achieved through sacrificing others on the altar of the greater good. Still, the outcome would be net happiness. The social contract envisions a world of conflict that can be mediated through laws that regulate our behavior. Egoists insist that in a world where people follow their own self-interest, each individual can achieve his or her own personal happiness. Virtue ethics offers a path to happiness and fulfillment that attempts to preserve individual choice, which thereby enhances the common good. But which of these theories actually produces the type of community in which you would want to live?

References

Allegretti, A. (2022, April 14). Fresh calls for Boris Johnson to resign over Partygate fines. *The Guardian*. https://www.theguardian.com/politics/2022/apr/14/boris-johnson-refuses-to-say-whether-he-will-resign-over-covid-fines. Accessed 12 Sept 2022.
Alon, T., et al. (2020). *The impact of COVID-19 on gender equality* (NBER working paper series). National Bureau for Economic Research. https://www.nber.org/system/files/working_papers/w26947/w26947.pdf. Accessed 5 Feb 2023.
Aristotle. (350 BCE). *Nicomachean ethics*. Trans. W. D. Ross. The Internet Classics Archive. 2009. http://classics.mit.edu/Aristotle/nicomachaen.html

COVID-19 National Preparedness Collaborators. (2022). Pandemic preparedness and COVID-19: An exploratory analysis of infection and fatality rates, and contextual factors associated with preparedness in 177 countries, from Jan 1, 2020, to Sept 30, 2021. *The Lancet, 399*, 1489–1512. https://doi.org/10.1016/S0140-6736(22)00172-6

Cullen, P., & Murphy, M. (2020). Responses to the COVID-19 crisis in Ireland: From feminized to feminist. *Gender, Work and Organization: Feminist Frontiers Supplement., 28*(52), 348–365. https://doi.org/10.1111/gwao.12596

Davies, C. (2010, November 12). Mother loses appeal against conviction for mercy killing of brain-damaged son. *The Guardian.* http://www.theguardian.com/uk/2010/nov/12/frances-inglis-mercy-killing-appeal. Accessed 6 Sept 2022.

Epictetus. (c. 135). *Enchiridion.* Trans. T. W. Higginson. Project Gutenberg. 2014. https://www.gutenberg.org/files/45109/45109-h/45109-h.htm

Estivariz, C. F., Link-Gelles, R., & Shimabukuro, T. (2021, August 18). Poliomyelitis. *CDC.gov.* https://www.cdc.gov/vaccines/pubs/pinkbook/polio.html. Accessed 6 Sept 2022.

Fadulu, L. (2022, September 9). Hochul Declares Polio State of Emergency for New York. *New York Times.* https://www.nytimes.com/2022/09/09/nyregion/new-york-polio-state-of-emergency.html. Accessed 12 Sept 2022.

Feder, S., et al. (2021). "Why couldn't i go in to see him?" Bereaved families' perceptions of end-of-life communication during COVID-19. *Journal of the American Geriatric Society, 69*(3), 587–592. https://doi.org/10.1111/jgs.16993

Fink, S. (2020, March 28). U.S. Civil Rights Office rejects rationing medical care based on disability, age. *New York Times.* https://www.nytimes.com/2020/03/28/us/coronavirus-disabilities-rationing-ventilators-triage.html. Accessed 13 Sept 2022.

Fitzpatrick, M. (2006). The cutter incident: How America's first polio vaccine led to a growing vaccine crisis. *Journal of the Royal Society of Medicine, 99*(3), 156. https://www.ncbi.nlm.nih.gov/pmc/articles/PMC1383764/

Gilligan, C. (1982). *In a different voice: Psychological theory and women's development.* Harvard University Press.

Gilson, E. (2021). What isn't new in the new normal: A feminist ethical perspective on COVID-19. *Les ateliers de l'éthique/The Ethics Forum, 16*(1), 88–102. https://doi.org/10.7202/1083647ar

HHS. (2022, May 2). *Mental health and coping during the Coronavirus (COVID-19) Pandemic.* https://www.hhs.gov/coronavirus/mental-health-and-coping/index.html. Accessed 12 Sept 2022.

Hursthouse, R., & Pettigrove, G. (2018). Virtue ethics. In E. N. Zalta (Ed.), *The Stanford encyclopedia of philosophy* (Winter 2018 Ed.). https://plato.stanford.edu/archives/win2018/entries/ethics-virtue/. Accessed 6 Sept 2022.

Jöbges, S., et al. (2020). Recommendations on COVID-19 triage: International comparison and ethical analysis. *Bioethics, 34*(9), 948–959. https://doi.org/10.1111/bioe.12805

Marcus Aurelius. (c. 170 CE). *Meditations.* Trans. M. Casaubon. Project Gutenberg. 2021. https://www.gutenberg.org/files/2680/2680-h/2680-h.htm

McRobbie, L. R. (2020, May 26). The man in the iron lung. *The Guardian.* https://www.theguardian.com/society/2020/may/26/last-iron-lung-paul-alexander-polio-coronavirus. Accessed 6 Sept 2022.

Mill, J. S. (1863). *Utilitarianism.* Project Gutenberg. 2004. https://www.gutenberg.org/cache/epub/11224/pg11224-images.html

Norlock, K. (2019). Feminist ethics. In E. N. Zalta (Ed.), *The Stanford encyclopedia of philosophy* (Summer 2019 Ed.). https://plato.stanford.edu/archives/sum2019/entries/feminism-ethics/. Accessed 5 Feb 2023.

Pidd, H. (2010, October 20). Mother who killed brain damaged son challenges conviction. *The Guardian.* http://www.theguardian.com/uk/2010/oct/20/frances-inglis-mercy-killing-appeal. Accessed 5 Sept 2022.

Porat, T., et al. (2020). Public health and risk communication during COVID-19—Enhancing needs to promote sustainable behavior change. *Frontiers in Public Health, 8*, 1–15. https://doi.org/10.3389/fpubh.2020.573397

Reardon, S. (2022, August 19). First U.S. Polio case in nearly a decade highlights the importance of vaccination. *Scientific American.* https://www.scientificamerican.com/article/first-u-s-polio-case-in-nearly-a-decade-highlights-the-importance-of-vaccination/. Accessed 27 Sept 2022.

Snowden, F. M. (2019). *Epidemics and society: From the black death to the present.* Yale UP.

Sola, A. (2009). The enlightened grunt? Invincible ignorance in the just war tradition. *Journal of Military Ethics, 8*(1), 48–65. https://doi.org/10.1080/15027570902782068

Voina, A., & Stoica, M. (2023). Reframing leadership: Jacinda Ardern's response to the Covid-19 pandemic, *11*(1). https://doi.org/10.17645/mac.v11i1.6045

Walker, J. S. (2005). Recent literature on Truman's atomic bomb decision: A search for middle ground. *Diplomatic History, 29*(2), 311–334. https://doi.org/10.1111/j.1467-7709.2005.00476.x

WHO. (2022, August). Polio today. *Polioreadication.org.* http://polioeradication.org/polio-today/polio-now/this-week/. Accessed 7 Sept 2022.

Chapter 8
Toward a Pragmatic Ethics in an Age of Pandemics, Environmental Crisis, and Social Disorder

8.1 Where Did We Come from and Where Are We Going?

Having taught ethics courses for over 20 years, I have learned that my students usually progress through five emotional phases throughout a typical semester. At the start of term, they often exhibit a mixture of enthusiasm and anxiety. They are enthusiastic because they are eager to explore ethics, and they are excited about having a forum to discuss their beliefs about the world and their place within it. The anxiety usually comes from fear about their grades, but also some are nervous about the intensity of the course and the difficulty of the reading. This first phase holds through the chapter on Immanuel Kant, since his theory provides a clear, albeit nuanced, assessment of ethics that is familiar, since most students already possess a fundamental knowledge of universal human rights and believe in the dignity of human beings.

The second phase begins during the chapter on utilitarianism and is characterized by conflict and debate both inside and outside the classroom. Since Kant's deontology and utilitarian consequentialism are directly opposed and, for the most part, wholly incompatible, battle lines can be easily drawn. Advocates of deontology hold to the view that dignity of human beings should never be violated, but advocates of utilitarianism, citing specific examples, hold that sometimes the greater good is worth the sacrifice of individuals. Furthermore, utilitarianism explicitly introduces the government's role in creating initiatives that increase happiness and decrease happiness, sometimes at the expense of individual human rights.

The third phase of the course begins with conflict engendered by the previous dispute and often ends in exasperation caused by the sheer scale and complexity of social contract theory. The deontology-consequentialism dispute pits the absolutists against those willing to grant exceptions to moral rules because life often presents complex problems that blind rule-following does not solve. Since establishing a clear set of rules for personal ethics seems to leave us in a dead end, one way out is

A. Sola, *Ethics and Pandemics*, Springer Series in Public Health and Health Policy Ethics, https://doi.org/10.1007/978-3-031-33207-4_8

to reject personal ethics entirely and focus on the establishment of societies with rules that set a *minimum* standard for appropriate behavior, in other words, the laws of the land. However, social contract theory proves to be exasperating because of its wide scope, as well as its admirable but impossible goal to harmonize all of the individual self-interests of everyone living in a society. Wandering through weighty themes like freedom, obedience, power, the ends of power, justice, equality, property, reason, self-interest, consent, and rebellion, it tries to establish certainty, but ends with the most frustrating of paradoxical questions: Should humans be forced to be free?

The frustration caused by the social contract theory finds its release for many students in the fourth phase, when egoism provides them with the opportunity to say, "Ethics is too complex. I'm doing whatever I want anyway." Indeed, the various forms of egoism provide simple solutions to the intellectual knots we have tied ourselves up in. The hedonist philosophy gives us permission to pursue enjoyment as much as we can before our candle burns out. The more refined forms of egoism tell us to embrace our selfish self-interest and pursue it rigorously because living the fullest life possible is our greatest moral responsibility to ourselves. Some people prefer to stay in this phase, and who can blame them?

However, others find egoism to be unsatisfying because they still have a feeling deep inside that ethics should challenge us to become our *better* selves—not our self-interested selves, which is easy to do because care-for-self is usually our default mode of living. And so we arrive at the fifth phase, which should hopefully come with the feelings of hope and personal agency that virtue ethics provides. Indeed, virtue ethics provides three important solutions to the problems we encountered previously. First, it avoids the strict rules and formulas imposed by Kant's deontology and utilitarian consequentialism. We can avoid the question of right or wrong action by looking at people's motivations. Second, it reframes the question raised by social contract theory—how do we create a good society?—with a different question: How do we create virtuous individuals, people who want to become their better selves? After all, if a society is full of virtuous people, then we have a much better chance of living in a good society, full of patient, charitable, tolerant, and kind people who are devoted to justice. Third, it completes egoism, which considers self-interest to be the only important rule to follow. Virtue ethics agrees that achieving happiness and becoming fulfilled is a perfectly acceptable goal, but it reminds us that there are other important aspects of fulfillment. Indeed, the virtues come in two forms: self-regarding and other-regarding. We should be proud about having successful careers, acquiring luxuries, going on holidays, and developing new skills. However, we should also be proud of being kind to others, tolerant of others, charitable to others, and faithful to others—in other words, we should try to imagine our better selves and become them.

And now we come to the final phase—leaving the classroom and living the rest of our lives. How should we live them? Maybe no one can answer that question. If anything, the history of philosophy teaches us that answers are hard to come by, and perhaps this book has not helped clarify ethics at all and simply confused issues even further. However, I think we can begin to answer the question by combining four distinctly human processes: an emotional process, an imaginative process, an intellectual process, and a lived process.

8.2   The Emotional Process: Pragmatism, Doubt, and Belief

As we look at the history of philosophy, we see that each philosophical school claims to offer ideas that will lead to better, happier, more enriched lives: "Follow the laws of reason," says one. "Seek sensual pleasure," says another. "No, cultivate the virtues," says yet another. The proliferation of options leads to confusion. Perhaps the only conclusions to be drawn from the variety of choices in philosophy are three purely descriptive, fact-based assertions:

- Different philosophies tell us there are different ways to achieve happiness.
- Different philosophies have differing views of right and wrong, good, and evil.
- Different philosophies conceive of good societies in different ways.

Are these three statements the demoralizing terminus of philosophical analysis? Can we only make factual statements about the existence of a variety of viewpoints? Do we conclude that philosophy only provides options, but no concrete conclusions—only different concepts of Right, Wrong, Reason, and Truth, but no definitive and universal agreement on what these concepts really mean?

Faced with the reality of this hodgepodge of contradictory worldviews, a distinctly American version of philosophy was formed in the nineteenth century called pragmatism. Forged in the crucible of three powerful emotions—namely, doubt, belief, and hope (since we have free will)—the founders of pragmatic philosophy were two close friends, Charles Sanders Peirce (1839–1914) and William James (1842–1910). Peirce, who is considered by some to be one of the greatest American thinkers, was born into a well-to-do and scholarly family; his father was a Harvard professor. However, like many philosophers, Charles was eccentric, and he struggled to establish a career and find steady work. His wife left him, and he was fired from the only academic position he ever had at Johns Hopkins University. He never became famous while living and died in poverty. The most positive part of his life was his close friendship with William James, the brother of the novelist Henry. Like the Peirce family, the James family was wealthy, cosmopolitan, and studious. William was raised in Switzerland, England, and France, before he returned to the United States to earn his medical degree at Harvard, where he remained as a professor of philosophy and psychology. But his life was not wholly an unalloyed success story. Like John Stuart Mill, who suffered a mental breakdown because his father wanted him to become an emotionless, utilitarian calculating machine (see Chap. 4), James also suffered a severe depressive episode while at Harvard. Mill recovered through the influence of his caring partner, Harriet Taylor, who taught him how to balance the cold of abstract reason with the warmth of human emotion. James dragged himself out of his depression, he claims, through the power of his will. He recognized that he had free will, and with that gift comes the ability to shape his mental attitude. (This is an idea that echoes Stoicism as we saw in Chap. 7.) Our free will can either make us happy or sad; mastering our free will can also give us hope, and this is one pillar of pragmatism.

The second pillar is that ideas (or philosophical theories, ideologies, beliefs, or worldviews) only matter insofar as they make a difference in our real lives. James (1907) states in his lecture "What Pragmatism Means," "The whole function of philosophy ought to be to find out what difference it will make to you and me, at definite instants of our life, if this [idea] or that [idea] be the true one" (para. 9). If ideas do really make a significant difference in our lives, then they have value; if they make no impact, then they do not matter. Ideas must pay out; if not, they are bankrupt and should be discarded.

This pragmatic claim is quite remarkable, and it helps us to evaluate further the smorgasbord of ethical theories presented in this book. Does following Kant's system make a difference in your life? What about Bentham's or Mill's? Or how about the ideas of Hobbes, Locke, or Rousseau? Do Ayn Rand and Aristotle have ideas that pay out? If ideas make no difference, then a pragmatist would urge us to ignore them and find, instead, ideas that do make a difference.

In order to find ideas that make a difference, one must first have a desire to find them. Pragmatists argue that there is no emotional drive to inquire about the various options if we do not have the urge to inquire. Indeed, contented individuals who are comfortable in their beliefs have no reason to tear down their whole worldview and construct a new one. For the most part, believing what we already believe is the most comfortable way to live one's life. However, life does not lead to endless periods of calm, comfort, and unchallenged belief. Life throws up obstacles, some great and some small. When faced with new experiences that undermine our worldview, we begin to doubt, and understanding the psychology of doubt and belief is the third main pillar of pragmatic thinking.

Charles Sanders Peirce argued that human beings alter between two modes of being, belief and doubt. The mode of belief is pleasant and comfortable. Emotionally speaking, it is a safe place to be. Doubt, on the other hand, is uncomfortable and insecure. It disorients us and makes us yearn for the comfort of belief. When faced with doubt, we are forced to identify new ideas that make us safe in belief again— new ideas that pay, new ideas that make a difference. Crucially, Peirce does not argue that the new beliefs have to be true. Truth as such is merely "a belief that we think shall be true." He describes the doubt-belief relationship in his essay "The Fixation of Belief" (1877), which is quoted at length to illustrate the complex phases of the process:

> The irritation of doubt causes a struggle to attain a state of belief. I shall term this struggle inquiry, though it must be admitted that this is sometimes not a very apt designation. The irritation of doubt is the only immediate motive for the struggle to attain belief. It is certainly best for us that our beliefs should be such as may truly guide our actions so as to satisfy our desires; and this reflection will make us reject any belief which does not seem to have been so formed as to insure this result. But it will only do so by creating a doubt in the place of that belief. With the doubt, therefore, the struggle begins, and with the cessation of doubt it ends. Hence, the sole object of inquiry is the settlement of opinion. We may fancy that this is not enough for us, and that we seek, not merely an opinion, but a true opinion.

But put this fancy to the test, and it proves groundless; for as soon as a firm belief is reached we are entirely satisfied, whether the belief be true or false. And it is clear that nothing out of the sphere of our knowledge can be our object, for nothing which does not affect the mind can be the motive for mental effort. The most that can be maintained is, that we seek for a belief that we shall think to be true. But we think each one of our beliefs to be true, and, indeed, it is mere tautology to say so. (p. 6)

The pragmatic concept of belief, then, has no relationship to Truth. Indeed, the pragmatists were careful not to advocate any absolute concepts like Truth, the Good, or Reason since those concepts are merely another variety of belief that must be tested in the pragmatic way—through testing their usefulness in the real world.

This pragmatic theory of belief neatly explains the tribalism that pervades contemporary politics as well as the psychological forces that social media uses to reinforce our comforting beliefs. For the vast majority of people, belonging to a tribe is comforting. Teenagers might be goths, skaters, punks, hippies, mods, or jocks. It makes them feel more secure. As we develop through life, we still join tribes. Adults just call these tribes political parties, charitable associations, churches, or professional associations, but these institutions provide the same feelings of security and belonging. Belief, in short, is a powerful phenomenon, and it is very difficult to convince people to move to a state of doubt because doubt is uncomfortable. In the pragmatists' view, belief is even stronger than science, logic, and reason. No amount of effective argumentation will change a person's mind if he or she feels safe in a belief. (Just try having a patient discussion with extremists—racists, terrorists, homophobes, or members of a cult—about their beliefs.) However, it is not only extremists who are tenacious about their beliefs; so-called mainstream, middle-of-the-road moderates are also subject to the same forces. It is, therefore, no surprise that politicians rarely change parties, that voters rarely become non-voters or vice versa, that bankers rarely give up their careers to become mendicant friars, that professional soldiers rarely become conscientious objectors, that people rarely convert to other religions, and that citizens of one nation rarely renounce their citizenship and join another nation's social contract. These life changes do happen, but they are few and far between. The pragmatists tell us why: Doubt is uncomfortable and belief is comfortable.

Although the pragmatists created their theory of doubt and belief in the nineteenth and twentieth centuries, social scientists have confirmed the general outlines of this pragmatic thesis through studies that show that human beings are particularly susceptible to cognitive bias (Kahneman, 2011). Cognitive bias takes many forms, but it basically means that we are habituated to overlook or minimize pieces of evidence that contradict our worldview. Let's just examine one obvious example of bias: confirmation bias in social media. Social media companies use cognitive bias—maybe nefariously, maybe not—to generate engagement and clicks (thereby increasing advertising revenue) by recommending links to products, ads, news stories, or groups that share a user's worldview (Modgil et al., 2021). One way of achieving this is through working on people's confirmation bias, the tendency to be attracted to ideas that confirm our preconceptions (or beliefs, as pragmatists would argue). Hence, if you have been identified by an algorithm as a young

African-American who likes Killer Mike and NWA, you might be sent ads that support the political campaigns of a progressive Democrat. On the other hand, if you are identified as a white construction worker who likes country music and guns, you might be sent ads that support a conservative Republican. Alternatively, if you have a tendency to read postings about conspiracy theories, you will be given recommendations to follow groups that advocate similar conspiracies. The overall effect is that your preconceptions are reinforced through thousands and thousands of digital interactions. Suddenly, your entire worldview congeals into a comfortable state of belief. Pragmatists argue that when beliefs are fixed so thoroughly, it is nearly impossible to change them.

Occasionally, however, the world throws a spanner in the works. Sometimes something happens to shake those beliefs, and doubt begins to creep into our minds. These events can be world-historical, such as the end of the Cold War, the 9/11 attacks, the COVID-19 pandemic, or the Russian invasion of Ukraine, or they can be deeply personal, such as the death of a loved one, divorce, a natural disaster, or the loss of one's job. These events shake our belief system and lead to doubt. Pragmatists argue that doubt is unpleasant, so we are compelled to return to a comfortable state of belief. When we truly experience doubt, we feel it first in our hearts and then our reasoning is reactivated. At this point we enter into a state of *inquiry*.

If the COVID-19 pandemic or another crisis made you feel *uncomfortable*, then a pragmatist would argue that your beliefs about the world were no longer adequate—they no longer paid out. Indeed, the pandemic made people uncomfortable about a huge number of previously held beliefs. For example, they may have begun to doubt the advice of medical experts. They may have begun to doubt the resilience of the global supply chain. They may have begun to doubt the safety of the air on cruise ships, in airplanes, or on public transportation. They may have begun to doubt the goodness of their fellow human beings. They may have begun to doubt the honesty, transparency, and competence of politicians, the news media, or their teachers.

These uncomfortable feelings can be useful because they provide an emotional impulse to *inquire* further. Here we have some options. We could turn back to the marketplace of ideas. We could read some more philosophy and find another theory that pays. We could change political parties or careers. We could find new friends. All of these methods of inquiry help us to return to the state of belief. Pragmatists suggest that *we should choose a difference that makes a difference in our real lives*.

However, a pragmatist would also argue that if everything is going well for us, then there is no reason to turn to other ideas to change that happy and comfortable scenario. As Peirce (1868) states, "Let us not pretend to doubt in philosophy what we do not pretend to doubt in our hearts" (p. 140). In other words, let us not reject the emotional aspect of our lives. If you feel good, then pragmatists suggest that you have the permission to continue to feel good believing whatever it is you believe. However, if you feel uncomfortable—because sea levels are rising, because poverty is increasing, because people are losing their livelihoods, because people of color are still subject to racism and abuse, because women still suffer discrimination, because nuclear weapons still exist, because conflicts still rage in much of the world, because senior citizens receive substandard care in nursing homes, because people are dying of COVID-19 and other preventable diseases, and because, in your heart, you cannot ignore any of these facts—well, maybe then it is time to inquire further. And so we can turn Peirce's formula on its head and also proclaim, "Let us not pretend to believe in philosophy what we do not pretend to believe in our hearts."

8.3 The Imaginative Process: Pragmatic Imagination and Hope

Pragmatism is an approach that forces us to acknowledge the powerful emotions of belief and doubt. It also forces us to engage in the world. We exist in a world with lots of good things and lots of bad things happening. Most of the time, the comfort of belief prevents us from inquiring further. However, sometimes bad things happen, and we experience doubt in our hearts, which leads to doubt in our minds. This, in turn, leads us to the activity of inquiry. But what is the goal of inquiry? Is it to find a pre-existing theory in the marketplace of ideas that fits with our current emotional state? Is it to create a new theory that explains the Truth about the world in a better way? The famous twentieth-century pragmatic philosopher Richard Rorty (1931–2007) had a simple answer. The *only* reason why we should inquire, compare, justify, analyze, evaluate, and assess the different options in the marketplace of ideas is "to contrast a possible future with the actual present" (1999, p. 39). In order to perform the contrast, one needs to imagine a possible future. For Rorty, imagination provides us with the tool we need to envision a future. And we are naturally inclined to imagine a better future because imagining a worse future seems to be, frankly, counterproductive.

We have seen in the previous section that in pragmatism only ideas that make a difference matter. Those ideas matter by leading to change in the actual world in which we live. We can use the pragmatists to evaluate all sorts of ideas, from the silly to the serious. Let's take the flat-earth conspiracy theory—which is admittedly very imaginative, but not pragmatic—as an example. How would pragmatists assess the theory? First, they would not try to establish if the theory were true or false. Pragmatists do not really concern themselves with absolute concepts like Truth. Instead, they would try to see if the theory is useful. Does it help us do things in the world in a better way? For example, can we travel more easily if we believe that the earth is flat? Does it help us communicate with satellites better? What is the use of the theory? Pragmatists argue if a theory is not *useful*, it will perish on its own, without the need for scientists, philosophers, or politicians to prove that it is false. Indeed, Rorty was opposed to most forms of truth-seeking and wished to avoid debate about the tactics people use to justify their beliefs. (Again, pragmatists understand how difficult it is to persuade people to change their ideas once they have become attached to their comfortable beliefs.) Rorty (1999) writes, "The purpose of inquiry is to achieve agreement among human beings about what to do, to bring about consensus on the ends to be achieved and the means to be used to achieve those ends. Inquiry that does not achieve coordination of behavior is not inquiry but simply word play" (p. xxv). Therefore, if the earth were indeed flat, then there would not need to be websites and activist groups devoted to justifying it. Instead, *flat-earthism* would be a belief that pays, a belief that makes a difference, a belief that requires no special justification or proof. Logistics firms, airlines, aerospace companies, astronomers, physicists, and engineers would operate according to that belief without any need for special justification because the belief pays off. So, one of the best ways to think about conspiracy theories, in general, is that they are simply word play because they do not lead to coordination of behavior to achieve specific ends in the world. Other theories, however, do lead to coordination of behavior and do seek to change the world. These are ideas that truly make a difference.

While disputes about facts like the shape of the earth tend to be easy to resolve, there are other disputes that are not so easy to resolve. For example, some people believe that women should not drive cars or leave the house without a male relative; others believe that one race is superior to another; still others believe that eating animals is immoral. Are disputes about morality the same as disputes about scientific facts? After all, if, as pragmatists suggest, all beliefs should only be evaluated by their usefulness, then sexism, racism, and speciesism exist because they are *useful* in the real world in much the same way that the belief in earth's roundness exists because it is useful. Like round-earthism, sexism, racism, and speciesism coordinate behavior and seek to achieve specific ends in the real world, presumably the maintenance of male, white, or human privilege. This seems like a troubling and evil conclusion to draw from pragmatism.

How do pragmatists respond to this criticism? Despite the potentially immoral consequences of this position, pragmatists insist that moral beliefs and scientific beliefs are the same. Rorty (1999) maintains, "To say that [moral] values are more subjective than facts is just to say that it is harder to get agreement about which things are ugly or which actions evil than about which things are rectangular" (p. 51). This statement is perfectly in keeping with the pragmatic belief that the only ideas that matter are ones that make a difference. However, we may still be left with the uncomfortable feeling that such an approach to ethics leaves ample room for justifying evil, because evil ideas might still pay off in the real world. And we have plenty of evidence of the persistence of useful ideas that are evil as can be seen in the prevalence of sexism, racism, and speciesism in the world today.

However, pragmatists disagree with the charge that their philosophy condones evil. Indeed, pragmatists believe in moral progress through the development of our sensitivity, the free play of our imagination, and the cultivation of hope. Richard Rorty, for one, was an ardent believer in moral progress, the belief that human beings can become their better selves together, and he suggested the one method of doing this was to increase the size of the moral community to include more and more individuals who had been excluded from the moral community by previous generations. Pragmatists, he writes, "think of moral progress as a matter of increasing *sensitivity*, increasing responsiveness to the needs of a larger and larger variety of people and things [...] of taking the needs and interests and views of more diverse human beings into account" (pp. 81–2). *Sensitivity* here stands in for imagination and hope. Being more sensitive to the pain and suffering of other people and things is an imaginative act. The imaginative act is also a hopeful act, because being sensitive about the suffering of another correlates with the mental process of contrasting the actual present of suffering with a possible future in which that suffering is eliminated—this idea echoes utilitarianism. On the other hand, not being sensitive to the suffering of others implies both a lack of imagination as well as the absence of hope.

Imagining a better future for oneself and for others is, according to pragmatists, the right way to live one's life. Let's look at three examples of recent major social problems in order to illustrate the importance of imagination and hope in our response to them: first, the COVID-19 pandemic; second, the climate crisis; and third, the race crisis precipitated by the killing of George Floyd in the United States on 25 May 2020.

If anything, the COVID-19 pandemic exposed the inadequacies of the people and institutions that we rely on for guidance, order, and security in times of crisis. In pragmatic terms, the virus and the global response led many people into a state of uncomfortable doubt. During the pandemic, public health experts were frogmarched into press conferences to answer journalists' questions, but their answers differed from day to day, city to city, and nation to nation. Leaders changed their minds about their priorities. Medical firms announced breakthroughs in treatment that turned out to be fraudulent. Scientists published faulty studies that they were then forced to retract. One day, they said that we could go out to restaurants, but the next day we couldn't, only to be told that it was safe to go out once again.

As the public began to doubt the competence of their leaders, those leaders felt the political pressure to respond with unimaginative initiatives that blamed the Other. These responses were not new in the history of pandemics (see Chap. 5 on the Black Death); indeed, they are as old as our prejudices. Some leaders proclaimed, "We were disease free until foreigners brought it to our lands," as if novel zoonotic respiratory viruses in an age of globalization, international travel, and global supply chains could be stopped at a national border. However, the knee-jerk reaction from many politicians required leaders to shrink the scope of the moral community. They said that we must care for ourselves, reinforce our borders, hoard supplies for ourselves, and be less sensitive to the pain and suffering of others.

Richard Rorty was quite prescient about these types of community-shrinking responses. Writing in 1994, well before the COVID-19 pandemic, he noted, "It is neither irrational nor unintelligent to draw the limits of one's moral community at a national, or racial, or gender border. But it is undesirable—morally undesirable. So it is best to think of moral progress as a matter of increasing *sensitivity*, increasing responsiveness to the needs of a larger and larger variety of people and things" (1999, p. 81). The pragmatic moral response to the COVID-19 pandemic would have been to use it as an opportunity to expand our imagination and our sensitivity to more people and things, not to fewer; to imagine more inclusive responses, not more exclusive ones; to forge more global responses, not more localized ones.

Traditional responses to the environmental crisis also exhibit a lack of sensitivity to the plight of humans, non-human animals, and other organisms that make up the earthly community. Many individuals and interest groups still refuse to contrast a possible (better) future of the planet with the actual present. Despite the prevalence of air and water pollution, the plasticization of the planet, the extinction of species, the melting of glaciers, and the destruction of the remaining wildernesses, it is still difficult to reach agreement on both the facts of climate change as well as the moral value of doing something about it. A pragmatist would note that the lack of sensitivity to the environmental crisis stems from two factors. First, some people are still comfortable in their belief that everything is okay. They have not yet been shocked into doubt. Second, the lack of sensitivity arises from the same narrow conception of the moral community that prevented a more effective global response to the COVID-19 pandemic. By closing off the moral community to include only humans and to exclude the natural world, pragmatists would argue that we show a lack of imagination in understanding our place in nature as well as an inability to contrast the present with a better future. Indeed, air pollution, water pollution, and climate change—much like COVID-19—have no interest in or respect for national borders, so it is curious that national interests should be prioritized over planetary interests. On the bright side, the growing environmental consciousness in the younger generation reveals an increase in sensitivity to the people and things affected by the climate crisis, an abundance of imagination in thinking about ways we can reverse climate change in order to create a healthy and sustainable planet, and lastly the presence of the pragmatic hope that we have the agency to achieve our aims.

Finally, the prevalence of racism throughout the world illustrates some important points about pragmatism. First, racism is, unfortunately, an idea that still pays. However, racism, like sexism, rests upon exclusion rather than inclusion. It rests on a lack of sensitivity to the needs of others. It rests on a lack of imagination to conceive of a better future. However, there is some hope. The murder of George Floyd by a white police officer, a shocking act that was caught on video, led to one of those instances of doubt that shake our beliefs to the core. The murder led to outrage, but it also led people around the world to *inquire* further about the presence of systemic racism and the role of the police in our communities. The event—coupled with the pragmatic act of contrasting a potential future with the actual present—also forced people to use their imaginations to contrast a better future with the present. These are pragmatic responses, moral responses. But how would a pragmatist evaluate the action of the ex-policeman who killed Floyd? Again, Rorty (1989) is prescient here:

> An immoral action is, on this [pragmatic] account, the sort of thing which, if done at all, is done only by animals, or by people of other families, tribes, cultures, or historical epochs. If done by one of us, or if done repeatedly by one of us, that person ceases to be one of us. She becomes an outcast, someone who doesn't speak our language, though she may have once appeared to do so. (p. 59)

The Black Lives Matter protests show that many people no longer recognize certain policing behaviors as actions that should be done in *our* nations, in *our* communities, in *our* homes. Pragmatists would view Floyd's murderer as someone who does not belong in our community. Furthermore, the public response to Floyd's killing reveals the reality of moral progress. It reveals the enlargement of the moral community and an increasing sensitivity to the suffering of those who have been excluded for too long.

Pragmatists remind us that arguing with conspiracy theorists, climate deniers, or racists is a waste of our time. People believe what they believe, and it is practically impossible to change their minds using science, reason, or logical argumentation. However, the three examples above show us that there are glimmers of hope. All we need is our moral imagination, the ability to contrast the actual present with a potential future, and the desire to inquire. Lastly, we require the courage to start believing in ideas that make a difference in the real world. If we do this, then perhaps we can still be hopeful.

8.4   The Intellectual Process: Constructing a Pragmatic Ethics that Makes a Difference

Having considered five of the major options in ethics in this book as well as the pragmatic approach above, you are in a position to start conceiving of your own ideal ethical theory—a theory that pays out. So, how can you go about creating your ideal theory? If you follow the guidelines of the book, you should be able to construct a sound system of ethics that makes a difference. There are two ways of approaching this task—you can work forward or backward. Working forwards is a traditional method that allows you to build a theory on fundamental principles. However, it is also appropriate to work backward, beginning with imagining the world you would like to live in. These two approaches are described below and are followed by a third, more discipline-specific approach that specifically addressed pandemics and public health.

Approach 1: Working Forward from Principles

Step 1: First, you can anchor your analysis in some of your fundamental views about human nature which were covered in the introduction of the book:

1. Are human beings selfish and egotistical or unselfish and altruistic?
2. Are humans driven primarily by biological impulses or by reason?
3. Will human beings be forever alienated from each other or do we have the ability to reconcile our religious, social, economic, and political differences?

Step 2: By establishing your positions on some of these fundamentals, you can begin to assess each ethical theory according to the 12 evaluation criteria that we established in each chapter. You might not think that all of these criteria are valuable, but some should stand out as being essential to your way thinking:

1. Does the theory have an appropriate scope for who belongs in our moral community?
2. Does the theory exhibit an appropriate degree of rational consistency?
3. Does the theory align with "common sense"?

4. Does the theory adequately explain issues about moral distance?
5. Does the theory have an appropriate *telos* or ultimate goal?
6. Does the theory clearly delineate obligatory actions and supererogatory ones?
7. Can the theory adapt to and account for the emergence of new technologies?
8. Can the theory be easily applied to different situations by providing clear-cut solutions?
9. Does the theory account for conflicts of interest?
10. Does the theory explain the importance of motivation in assessing ethical decisions?
11. Does the theory include personal happiness or personal fulfillment as a central concern?
12. Does the theory envision the creation of the kind of world you want to live in?

Step 3: As you establish your key criteria, you will begin to see connections between these criteria and some key concepts from other philosophers. Make sure you connect your thoughts to the history of philosophy.

Step 4: Next, it is important to use examples to anchor your theory in the real world. Have you seen anything in the news that made you think about ethics? Have you experienced anything in your personal life that might illustrate some points? Concrete examples will help you convey your key ideas more clearly.

Once you have identified your core beliefs, established your key criteria, noted the connections between your ideas and those of other philosophers, and provided examples to illustrate your points, you have created your own ideal ethical theory.

Approach #2: Working Backward from an Ideal World

Step 1: Richard Rorty reminds us that we can use our imaginations to envision a better future which contrasts with the imperfect present. So begin with the last evaluation criterion (12) from Step 2 above and describe the type of world you want to live in.

Step 2: Next, describe your moral community (criterion 1 from the list). Who or what belongs in the moral community?

Step 3: Identify additional criteria from the remaining eleven criteria that would help to achieve the goal. Explain how the other criteria help us imagine the better future, providing examples where appropriate.

Step 4: Identify which elements of the five ethical theories that support the achievement of that goal. Provide examples that illustrate your point. You may also here identify the elements in the theories that prevent the achievement of that goal and provide examples to illustrate the point.

Step 5: Identify practical steps that can be implemented by both individuals and communities that would help us achieve your imagined better future.

8.5 Creating an Ethical Public Health System for the Next Global Pandemic

The two approaches described in the previous section will help you develop a broad ethical theory for your life, in general. However, it is appropriate now to focus more specifically on the development of a specific system of pandemic and public health ethics. How can we create a robust and ethical public health system that will guide us safely through the next global pandemic? I suggest that the two basic approaches outlined above would also be useful for addressing this more specific problem. So, you can start by working forward from principles or you can work backward from you conception of an ideal, pandemic-resilient public health system.

Approach 1: Working Forward from Principles

Step 1: First, anchor your analysis in some of your fundamental views about human beings. Are human beings selfish or altruistic or some mixture of the two? Depending on your answer, you might need to envision public health institutions with broad powers that can coerce people to behave in appropriate ways; alternatively, public health institutions might only require limited powers that preserve individual freedoms. After all, if people are altruistic, we can rely on their good behavior.

Next, ask yourself if human beings are driven primarily by biology, reason, or some mixture of the two? Again, your answer here will lead to a number of different public health approaches. Should we use public shaming to enforce compliance with pandemic regulations? Should public health communication be focused on rational arguments? And, again, how much raw power should public health institutions have in order to enforce compliance?

Lastly, is your broad perspective on the future of humanity optimistic or pessimistic? Can we learn from our mistakes, or are we doomed to repeat them over and over again? Your answer to this question will determine the relative strength or weakness of public health powers.

Step 2: By establishing your fundamentals, you can begin to build out your theory. Review the list of twelve criteria that ought to be included in an ethical public health system. For example, what should the ultimate purpose or *telos* of a public health system be? Who and what should we include in the moral community? How should conflicts of interest be resolved—for example, between the welfare of individuals and the health of the community?

Step 3: As you establish your key criteria, you will begin to see connections between these criteria and some key concepts from other philosophers. Make sure you connect your analysis to the history of philosophy. How do your ideas echo those of the great philosophers from Plato to the present?

Step 4: Next, it is important to use examples to anchor your theory in the real world. This book has covered both the COVID-19 pandemic and a number of historical pandemics. What lessons can we learn from these specific examples?

- Typhus
- Smallpox
- The Black Death
- HIV/AIDS
- Polio
- COVID-19

Which public health systems performed better than others? Which public health measures were successful and which were misguided? Concrete examples will help you convey your key ideas more clearly.

Step 5: A number of practical problems are raised when a global pandemic strikes. Solutions to those problems involve weighing a variety of different ethical trade-offs. During the COVID-19 pandemic, for example, politicians were forced to weigh the risks and benefits of lockdowns, testing, and vaccination. On an individual patient level, medical professionals had to make difficult decisions about resource allocation to patients. How should we integrate these specific issues into our theory of pandemic ethics?
Below is a table summarizing 20 practical problems raised in this book.

Once you have identified your core beliefs, established your key criteria, noted the connections between your ideas and those of other philosophers, and provided examples to illustrate your points, you will have created—at least theoretically— an ethical public health system that will lead to better outcomes when we face the next global pandemic.

Approach #2: Working Backward from an Ideal World
Step 1: Richard Rorty reminds us that we can use our imaginations to envision a better future that contrasts with the imperfect present. So, begin by carefully describing a public health system as well as a pandemic management system that would have managed COVID-19 in an ideal way. You may wish to note both specific successes and failures of key public health decisions throughout the pandemic.
Step 2: Next, identify some specific criteria from the list that would help to achieve your ideals. For example, describe your moral community (criterion 1 from the list). Who or what belongs in the moral community? Do global pandemics require that we envisage a global moral community? Explain how the other criteria help us imagine a better future, providing concrete examples where appropriate.
Step 3: Identify which elements of the five ethical theories that support the achievement of that goal. Provide examples that illustrate your point. You may also here identify the elements in the theories that prevent the achievement of that goal and provide examples to illustrate the point. For example, does Kant provide a solid framework for ensuring that the dignity of all people is respected? Or do you take a utilitarian approach that requires us to sacrifice some innocent people for the greater good?
Step 4: Anchor your analysis by providing specific examples from COVID-19 and the historical pandemics we have discussed throughout the book. What lessons can we draw from the successes and failures of history?

Step 5: Using some of the 20 practical pandemic problems from Table 8.1, identify practical steps that can be implemented by governments and public health authorities that would ensure that our response to the next global pandemic is more effective than our response to COVID-19.

Table 8.1 20 Practical pandemic problems from 20 interdisciplinary perspectives

Problem	Interdisciplinary Perspective	Description
#1: Age-specific regulations during pandemics	2.1	Different diseases affect different age-groups differently. How should public health authorities use this data to target specific groups? Is age-targeting ethical? Should everyone be required to follow the pandemic restrictions?
#2: Public shaming and other coercive strategies as public health tools	2.2	Public shaming has been used throughout history in order to compel behavioral changes during pandemics. However, other coercive strategies have been used to encourage healthier behaviors, as seen with efforts to reduce smoking. How can we frame ethical public health communication strategies that work?
#3: Pandemics and the environment	2.3	All of the data show that we are facing a new normal of zoonotic disease. The next global pandemic will likely be caused by a problematic interaction between a human and an animal. To what extent do we need to address environmental concerns in our pandemic preparedness?
#4: Medical technology and intellectual property in an age of global pandemics	3.1	Current international rules prevent the rapid sharing of intellectual property even during global pandemics. To what extent do these rules need to be rethought in order to ensure the swift development, manufacture, and distribution of lifesaving medical technologies?
#5: Enforced quarantines and the importance of valuing human dignity during pandemics	3.2	The case of Typhoid Mary raises questions about enforced quarantines and human dignity. Is it ever appropriate to quarantine (imprison) individuals for health reasons and through no fault of their own?
#6: Vaccine equity	4.1	Although COVID-19 vaccines were produced in large enough numbers to vaccinate everyone on the planet, structural problems prevented that from happening. How can we develop programs that ensure vaccine equity when the next global pandemic strikes?
#7: Healthcare economics and the value of a statistical life (VSL)	4.2	Resource allocation in healthcare is always a challenge, particularly during medical emergencies. The ethical problem here is that mathematical analysis of a patient's healthcare costs immediately reduces the dignity and priceless value of a human being into a monetized quantity. What are some ways to navigate these trade-offs in a more ethical way?
#8: Involuntary medical testing during pandemics	4.3	Edward Jenner tested his first smallpox vaccine on an 8-year-old boy. Some people would find this decision to be ethically dubious. Others would justify it due to the positive consequences of the action—namely, the eradication of the disease. Is it ever right to test new lifesaving technologies on unwilling people?

(continued)

Table 8.1 (continued)

Problem	Interdisciplinary Perspective	Description
#9: Managing human nature during pandemics	5.1	Thomas Hobbes argued that human beings are vicious creatures. Therefore, strong governmental powers are required to check our evil nature and force us to comply with rules that benefit the whole. To what extent should emergency powers be granted to public health authorities during global pandemics in order to check our vicious behaviors?
#10: Rebelling against excessive emergency powers during pandemics	5.2	John Locke insisted that citizens must always consent to legitimate power, but he did not argue that all power is legitimate. When a government fails to meet its obligations to secure the peace, welfare, and property of its citizens, it loses legitimacy. During COVID-19 many people protested because lockdowns prevented them from earning the money they needed to live. Under what circumstance are public health powers unjustified? How can we balance the good of public health with the good of a functioning economy?
#11: Compulsory vaccination during pandemics	5.3	Jean-Jacques Rousseau argued that all citizens should be compelled to follow the same rules as everyone else. Since everyone in a civil society benefits from living in that society, we must also accept the same burdens, from paying our taxes to following traffic laws. In a pandemic, he would argue that all citizens should be compelled to be vaccinated as well. How would you address this issue?
#12: Evaluating specific public health powers during pandemics	5.4	The Black Death led nation states to expand their public health powers dramatically. Today, in the modern world, we have inherited many of these structures and procedures. The Italians established quarantine centers and militias to compel obedience centuries ago, and the same was done around the world during COVID-19, particularly in China. How do you evaluate these powers? When are they excessive? When are they justified?
#13: Relational ethics and the inadequacy of traditional medical ethics during global pandemics	6.1	The four traditional principles of medical ethics have proven to be appropriate for the vast majority of situations that healthcare professionals face. However, pandemics strain the relationship between the healthcare provider and the patient. Relational ethics provides one corrective to the hierarchical relationship between the carer and patient. How should the four principles be revised to account for relational considerations, especially during pandemics?
#14: Evaluating pandemic nationalism and international cooperation	6.2	One of the biggest challenge facing political leaders during global pandemics is nationalism. Politicians have to protect their own citizens, while at the same time the very definition of a *global pandemic* requires them to consider the interests of rest of the world. How should politicians navigate the tricky issues of vaccine hoarding and export controls on medical supplies, on the one hand, and international aid and support for other countries, on the other?

(continued)

Table 8.1 (continued)

Problem	Interdisciplinary Perspective	Description
#15: Evolutionary biology and the science of egoism and altruism during global pandemics	6.3	Assumptions that humans are fundamentally egotistical or altruistic cloud much of our history and inform many pandemic policy decisions. But what does evolutionary biology teach us? Does it confirm a biological urge to care only for our own kinship groups? If so, this would justify pandemic nationalism. If not, we might consider a more international humanitarian approach. Evaluate this dichotomy.
#16: Legal lessons and public health outcomes from HIV/AIDS	6.4	A comparison between HIV and COVID-19 reveals important insights about countless facets of pandemic management, including criminal law, international travel regulations, and medical privacy and disclosure rules. What were some unethical HIV and COVID-19 policies? How can we ensure that future public health rules do not discriminate against people with pandemic-related medical conditions?
#17: Feminist ethics and a care-based approach to pandemic management	7.1	The feminist critique of traditional ethical theories is profound for a number of reasons. It reminds us that our fundamental condition as human beings is our vulnerability. Also, it provides a clear path toward achieving a more just and equitable society, a society that protects the vulnerable, and a society that is pandemic resilient. Criticisms of well-intentioned COVID-19 rules like lockdowns proved that some prevention measures harmed the vulnerable more than the powerful. This fact forces us to reevaluate many of those rules. So how can we create more care-focused pandemic management strategies?
#18: Moral character and ethical triage policies during pandemics	7.2	In contrast to many other ethical theories, virtue theory argues that a patient's moral character should be used to determine whether or not they deserve treatment, especially when resources are limited. Therefore, it would be acceptable to deny treatment to a young criminal in favor or a senior citizen who has lived a good and moral life. This is a controversial claim. However, why should bad healthy people be given preferential treatment over good unhealthy people? Should the evaluation of a patient's moral character be included in triage policies?
#19: Vaccine skepticism and polio	7.3	The global fight against polio has been very successful by many measures, but it has yet to be eradicated. One reason for this is vaccine skepticism, caused in part by the Cutter Labs polio vaccine catastrophe which led many people to distrust vaccines. What are some ways that public health authorities can continue to build trust in the public while acknowledging legitimate concerns about the safety and efficacy of vaccines?
#20: Reinforcing interpersonal and governmental trust before, during, and after pandemics	7.4	Preliminary studies about COVID-19 seem to show that the level of social trust has a direct effect on pandemic outcomes. High-trust societies fare better than low-trust ones. Given the diversity of opinions in all societies, what can political leaders and public health authorities do to increase social trust before, during, and after pandemics? How can public health messaging be improved to create the conditions needed to combat the next global pandemic more effectively?

8.6   The Lived Process: Joining Emotions, the Imagination, and the Mind

Having reached the end of this book on understanding ethics during the COVID-19 pandemic and beyond, we can take a moment to survey the scene. We have examined some fundamental beliefs about human nature, covered five of the main options in the history of ethical theory, evaluated the strengths and weaknesses of the theories, and applied those theories to a variety of situations related to ethical life during pandemics. We have introduced 20 interdisciplinary perspectives to help us broaden and deepen our understanding of ethics and pandemics. To be sure, there are many other options and viewpoints to consider and even more perspectives to consider—and all of these ought to have been discussed. However, there must be an end point to speculation so we can return to the process of living our lives.

One philosopher whom I regretfully excluded was the brilliant Scottish philosopher David Hume (1711–1776), who was one of the fathers of skepticism, the idea that we can never really know anything despite our pretensions to knowledge. Indeed, he showed quite convincingly that we do not even *know* that the sun will rise tomorrow. We only think we know because we are in the *habit* of thinking we know stuff. One takeaway from this book might be the skeptical idea that we do not know much about ethics, despite the fact that we've been pretending to know for thousands of years. This is how Hume handled the emotional consequences of his skepticism, as described in *A Treatise of Human Nature* (1739):

> The intense view of these manifold contradictions and imperfections in human reason has so wrought upon me, and heated my brain, that I am ready to reject all belief and reasoning, and can look upon no opinion even as more probable or likely than another. Where am I, or what? From what causes do I derive my existence, and to what condition shall I return? [...] I am confounded with all these questions, and begin to fancy myself in the most deplorable condition imaginable, invironed with the deepest darkness, and utterly deprived of the use of every member and faculty.
>
> Most fortunately it happens, that since reason is incapable of dispelling these clouds, nature herself suffices to that purpose, and cures me of this philosophical melancholy and delirium, either by relaxing this bent of mind, or by some avocation, and lively impression of my senses, which obliterate all these chimeras. I dine, I play a game of backgammon, I converse, and am merry with my friends; and when after three or four hours' amusement, I would return to these speculations, they appear so cold, and strained, and ridiculous, that I cannot find in my heart to enter into them any farther.
>
> [...]If I must be a fool, as all those who reason or believe anything certainly are, my follies shall at least be natural and agreeable. (I, VII, para. 8–10)

Hume provides one jolly perspective on the activity of thinking about ethics and philosophy too seriously: It can make us disagreeable. Therefore, it's best to remember that other activities are available to dispel the clouds of doubt, lighten our mood, and make us agreeable members of the human community again.

I would also like to return to a second great thinker Epictetus, the Stoic, whom we met in Chap. 7. He highlights some troubling tendencies in our day-to-day ethical thinking. He cautions us about the tendency of clever thinkers to justify their bad behaviors through the use of fancy philosophical language and argumentation. In the *Enchiridion*, Epictetus (c. 135) notes:

> The first and most necessary topic in philosophy is the practical application of principles, as, *We ought not to lie*; the second is that of demonstrations as, *Why it is that we ought not to lie*; the third, that which gives strength and logical connection to the other two, as, *Why this is a demonstration*. For what is demonstration? What is a consequence? What a contradiction? What truth? What falsehood? The third point is then necessary on account of the second; and the second on account of the first. But the most necessary, and that whereon we ought to rest, is the first. But we do just the contrary. For we spend all our time on the third point and employ all our diligence about that, and entirely neglect the first. Therefore, at the same time that we lie, we are very ready to show how it is demonstrated that lying is wrong. (para. 51)

Like Hume's comments above, we can often focus on the complexities of ethical thinking and avoid the key principles of ethical behavior. Perhaps, we should heed Epictetus' word of caution since there is some value in doing the things that we know to be right with little additional thought.

Returning to pragmatism, it is important to remember that life involves a lot of choices and decisions. We might believe that our individual choices are the best choices and that everyone else ought to choose as we do. However, pragmatists remind us that beliefs which might pay off for you may not necessarily pay off for others. Indeed, one enormous topic I have almost entirely neglected in this book is religion. Pragmatists remind us that beliefs only matter if they make a difference in our lives, and religion is one such important idea that clearly makes a difference. However, not believing in a religion also makes a difference in people's lives, so being non-religious is also pragmatic. In sum, as Richard Rorty (1999) reminds us, "There is a potential infinity of equally valuable ways to lead a human life" (p. 268). Aristotle would most certainly agree. Accepting this fact in your own life as well as in others' lives will probably keep you happy and agreeable.

The final takeaway has to do with individual free will and human destiny. It might seem that we are careening down a path that is taking our species and the planet to a single, inevitable destination. If we believe that we have no agency to change the path, then we have lost hope. I'm not entirely sure that such an idea is one that makes a difference. Therefore, it may be worthwhile to consider an alternative. Maybe the human species is not destined to end at any specific terminus. After all, we can be extinguished through no action of our own—a cosmic collision, the arrival of genocidal aliens, or an extinction-level pandemic. If that's how the human species is destined to end, what was the point of all this word play about Truth and Reason and the Good? We might also be the agents of our *own* destruction through nuclear Armageddon, human-caused environmental catastrophe, or the creation of a new bio-weapon that ends all life on earth.

The pragmatic approach to this uncertainty about our destiny as a species is to remind us that believing in destiny might not pay off in the real world. Richard Rorty (1999) said that if the human species does indeed perish, we "will simply have missed a chance to be happy" (p. xxxii). No tears. No sadness. No woe. Our extinction will not have been right or wrong, rational or irrational, good or evil; it will just be what happened to a sad, little, insignificant species on a lonely planet in an infinite universe.

Nevertheless, until we perish, we have all been given at least this one chance to be happy—as individuals, as members of the human community, and as organisms on our shared planet.

Maybe it would make a difference to take that chance.

References

Epictetus. (c. 135). *Enchiridion*. Trans. T. W. Higginson. Project Gutenberg. 2014. https://www.gutenberg.org/files/45109/45109-h/45109-h.htm

Hume, D. (1739). *A treatise of human nature*. Project Gutenberg. 2022. https://www.gutenberg.org/files/4705/4705-h/4705-h.htm

James, W. (1907). What pragmatism means (lecture II) in *pragmatism: A new name for some old ways of thinking*. Project Gutenberg. 2013. https://www.gutenberg.org/files/5116/5116-h/5116-h.htm

Kahneman, D. (2011). *Thinking, fast and slow*. FSG.

Modgil, S., et al. (2021). A confirmation bias view on social media induced polarisation during Covid-19. *Information System Frontiers*. https://doi.org/10.1007/s10796-021-10222-9

Peirce, C. S. (1868). Some consequences of four incapacities. *Journal of Speculative Philosophy*, *2*, 140–147. https://arisbe.sitehost.iu.edu/menu/library/bycsp/conseq/cn-frame.htm

Peirce, C. S. (1877, Nov). The fixation of belief. *Popular Science Monthly*, *12*, 1–15. The Internet Archive. https://archive.org/details/1877-peirce-fixation-of-belief.

Rorty, R. (1989). *Contingency, irony, and solidarity*. Cambrige University Press.

Rorty, R. (1999). *Philosophy and social hope*. Penguin.

Index

Printed in the United States
by Baker & Taylor Publisher Services